JOHN WESLEY
CHRISTIAN PHILOSOPHER AND
CHURCH FOUNDER

JOHN WESLEY.
IN HIS MATURITY.
From the painting by John Russell, R.A.

*Now in Kingswood School,
Lansdown, Bath.*

(See note in appendix)

JOHN WESLEY

CHRISTIAN PHILOSOPHER
AND CHURCH FOUNDER

BY
GEORGE EAYRS
Ph.D. (Dunelm), F.R.Hist.S.

HONORARY SECRETARY OF THE INTERNATIONAL
METHODIST HISTORICAL UNION (EASTERN SECTION)

WITH WESLEY PORTRAITS BY RUSSELL AND HONE,
AND COPIES OF
METHODIST ORDINATION CERTIFICATES

WIPF & STOCK · Eugene, Oregon

Wipf and Stock Publishers
199 W 8th Ave, Suite 3
Eugene, OR 97401

John Wesley
Christian Philosopher and Church Founder
By Eayrs, George
ISBN 13: 978-1-60899-981-1
Publication date 9/21/2010
Previously published by Epworth, 1926

PREFACE

THE title and sub-title of this work indicate its two-fold purpose. It is designed to claim for Wesley his rightful place among constructive thinkers, and to show his work as a Church Founder which issued from his Christian philosophy.

It is believed that this is the first time that Wesley has been regarded chiefly as a Christian Philosopher. As an evangelist, a teacher and social reformer, and as the human founder of a Christian Church, he is well known. The People called Methodists are now in every country. References to Wesley's contributions to Thought are, however, few and meagre, although he was an influential thinker in his period on Baconian principles, and a modern pioneer in the field of Christian Experience which now engages much attention. It is true that only lately have Wesley's cipher diaries been deciphered and become available, with other material, for an accurate estimate of his personality, philosophy, and work. A new Wesley has emerged. His mental and spiritual development demands fresh and full study, especially in view of the persistence of his philosophy, theology, and church polity, and their spread throughout the world. I have here endeavoured to study Wesley with the help of the new materials, available by the efforts of many workers, and my own investigations. A new statement of the facts is needed. The Methodist Churches in Britain and America are moving towards Union; and

Wesley, their first human Founder, is often misunderstood and misrepresented.

Considerable portions of this statement of Wesley's Thought were used in my thesis on the Philosophy of Religion which was accepted by Durham University some years ago. It is understood that this was the first occasion on which Wesley's philosophy of Christian experience was considered in this way in a British University. There was appropriateness in this association with Durham, as the Thought of Wesley, through his Methodist work and writings, was singularly influential and beneficent in northern England. Its importance is now acknowledged everywhere. As Honorary Secretary of the International Methodist Historical Union (Eastern Section), I have associated this writing with Wesley's Day, the anniversary of his evangelical conversion. This is now widely observed every year.

My indebtedness to previous workers is acknowledged in the text and the Appendix of *Additional Notes and Literary Authorities*. This section represents much labour, and will, I hope, be of service. Attention is invited to the unique Wesley portraits and illustrations. Without invaluable help from many friends this volume could not have been prepared. Several ministerial and lay friends in the United Methodist Church, by their generous appreciation of my endeavours to serve them and Methodism and their manifest pleasure at the recognitions received, heartened me greatly during more than thirty years of work in this field, chiefly in my scanty leisure. Earlier than that, the late Professor Robert Adamson and Professor J. S. Mackenzie, M.A., Litt.D., LL.D., then of Manchester University, made me their debtor for

PREFACE 7

direction and stimulus along these lines of study. As an Advanced Student for Research work during three years at Armstrong College, Newcastle-upon-Tyne, in Durham University, I am under deep obligation to the Professor of Mental and Moral Philosophy, Mr. R. F. Alfred Hoernlé, M.A., B.Sc., for encouragement and teaching. It was my privilege to hear at first hand much of the contents of two important works by him, *Idealism As a Philosophical Doctrine*, and *Matter, Life, Mind, and God*. Nor can I forget the kindness of the Vice-Chancellor of Durham and Master of Hatfield Hall, (Professor Arthur Robinson, M.A., D.C.L.), the Principal of Armstrong College (Sir Theodore Morison, M.A., D.C.L.), the Principal of Mansfield College, Oxford (Rev. W. B. Selbie, M.A., D.D.), the Librarians (Mr. F. Bradshaw, M.A., D.Sc., and Mr. A. V. Stocks, M.A.), and that of the Dean of Durham Cathedral (Bishop J. E. C. Welldon, D.D.). The Lord Bishop of Durham (Dr. H. Hensley Henson), stimulated my renewed study of Bishop Butler, his illustrious predecessor. I have ventured to quote from his letter. In London, invaluable information was made available by the help of the staff of the London Library, and especially of the Guildhall Library. Membership of the Aristotelian Society, and access to the unique collection of Wesley manuscripts and portraits at the Methodist Publishing House were of much assistance. It is a pleasure to record the continued help I received from the Wesleyan Methodist Book Steward (the Rev. J. Alfred Sharp, D.D.), and the Editor (the Rev. John Telford, B.A.). The Rev. John Elsworth kindly read the proof sheets of Book II, and offered valuable suggestions. The late Sir Alfred Jermyn, of King's Lynn, with his friends, helped me by presenting a collection of Wesleyana. As in other works, I have been much helped by the *Proceedings* of the Wesley Historical Society. The United Methodist Church readily lent some literary treasures, through the Hon. Librarian of the Hobill Collection (the Rev. John S. Clemens, B.A., D.D.). None of these friends is, however, responsible for the work they have aided. Would it were worthier!

It remains to name the sustained helpfulness to me in this matter, of my nephew, the Rev. Alfred J. G. Seaton, B.D., and Mrs. Seaton; and of the Westminster College Vice-Principal (the Rev. Archibald W. Harrison, B.Sc., D.D.). Our daughter, Miss Winifred S. L. Eayrs, has again been an efficient amanuensis, and our sons, Mr. Hugh S. Eayrs and Mr. Charles W. Eayrs, of Toronto, have done all they could, as with my other works. My wife has done more than any by her sacrifice and keen interest. I wished to dedicate this book to her; but we decided to use the page for an ancient beloved Prayer.

GEORGE EAYRS.

Wesley's Day (May 24).

CONTENTS

                                      Page

INTRODUCTION
CHRISTIAN PHILOSOPHY AND THE CONDITION OF ENGLAND IN THE EIGHTEENTH CENTURY . . **15**

BOOK I
WESLEY AS A CHRISTIAN PHILOSOPHER

I. THE NEW LIGHT ON WESLEY AND HIS QUEST FOR GOD **37**

II. WESLEY'S LIFE AND WORK OUTLINED, WITH HIS QUALIFICATIONS AS PHILOSOPHER . . **44**

III. THE LITERARY DOCUMENTS OF WESLEY AND HIS CHRISTIAN EXPERIENCE **63**
    i. Wesley's 'Journal.'
    ii. 'Appeals to Men of Reason and Religion.'
    iii. Letters to 'John Smith.'
    iv. 'Rules' for Methodists.
    v. Hymnology.
    vi. Standard 'Sermons' and 'Notes on the New Testament.'
    vii. 'Philosophy'—Natural History and Metaphysics.

IV. CHRISTIAN EXPERIENCE AS SEEN IN WESLEY AND OTHER TYPES OF HIS PERIOD AND SINCE **82**
    i. Wesley and his Evangelical Conversion in 1738.
    ii. Other Eighteenth-Century Types—Asbury, Brackenbury, Silas Told, Lady Maxwell. Collections of Experience.
    iii. Later Typal Instances—Gladstone, Westcott, William Booth, George Cadbury, Alexander Whyte

V. WESLEY'S IMPLICATIONS OF CHRISTIAN EXPERIENCE **129**
    i. The Implications concerning God.
    ii. Confirmations of these Implications by their congruity with the Nature of Man.

CONTENTS

Page

VI. CRITICISM OF THE PHILOSOPHY OF CHRISTIAN EXPERIENCE 165
i. That it is limited in its Appeal.
ii. That Emotion is its chief Element.
iii. That it is Self-suggested.
iv. Criticism of Wesley's use of it.

VII. THE PHILOSOPHY OF CHRISTIAN EXPERIENCE SINCE WESLEY 181

Schleiermacher; 'The Varieties of Religious Experience'; 'The Religious Consciousness'; 'The Spirit: the Relation of God and Man'; 'Jesus in the Experience of Men.'

BOOK II
WESLEY AS A CHURCH FOUNDER

I. WESLEY'S THOUGHT AS RELATED TO HIS CHURCHMANSHIP 201

II. WESLEY'S ACTS AS CHURCH FOUNDER . . 206
i. Unauthorized Religious Services.
ii. A New Fellowship Instituted.
iii. Separate Church Buildings Erected.
iv. Church Workers Appointed.
v. A Supreme Court Constituted.
vi. Legal Acts to Secure Continuity.
vii. A Church Constitution for American Methodists.
viii. Ministers Ordained for British Methodism.

III. WESLEY'S REGULATIVE PRINCIPLES AS CHURCH FOUNDER 227
i. The Primacy of Spiritual Intuition and Moral Consciousness.
ii. Divine Guidance through Holy Scripture.
iii. The Verdict of the Common Sense of Christians.
iv. Value as discovered by Use.

APPENDIX

ADDITIONAL NOTES, WITH LITERARY AUTHORITIES USED IN THIS WORK 248
I. Notes on the Illustrations.
II. Additional Notes and Literary Authorities

INDEX 285

ILLUSTRATIONS

I. John Wesley in his Maturity. A study of his face, as in the Portrait by John Russell, R.A. . . *Frontispiece*

To face page

II. Wesley the Teacher-Evangelist. After the painting by Nathaniel Hone and the engraving by Greenwood . 34

III. & IV. Methodist Certificates of Ordination to the Office of Minister 198
    A. Of Robert Gamble, by Wesley, in 1788.
    B. Of Alexander Kilham, by Joseph Cownley and Charles Atmore, in 1792.

V. Sketch Plan of Aldersgate Street and Little Britain, London, indicating sites of buildings associated with the Evangelical Conversion of John and Charles Wesley 264

A PRAYER
OF ONE WHO WOULD LOVE GOD WITH THE MIND

GOD be in my head
    and in my understanding;
GOD be in mine eyes
    and in my looking;
GOD be in my mouth
    and in my speaking;
GOD be in my heart
    and in my thinking;
GOD be at mine end
    and at my departing.

From the blackletter edition of The Prymer in English and Latin, *after Sarum (Salisbury) use,* 1558.

INTRODUCTION

CHRISTIAN PHILOSOPHY AND THE CONDITION OF ENGLAND IN WESLEY'S CENTURY

> What a fathomless wealth lies in the wisdom
>   and knowledge of God!
> How inscrutable His judgements!
> How mysterious His methods!
> 'Who ever understood the thoughts of the Lord?
>   Who has ever been His counsellor?
> Who has first given to Him and has to be repaid?'
>   All comes from Him,
>   All lives by Him,
>   All ends in Him.
> Glory to Him for ever, Amen!
>   ST. PAUL, *Romans* xi. 33–36 (Moffatt's translation).

Religion and Philosophy have close and intricate mutual relations.

Religion *provides* the solution which philosophy *seeks*. That which is the quest of Philosophy is the realized experiences of Religion, a unity in which the profoundest differences in Life are actually reconciled, which leaves nothing beyond itself to confound the human spirit, but brings all elements of experience into a perfect spiritual harmony.

Philosophy vindicates the validity and reasonableness of Religion. It provides 'a vindication of the religious consciousness.' Philosophy at the same time has to consider the form in which this religious experience at any particular epoch clothes itself. And if it shall appear that the form contradicts the universality and comprehensiveness of the experience of which it is the expression, and is, therefore, falsifying and imperilling that experience, Philosophy must ruthlessly assail that form, and break it up, in the name of that principle of reconciliation which is the inspiration and the goal of thought and action.

PROFESSOR T. B. KILPATRICK, M.A., D.D.
(Hastings, *Bible Dictionary*, iii.)

I trust my heart will always say, both to God and man, 'What I know not, teach Thou me.'
JOHN WESLEY, *A Survey of the Wisdom of God in the Creation*, v. 3.

CHRISTIAN PHILOSOPHY AND THE CONDITION OF ENGLAND IN WESLEY'S CENTURY

THOSE who watch for signs of true progress more than those who watch for the morning are encouraged by the growing recognition, in this age, of moral values. Worth seems to be more generally reckoned in terms of Goodness, Truth, and Beauty, rather than in those of size, material possessions, physical energy or mental equipment.[1]*

Recent Estimates of Wesley

The place and rank now given to John Wesley is an instance of this advance. Even in his own century, towards its close, he was esteemed very highly for his work's sake as Evangelist and Social Reformer. A century later, the *Spectator* ranked Wesley with Shakespeare, and indeed higher. W. T. Stead styled Wesley ' St. John of England.' If the words, ' and the English ' be added, this may stand. The English-speaking peoples have no nobler representative than Wesley in the files of their history; neither King Alfred, nor Roger Bacon, nor Milton, nor Cromwell, with all of whom Wesley has been compared. President Woodrow Wilson described Wesley as ' poised in spirit,

---

* Numbers like this throughout the text refer to Notes in the Appendix.

deeply conversant with the natures of his fellow-men, studious of the truth, sober to think, prompt and yet not rash to act : a sort of spiritual statesman, a politician of God, speaking the policy of a Kingdom unseen.' (*John Wesley's Place in History*).* Public memorials also indicate his growing significance. A catholic historical scholar and churchman, Dean Stanley, welcomed to Westminster Abbey in 1876 a memorial to John Wesley and his brother Charles, the chief modern hymn-writer of Christendom. A philosopher of the Christian religion and a representative of ancient English Dissent, Dr. A. M. Fairbairn, erected Wesley among the statues of Wycliffe, Calvin, and other Church leaders in Mansfield College Chapel, Oxford. In the latest and most impressive building of Protestant Christianity, Liverpool Cathedral, Wesley is commemorated along with St. Francis of Assisi, Wycliffe, Savonarola, Cranmer, Butler, and Westcott.† Finally, Wesley has been lately acclaimed as the best representative of the seventh age of man upon earth. The six earlier ages have as their representatives Socrates, Aristotle, Jesus, Augustine, Erasmus, and Cromwell.*

As Christian Thinker and Church Founder

Wesley is placed in the last list among thinkers, as well as world leaders.‡ The fineness of his mind

---

*Wilson was earlier the Professor of History in Wesleyan University, Middletown, Conn.

† The figure of Wesley is in a stained-glass window. His mother, Susanna Wesley, is included in the Women's Window.

‡ It must be said that Wesley's religious convictions would not have permitted his name, or that of any man, to have ranked alongside that of Jesus Christ our only Lord and Saviour.

IN THE EIGHTEENTH CENTURY 17

as well as the beauty of his character, is noticed. Recognition of his mental eminence is almost a new feature in estimates of Wesley and his work, although Lecky regarded Wesley's intellect as ' one of the most powerful and active in England.' While abating not one jot of the claim for Wesley as Evangelist and Social Reformer, we here consider Wesley's Thought, together with his work as the human instrument in forming a new church organization. He was a Christian Philosopher and Church Founder. These aspects of his work are closely related. All his work for man grew out of his knowledge of, and conscious relation to God. It was given to Wesley to state afresh the Christian view of God and the universe, with the relation of God to man and of man to God. This he did with remarkable power and attractiveness. His teaching contained truth, universal and enduring. Its essence is as vital and vitalizing as when he lived, and stated it by voice and pen, a century and a half ago.

Wesley's knowledge of God was experiential. He was a mystic, a practical mystic. He had mystic certitude as to spiritual reality. In his awareness of and dependence upon God, Wesley equalled Cromwell and George Fox. Sometimes he seemed more sure of God than he was of himself. It was the action of the Ineffable upon the imperfect human being Wesley, causing his reaction towards God, which was the centre and soul of Wesley's teaching and the master-light of all his seeing and serving. His experience was akin to that of St. Paul. God ' revealed Himself in him.' Like that apostle, he could declare of his message that ' it is not a human affair, no man put it into my hands, no man taught me what it meant; I had it by a revelation of Jesus Christ.' These are the central facts concerning Wesley, although, as will be shown, he made full use of divine teaching to men who spoke in the Scriptures and in the days before his own. He constantly corrected his understanding and interpretation of divine truth by comparison with that given to others. Wesley was a catholic teacher. In essence his faith was that of all good men. He appealed for confirmation to the common sense of all who are faithful to the moral ideal; and he tested his teaching and methods by their results in the individual and in society.

Wesley was a Christian Idealist, and also a Pragmatist. He is clearly distinguished by his combination of these capital qualities. The mystical and the practical both appealed to him. Here again, as will be shown, he is misunderstood and misrepresented. In his *Prophets, Priests, and Kings*, Mr. A. G. Gardiner contrasted Wesley unfavourably with Booth, the first General of the Salvation Army. He praised the latter because he was a social reformer who had a practical purpose behind his spiritual emotion, whereas 'Wesley saw only the celestial city.' This is a grave mis-statement. Similarly, another writer, who is generally accurate and sympathetic, Mr. C. Grant Robertson, describes Wesley in his *England under the Hanoverians*, as 'aloof alike from politics and the speculations of the schools.' The fact is that Wesley was continuously interested in political matters and social reform, and frequently active in them. He advised Bristol Methodists for whom to vote in a parliamentary election, published a booklet on the American Revolution, which was sold at the London church doors and roused England, and brought a representative of the Government to ask him what he wished in recognition of his services. When provisions ran short, he offered shrewd and valuable proposals for meeting the problem. As to his aloofness from 'the speculations of the schools,' we shall show that Wesley studied and wrote upon the theories of Locke, Berkeley, Clarke, Butler, Peter Browne and the theory of Evolution. Wesley was aloof from nothing human, least of all from speculation. The beatific vision was his supreme quest; but his was not 'a fugitive and cloistered virtue, unexercised and unbreathed, that never sallies out and sees her adversary.' Such statements are corrected by Mr. H. W. V. Temperley's reference to Wesley in the *Cambridge Modern History*. He states that more important than the work of politicians, poets, philosophers or divines, in universality of influence and range of achievements, were John Wesley and the religious revival to which he gave his name and his life.

Christian Thought and Moral Conditions in Wesley's Century

The features of Christian Thought and the moral conditions of England in Wesley's period, the eighteenth century, must be briefly noticed. Bishop Berkeley, Samuel Clarke, and Bishop Butler were the chief Christian thinkers. William Law is referred to later. Wesley, like a new planet, swam into the ken of devout watchers. To the basis of faith and the motives for conduct supplied by the brilliant thinkers named, Wesley added those supplied by experience of God in

Christ by the Holy Spirit. Moral conditions in that period cried aloud for the restatement of truth and the rediscovery of sources of spiritual energy. Thomas Arnold's characterization of the eighteenth century as a misused seed-basket must not be accepted without qualification. Nevertheless, it is true that the need was urgent for the experience and restatement of faith in God as an intellectual and emotional possession with appropriate ethical results. In his *Religious Thought in England*, Mark Pattison noted the period from 1714 to 1744 as characterized by decay of religion, licentiousness of morals, public corruption, and profaneness of languge : ' It was an age whose poetry was without romance, whose philosophy was without insight, and whose public men were without character ; an age of light without love, whose very merits were of the earth, earthy.'

Testimony, which cannot be questioned, from writers of that period, abundantly supports this opinion. William Law (1686–1761) was only excelled by Wesley in his knowledge of the period and in anxiety for its reform. The incomparable literary portraits of imaginary characters which Law gives in his *Christian Perfection* and his *Serious Call* show the age. Sincerity is rarely drawn ; moral earnestness almost never. ' Ouranius ' and ' Miranda ' are almost solitary, and shine by contrast among Law's studies drawn from life. That Mandeville found material for his satire, *The Fable of the Bees ; or Private Vices, Public Benefits*, and secured acceptance for his theory that ' the moral virtues are the political offspring which flattery begot upon pride,' is sad evidence of general corruptness. Berkeley said, in 1721, that it was fashionable to decry religion and spend upon it ' that little

IN THE EIGHTEENTH CENTURY 21

talent of ridicule.' Writing in 1736, Bishop Butler stated that people of discernment generally agreed to treat religion as if it were fictitious and merely a subject for mirth and ridicule. There is evidence for the statement that he declined nomination to the Primacy in 1747, as he judged that 'it was too late for him to try to support a falling church.' The facts detailed by Wesley in his *Appeals to Men of Reason and Religion* concerning the ignorance, immorality, and irreligion of all classes, at least during the first half of the century, have never been seriously challenged. In 1745 he declared that 'our nation stands on the very brink of destruction. And why are we thus, but because the cry of our wickedness is gone up to heaven? Because we have so exceedingly, abundantly, beyond measure, corrupted our ways before the Lord.' Mr. Abbey, in his *English Church and Its Bishops*, 1700–1800, acknowledges the earnestness of some church leaders; but he is compelled to include most of them in a stern, sad summary: they 'left Wesley and his followers struggling bravely but alone, amid insult and obloquy, to revive the power of Christianity amid a godless and perverse generation.' The English Free Churches, —Baptists, Independents, Presbyterians, and Quakers—had grown considerably since the Revolution of 1688. At the death of Queen Anne they had fifteen hundred church buildings. Some of their leaders were of such social standing as to secure nomination as sheriff of London, and were brave enough to suffer heavy fines and much odium rather than accept that office and honour on conditions which violated their religious convictions. But by 1729 they had to bemoan decline in numbers and spiritual efficiency. Arianism had silenced the evangelist among them ; he was almost unknown in the Establishment also. ' Men talked their father's language after they had lost their father's faith.'

Leaders of Thought : Berkeley

Privilege and opportunity made the Established Church the home of the intellectual leaders of the period. Wesley was also one of its clergy. We refer, briefly, and in a popular manner, to the contributions of Berkeley, Clarke, and Butler, before considering those of Wesley.

George Berkeley (1685-1754)* was a bishop of the English Church in Ireland. He designed to help truth and virtue by restating the Idealism of Plato* and the Spiritual Realism of St. John (*Works*, iii. 295). In his early, brilliant treatise, *The Principles of Human Knowledge*, with the novel features of his philosophy, he declared his life-long purpose. He said, ' What deserves first place in our studies is the consideration of GOD and our DUTY ; which to promote, as it was the main drift of my labours, so shall I esteem them altogether useless, if by what I have said I cannot inspire my readers with a pious sense of the Presence of God.'* Berkeley stood for Theistic Idealism. He argued against Deism, the foe of Christian teaching in that age, as Wesley found. Berkeley strove to establish Theism and practical belief in God, with the corresponding conduct and character. Deism generally defined God as a person, who is transcendent, and a determinate Being in determinate relations to the world and man. God was regarded by Deists as an object of worship, but He was thought of as isolated, remote from all

His creations, incapable of, or at least without concern for, or participation in their development or affairs, and unresponsive to His chief creation, man. Berkeley could not understand that any who believed the Holy Scriptures could speak of Nature as something distinct from God. Heathens did this. They credited Nature with the effects which the Scriptures ascribed to the immediate hand of God. Berkeley maintained that the First Cause is continuous active intelligence, living divine mind or power. The universe shows that there is a divine conservation, a continuous creation by divine mind.' All Nature would shrink to nothing unless maintained by the same force that created it. While Berkeley felt the need of a divine revelation and found his chief authority in Holy Scripture, he claimed that his philosophy was that of the Stoics and Platonists (*Works*, ii. 257–62), and of ancient poets also, as Virgil, who affirmed *mens agitat molem*—a mind moves the mass (*Works*, i. 282).' This mind, power, and will, which creates, sustains and governs all, we call God.

Wesley was to add much that is specifically Christian to Berkeley's idealistic and theistic teaching. He knew Berkeley's works. The earlier ones he had at Oxford in 1725 and 1726. From Berkeley's *Alciphron* (1732), a brilliant, trenchant apology for the Christian religion, Wesley probably borrowed Berkeley's stinging epithet, 'The Minute Philosopher.' This Wesley applied to Hume and his school of thought in 1772. Wesley strongly sympathized with Berkeley and all who condemned Deism and materialistic philosophy also, and followed his endeavours to show the reasonableness of Theism and Christianity. In several features Berkeley and Wesley are alike. As philosophers, both were much attracted by the works and theory of Malebranche. Both were modern in their references to elemental fire, or spirit, now called ether. It seemed to them as near to the immaterial as any substance known to man.* Both wrote of all phenomena as linked as by a chain. As public men, both of them made experimental ventures in America. Berkeley issued in 1725 his *Proposal for Converting the Savage Americans to Christianity*, and went to America on an educational missionary project. Wesley went as a missionary in 1735. Both were genuinely and continuously eager to find, and remove, the causes of social distress; and both became famous for the remedies they offered for diseases of the body. Berkeley's philosophical treatise entitled *Siris* (σειρά, σειρίς, a chain), surveyed Nature in progressive related stages. In this he advocated tar-water as a medicinal remedy. This brought him more immediate fame than his philosophy, or the speculations he linked by a chain of reasoning. From tar-water he proceeded to chemistry, then to physics, metaphysics and theology. Similarly, Wesley's preaching of the Christian gospel for spirit, mind, and body, made him known and beloved. His quaint volume entitled *Primitive Physic* made a wide appeal.

Clarke

Samuel Clarke (1675–1729) was eminent among philosopher-divines in the early part of Wesley's century. Although not destined to affect Christian thought permanently as did Berkeley, Clarke was the recognized champion of the claims of reason

* See later references to Wesley's frequent use of this metaphor; and *cf.* Sir Oliver Lodge's suggestive work (1925) *Ether and Reality.*

IN THE EIGHTEENTH CENTURY 25

in the department of theology. He was a leader in the academic discussions at the court of Queen Caroline, where Wesley presented his father's learned work in 1735—*Dissertationes in librum Jobi.** Clarke was the intimate friend of Sir Isaac Newton, and expounded the theological implications of Newton's epochal discoveries and theories. Clarke was a sound classical scholar and logician. His Boyle lectures, delivered in St. Paul's Cathedral, London, drew many listeners, gave him European fame, and were widely used by Christian thinkers. They are entitled *A Demonstration of the Being and Attributes of God.*

Clarke claimed that 'by one clear and plain series of propositions, necessarily connected and following one another,' the existence of God can be proved; and that the works of God reveal His attributes and character. Clarke used both the *a priori* and *a posteriori* arguments. He based his argument upon the fact of existence. This fact one cannot deny without contradicting his own consciousness. Since no finite existence is self-caused, there must be a necessarily self-existent Being. This Being Christians call God. We are therefore certain of the Being of a supreme independent Cause, Clarke contended, because it is strictly demonstrable that there is something in the universe actually existing without us, the supposition of whose non-existence plainly implies a contradiction. Clarke argued that the existence of an idea, as that two and two make four, implies the existence of that of which it is the idea. Here Clarke uses the traditional form of such reasoning which is known as the Ontological arguments.' Anselm, of Canterbury Cathedral, had formulated

* Adam Clarke's *Wesley Family*, 217.

this argument in the eleventh century. He stated it thus : God is that than which no greater can be thought. That God can be thought of, and is thought of, implies His existence. Descartes (1596–1690) followed upon this high and difficult line of reasoning.

Wesley knew Clarke's argumentation and quoted him as an authority. Wesley neglected no aid to faith. He was, however, being prepared to reopen to men the New Testament way by which the human spirit may gain experiential knowledge of God. Without this knowledge, philosophers and theologians alike admit that the idea of the existence of God cannot be validated, nor can it be of much service to reason or faith. Clarke's valuable treatise reached a tenth edition by the middle of the eighteenth century. It appealed to thinkers only, and to these chiefly as an intellectual exercise. It did little to dispel the moral darkness or stem the irreligion of the age.[10]

Butler

The contribution of Bishop Butler in the period of Wesley must receive fuller notice. Joseph Butler (1692–1752) was bishop of Bristol and later of Durham.[11] As already stated, he felt himself unable to lift the life of the nation and the Church or to arrest its decline. His character, work, and works were profoundly influential for good. In his kind, Butler was not for an age but for all time. No more characteristic contribution has been made to Christian ethics by any English thinker than by him. Butler interpreted man to himself. He led the mind from Nature up to Nature's God. Butler's service to his age and future ages has been often appraised as if limited to that of morals only.

He was a Christian philosopher. There was a coherent system of thought underlying his teaching. He sought to justify the ways of God to man and found in things seen an analogy of things unseen and eternal. He was a metaphysician as well as an apologist. Among Christian philosophers he is classed with those who have expounded the argument for the existence of God as inferred from the works of God. Wesley followed him in offering in popular form the facts of natural theology, in his *Survey of the Wisdom of God in Creation*, and uses the idea of a chain, or linked sequence, in the stages and progressive development of Nature by God (*Survey of Creation*, iv. 72). We refer to this work later. Before the eighteenth century closed, William Paley (1743–1802) published his work, *Natural Theology, or the Evidences of the Existence and Attributes of the Deity*. This elaborated and illustrated Butler's argument along the lines of teleology, with instances of divine design in phenomena.[18] Butler presented the more inclusive argument from Cosmology in its threefold aspect: from observed effects to the ultimate Cause; from an order perceived by man in phenomena and himself to an Orderer or Designer; and from the moral and spiritual nature of man as a creature to God as Creator, the first and final Cause, Author and Finisher. Butler's volume, *Fifteen Sermons*, on Human Nature, &c., which contains the germs of his later more famous work, appeared in 1726. His *Analogy of Religion, Natural and Revealed, to the Constitution and Course of Nature*, appeared in 1736.[19] Only a few elect spirits were affected, in that century, by Butler's profound, closely reasoned statements. Wesley was then labouring as a clergyman in Georgia.

It is when he deals with the moral nature of man, the conscience, that Butler displays his genius.[14] Wesley and Methodist preachers appealed to that court with unequalled power, and strikingly enforced Butler's argument. Butler claimed supremacy for conscience, that it has the highest value of all the parts of man's nature. None excels him in maintaining this august claim. Without consultation or advice, conscience majestically and magisterially exerts itself in man, and approves or condemns, says Butler (*Works*, i. 45). His impressive language takes on solemn splendour as he moves in the high court of Man-soul. He figures the principles of action standing together in the nature of man. As Shakespeare says, ' The genius and the mortal instruments are then in council.' One of these bears upon it the marks of authority over the others. It claims the absolute direction of them all, and allows, or forbids, their gratification. ' Neither can any human creature,' says Butler, ' be said to act conformably to his constitution or nature, unless he allows to that superior principle the absolute authority which is due to it (*Works*, i., Preface).[15] In the moral and spiritual nature of man Butler found also implications towards the existence of man after the cessation of his life on earth. There is the starting-point of the analogy he drew between religion and nature : ' I shall begin with that which is the foundation of all our hopes and of all our fears ; of all our hopes and fears, which are of any consideration ; I mean a future life.'

Butler was aware of the problems which his argument involved.[16] He knew, as few men have known, the imperfect, ruined condition of the nature of mankind, as seen in his day. He was amazed

and ashamed, as was St. Paul, and as Newman
was in the century succeeding that of Butler, at
the exceeding sinfulness of sinners. Butler's terse,
quiet literary style cannot prevent his exclamation
at the perfidy and guilt of Balaam and David. As
he knew them, men disappointed Butler; but man
as designed by God was, Butler held, God's noblest
work, made in His image and·a finite, faint resemblance of his Maker.[17]

Butler and Wesley

Wesley was much impressed by Butler's writings.
He thought the *Analogy*, read in 1746, ' a strong,
well-written treatise'; but he feared that it was
far too deep for the understanding of those to
whom it was primarily addressed. He read again
' that fine book,' as he styled it; but had still the
same fears for, as he said, ' *Freethinkers*, so called,
are seldom *close* thinkers.'

Earlier than this, however, in the first year of
his evangelistic journeyings (1739), Wesley had his
famous interview with Butler, then Bishop of
Bristol. In that year Wesley preached irregularly
in the open air at Bristol, and established a religious
society of Methodists in that city, as he had done
in London. The record of these interviews with
Butler existed for long in Wesley's handwriting.
The recently discovered Diaries of Wesley corroborate the well-known account (*Journal*, ii. 256).
This bears every mark of verisimilitude. Butler
and Wesley are completely characteristic throughout the records. Wesley had sought his advice
on his work as a clergyman, and Butler used the
opportunity to discuss the teaching and procedure
of Wesley. They could not agree as to the function

and power of the Holy Spirit in the mind of man, nor upon Wesley's work in the diocese which Butler ruled, where Wesley had no clerical appointment. 'I advise you to go hence,' said Butler. Wesley understood that his ordination as Fellow of a College (Lincoln, Oxford University), empowered him to preach in any part of the Church of England. He believed that he was obeying a divine prompting in ministering in Bristol. 'Therefore, here I stay,' said Wesley. Within a short time of the interview remarkable results followed upon his labours and those of his brother Charles. These were seen in the religious enlightenment of many, and in the moral reformation of not a few in the city and in the neighbouring colliery district of Kingswood. Butler knew well the need for this, there and elsewhere. He remained for eleven further years as Bishop of Bristol. Perhaps the exceptional progress of Wesley's work in that district during that period owed something to Butler's non-interference with the unconventional methods which the Wesleys were constrained to employ.

It is a pathetic and significant fact that the religious experience of Bishop Butler furnished evidence of the need of that experiential knowledge of God in Christ which Wesley then enjoyed, and was offering to man by his preaching and work, as we show in later chapters. Butler had not until his dying hours the spiritual confidence, the rest of faith in God, which is the chief gift of religion. Butler found the insufficiency of reasoning to sustain the human spirit when called to meet death, 'the shadow feared of man.' Butler said to his chaplain, Forster, 'Though I have endeavoured to avoid sin, and to please God to the utmost of my power, yet from consciousness of

IN THE EIGHTEENTH CENTURY 31

perpetual infirmities, I am still afraid to die.' 'My Lord,' said the chaplain, 'you have forgotten that Jesus Christ is a Saviour.' 'True,' said Butler, 'but how shall I know that He is a Saviour for me?' 'My Lord, it is written, "Him that cometh unto Me I will in no wise cast out."' 'True,' said Butler, 'and I am surprised that though I have read that scripture I suppose a thousand times over, I never felt its virtue till this moment. And now I die happy.'¹⁸

Typical Conditions in Wesley's England

Butler died at Bath. That city, like its neighbour, Bristol, then the largest English city except London, was a microcosm of English life, indeed of civilized life. There, and throughout the country and the world, men and women needed the light and comfort of Jesus Christ; and these, not for the hour and article of death alone, but for life, with its struggles and duties, sin and sorrow. A few people in each of those centres were intellectual, inquisitive, witty, and brilliant. With few exceptions, they were ignorant of the sources of spiritual light and power. Gay and fashionable people were more numerous. Their plight was worse in these respects. They wanted they knew not what. Around the intellectual and fashionable there were multitudes of neglected people for whom none seemed to care; they were without God and without hope in the world. Fear was the dominant motive. Gross superstitions swayed all classes. Few people could read. 'I offered them books, but they could not read,' Wesley wrote pitifully in his weekly London letter, concerning the mixed crowd at Bath when he had his encounter with the notorious Beau Nash in that city.¹⁰ 'It is time for Thee, O Lord, to work!' said the Hebrew psalmist, in like conditions. God wrought a wonderful work for England and the world in giving Wesley to enlighten and enliven men of reason and religion and the common people also. The latter heard him gladly. As Wesley moved onward to maturity and grand old age, he was certain that substantial improvement occurred in the nation as a whole. In love of neighbour, e.g. compassion and benevolence, in religious liberty, Christian tolerance and in civil liberty; above all, in the essential of real Christianity, which is love of God, Wesley recorded his convinced judgement that no former time since the Apostles left the earth had been better than his own, nor comparable to it in several respects (*Works*, vii. 165). He dared to claim (*circa* 1787) that Methodism was a signal instance of the goodness of God in that age (*Sermon* cii.).

This is not the place to describe general conditions of life in England when Wesley thought, and laid the foundations of world-wide Methodism.* A few further facts may be given, indicative of the conditions he had to face. Nearly half the land was uncultivated. Much was not used for any purpose, and was unenclosed. Large tracts were forest, undrained fen or wild waste land, without divisions, paths or roads. Made roads were very few. After the middle of the century, turnpike road acts were passed; but it was not until the nineteenth century that Macadam and such highway engineers built roads like those we know. Travelling—and Wesley was an incessant

* See Vol. V. *Social England*, by Traill and Mann. A summary is given in *A New History of Methodism*, I. chap. i.

traveller—was difficult, dangerous, and uncomfortable to a degree scarcely credible. The population was small and scattered. The people lived chiefly in hamlets, villages, and small towns. The population of England and Wales in 1742 was six millions and a half, say one-fifth of the present inhabitants, and fewer by a million than the present inhabitants of London and its suburbs.

In the pages which follow we consider Wesley in his unified activities of Christian Philosopher and Church Founder. These were closely related. He was neither of these without the other. His influence upon his age and since, in his own land and the world, arose from the use by God of the genius of Wesley in his combination of Christian thinker and church leader.

John Wesley, M.A. *Fellow of Lincoln College* OXFORD
Chaplain to the Right Hon.ble the Countess Dowager of BUCHAN.
Done from an Original Picture in the Possession of Thos. Wooldridge Esq.r of East Florida.
LONDON; Printed for ROB.T SAYER, Map & Printseller, N°.53 in Fleet Street. Publish'd as the Act directs, 20th Dec.r 1770.

(See note in appendix)

BOOK I

WESLEY AS A CHRISTIAN PHILOSOPHER

Christianity has penetrated more deeply into the essence of man than any agency previously offered to his mind; has opened up in him new depths; has added to him a new intensity. . . . The thought of man (through the Incarnation) has become habituated to the clearer and nearer contemplation of the Deity, and a new relation, mental as well as spiritual, and highly fertile in results, has been established between the Creator and the creature.—W. E. GLADSTONE, *Butler, Subsidiary Studies.*

Christ has revealed the glory of God which unfolds the meaning of the world, and has inspired the filial consciousness which responds to and manifests it. This twofold gift not only provides the only explanation of the universe, but shows how all the principles of successful thought and action in regard to it are fragments of the complete Truth and Life revealed to man in the incarnate Son of God.—THE REV. J. SCOTT LIDGETT, M.A., D.D. *Fatherhood of God in Christian Truth and Life.*

WESLEY AS A CHRISTIAN PHILOSOPHER

I

THE NEW LIGHT ON WESLEY AND HIS QUEST FOR GOD

WESLEY is now to be considered as a Christian thinker.[10] In this, and in all aspects, much about him has been learned recently.

Many persons become acquainted with Wesley through his incomparable *Journal*.[11] That great work, probably the best single account of English life in the eighteenth century, is largely occupied with Wesley's activities and his opinions on men and things and religious endeavour. It reveals much; but it leaves much untold as to the inner life and personality of the writer of the amazing record. Wesley knew that this was so. What he wrote in his seventy-fourth year had been true of him for thirty years, and was to be true for more than fourteen further years. He said that people did not understand his manner of life. 'It is true I travel four or five thousand miles a year; but I generally travel alone in my carriage, and consequently am as retired ten hours in a day as if I were in a wilderness. On other days I never spend less than three hours, frequently ten or twelve in a day alone.' This was as true of him when he travelled on horseback. It should be remembered that Wesley's 'day' had in it eighteen hours. He rose each morning at four, and retired at ten at night. Sometimes these hours varied; but the length of the day was almost never less, and this during about sixty years. Even this measure of retirement and solitude did not suffice him. He secured periods of deeper quiet, like Jesus Christ, of whom it is written that He retired to lonely places and prayed. There were several delightful country homes to which Wesley retired from travel and toil, like the residence of his chief lay friend, the London banker, Ebenezer Blackwell, at 'The Limes,' Lewisham. Even 'noisy thoughts' were forbidden to interrupt him. Wesley himself, the man behind the activities, can only be understood through his cipher or shorthand diaries. His religious vows were often literally fulfilled, as this : ' To dedicate an hour, morning and evening ; no excuse, reason or pretence ; to pray every hour, seriously, deliberately.'[11] The most frequent entry in this Methodist's record, sometimes six times in a day, is ' prayed ' ; ' sang ' is the next most frequently used ; 'meditated' occurs often. These items occur daily, and year by year. They prove, beyond doubt, Wesley's capacity for, and abundant use of, thought, and this in solitude —that mother country of the strong.'[12] 'No one lived nearer the centre than John Wesley,' says Mr. Augustine Birrell. It may be added that few men have lived so much at the centre. For Wesley this centre was God in Christ. There he gathered knowledge by experience ; there, also, he formulated his implications as to Reality.

The experience of Wesley included endeavours to find reasons for his own belief in God. He fought his doubts, and gathered strength ; he would not make his reason blind. He speaks

from his experience in this as on other matters.
In his early years he knew the wistful yearning
and agony of spirit which shakes every earnest
seeker for a reasoned faith. Of himself as such a
seeker, Wesley drew a vivid picture. 'After carefully heaping up the strongest arguments which I
could find either in ancient or modern authors for
the very being of God, and (which is nearly connected with it) the existence of an invisible world,
I have wandered up and down, musing with myself:
" What if all these things which I see around me,
this earth and heaven, this universal frame, has
existed from eternity? What if that melancholy
supposition of the old poet be the real case,

οἵη περ φύλλων γενεή, τοιή δὲ καὶ ἀνδρῶν ?

What if 'the generation of men be exactly
parallel with the generation of leaves'?—if the
earth drops its successive inhabitants just as the
tree drops its leaves? What if the saying of a
great man be really true,

Post mortem nihil est ; ipsaque mors nihil ?—
Death is nothing ; and nothing is after death?

How am I sure this is not the case? that I have
not followed cunningly-devised fables?"' Wesley
added, 'I have pursued the thought till there was
no spirit left in me, and I was ready to choose
strangling rather than life' (*Works*, vi. 356).
This desperate experience bred in Wesley tender
sympathy with all sincere seekers after truth.
The prayer which he composed for them (*Works*,
viii. 200) had been his own heart's cry : ' O Thou
Lover of men, is there no help in Thee?' This
help he found at length, and offered it to others in

experiential philosophy. He became that rare combination—an evangelical rationalist, a philosopher and an evangelist. His logic was on fire.

New Light on Wesley

These movements of Wesley's mind, with his attainment of steadfast peace and radiant gladness, can now be traced as never before. The decipherment of Wesley's cipher and shorthand diaries recently, the publication of new letters by him, and of important parts of others hitherto withheld,[14] and the disclosure of fresh facts, with closer study of manuscripts and documents written by or concerning Wesley, have given us what may be called a new Wesley. Perhaps he contemplated such a re-emergence. He burned many papers and letters in 1765; adding, ' Perhaps some of the rest may see the light when I am gone.' His diaries and original memoranda were written in curiously contracted words, a forgotten shorthand,[15] and an ingeniously constructed cipher, which he changed with irritating frequency. He left no complete key to his cipher and abbreviations. But he left the diaries in which he used all these devices for privacy.[16] This fact is a complete answer to those who think that Wesley's hiding-place of his deepest self should not have been violated. A penman so skilful as he was, and a reader so keen, knew well that what one man hides another can find. Any cipher can be deciphered. Wesley feared no disclosures. As was said of his later relative, the famous Duke of Wellington, ' Whatever record leaps to light, he never shall be shamed.' * Wesley published his thoughts as few

* The Wesleys and Wellesleys were of the same stock. The Duke of Wellington (Wellesley) styled himself Arthur Wesley for many years.

men have done. But he also left behind him the materials from which they were worked up; the records of the stages of his development; the scaffolding of his city of Mansoul. Curnock's decipherment of the diaries is a devout literary romance. Those of us who follow as his helpers are not such as would expose a father, or peep and botanize upon a mother's grave. The new Wesley is greater, more comprehensible and inspirational, than was the old. He is a more significant fact for our knowledge of God, of the mind of Christ, and the creating, renewing Spirit.

When Wesley is allowed in this way to utter the thoughts of his heart, and the *apparatus criticus* of the evolutionary method and the new psychology are applied to him and his character, a different impression of Wesley is received. There is no lessened sense of the divinity within him, in measure more than in most of the sons of men. Truly he was a religious genius. Moreover, the range and combination of his gifts and interests made him a citizen of the world,—

> A man so various that he seemed to be
> Not one, but all mankind's epitome.

His self-sacrifice and altruism have seldom been excelled. The new Wesley is all this. But he is now seen as completely human also: a man of like passions with all men. He was in all points tempted like they are; nor was he always without sin. He was strangely gullible, as even his earliest biographers admit; he was also very fallible, which some have hitherto scarcely allowed. In the light poured from his secret records, now made available, Wesley is not less impressive, but he is more lovable. He is better understood, more attractive as a personality, more helpful as a leader, than before. Some lives of him left one wondering how a man so sacrosanct, automatic, and autocratic, could secure anything more than cold respect and slavish obedience. When it is learned that Wesley had a frail body, with almost as many ailments as ' holy Mr. Baxter,' whom he admired, and was always fighting for health, and often for life ; that in early manhood he was sometimes guilty of practices which he bemoaned in deep penitence ; that he had several affairs of the heart, and was for thirty years the pure, but not always the wise and discreet, husband of the suspicious, jealous woman whom he chose, or accepted, so hastily ; that he lived nearly eighty-eight years, during more than fifty of which he discharged such a tale of toil and travel as is unequalled in world history ; that he became the embodiment of shining, happy serenity with incessant activity, and such utter truthfulness and unblamableness that a nation rested upon his words, and even his strange wife died ' in love and friendship ' towards him,—when these facts are revealed and remembered, Wesley takes on the charm of novelty, and fascinates all sorts and conditions of men. A distinguished Methodist historian, the late Rev. H. B. Kendall, B.A., uttered the experience of many general students. He said, ' I have had to unlearn Wesley that I might learn him better.'

This is not the place to enlarge upon Wesley's reasons and methods in thus hiding and also perpetuating himself by his cipher and shorthand, and the contracted words of his diaries. The handwritten little books—some of them used for several purposes, worked from front to back and back to front with impressive economy of space and paper

—fulfil Milton's description of a good book. They contain ' the precious life-blood of a master-spirit, embalmed and treasured up on purpose to a life beyond life.' For the purpose of this study of Wesley and his philosophy of Christian Experience they are invaluable. They contain and yield up to constant study the results of his verifications in religious and Christian experience and the implications which he drew therefrom. The experimental philosopher is there seen at work upon facts of the spiritual life. Wesley came to know many persons. Few have known so many, especially as to the thoughts of their hearts, with the stages and processes of their spiritual development. Of these he was indeed an interpreter, one among a thousand. He began with a painstaking study and understanding of himself, and the responsive beatings of his own spirit toward God in Christ."

II

WESLEY'S LIFE AND WORK OUTLINED, WITH HIS QUALIFICATIONS AS PHILOSOPHER

(*i.*) *Biographic Notes*

THE chief facts of the life, work, and character of Wesley as a Christian philosopher are of importance in a study of his experience. John Wesley was born at Epworth, Lincolnshire, in 1703, and died in London in 1791. His lengthy life almost covered the century, and was passed under four monarchs —Anne, and George I, II, and III. He was the son of Samuel Wesley, a clergyman of the Established Church, and his wife Susanna. He was their fifteenth child and fifth son. John Wesley graduated at Oxford, was Fellow of Lincoln College, Greek Lecturer and President of Disputations in that University; and the leader, though not the founder, of the Holy Club, a group of earnest students there. They were afterwards called Methodists. Ordained a clergyman, Wesley was his father's curate at Epworth and Wroot. Later, he was a missionary in Savannah, Georgia, U.S.A., then a British colony, for two years. He returned to England, where he passed through a spiritual crisis in London in 1738. He soon formed several religious societies of members of the Established

Church, and others who were unattached. These societies he drew into a connexion in 1739, as the United Society of Methodists. For more than fifty years he itinerated throughout the British Isles." He preached in the open air, in churches when permitted, and in chapels, and organized his followers for religious fellowship and redemptive service. London, Bristol, and Newcastle-upon-Tyne [10] were points of his almost ceaseless triangular evangelistic tours in the south, west, and north of England. Ireland and Scotland were frequently visited. In the cities above-named he held conferences with clergymen, his preachers, and lay leaders of religion. Each of these centres had its library of standard works in divinity, natural philosophy, and history. Wesley trained his preachers there, and was guide, philosopher, and friend to people of all ranks and conditions. He was consulted on almost every possible subject. In 1775 the British Government distributed his pamphlet (adapted from Dr. Johnson's *Taxation no Tyranny*), entitled by Wesley *A Calm Address to our American Colonies*. British colonial history would have been worthier had Lord North answered wisely the letter which Wesley addressed to him. ' Is it common sense to use force towards the Americans ? ' Wesley asked. His long-continued labours and noble character caused him to be venerated by all. To many he was truly a right reverend father in God.

With his brother, Charles Wesley, also a clergyman and evangelist, and the hymn-writer and poet of the movement, Wesley issued rules of membership and discipline for the Methodists. These rules were followed by standards of teaching for preachers whom he called out and appointed to Methodist chapels. Some of these preachers he ordained, first for the work in America, and later for Scotland and England. Thereby he violated ecclesiastical law, since he was only a presbyter of the Church of England. In 1784 he enrolled a deed in the High Court of Chancery, which constituted an annual conference of his preachers as the sole ecclesiastical authority for their work in Methodist circuits, and apart from the Church of England. At the time of his death his followers numbered one hundred and twenty thousand in England and America, with five hundred and eleven preachers, separated for the Methodist work.[11] Wesley was thus the chief human leader of the Evangelical Revival of Religion in the eighteenth century. A general moral and mental quickening, with social reforms, accompanied or resulted from the Revival. England was thereby saved from the horrors of the French Revolution, which occurred towards the close of that century. Such a catastrophe being avoided, the nation entered upon a period of rapid progressive development and world-wide expansion.

The chief facts of Wesley's physique and many ailments should be always borne in mind. They are significant in this present study. All accounts show that in his young manhood he was a prince charming. 'Who can be sad where you are?' wrote his sister Mary to him when he was twenty-five. In his prime his countenance was singularly impressive and arresting. In old age he was a picture of radiant serenity. Like all the Wesleys, he was short in stature and slight in build.[12] His father baptized him before he was a day old, fearing his very early death. At the Charterhouse School, London, and at Lincoln College, Oxford, he had all the signs of pulmonary decline. His was a little, frail, consumptive body." He had small-pox, and thrice suffered fever. A crisis occurred when he was fifty-one. He went to Bristol expecting to die there of consumption. When over seventy years old he was for days ' more dead than alive,' and only recovered after a surgical operation. Like his parents, he suffered frequently from gout, although he was always an abstemious man, and practised self-reverence and control. Sixty-nine attacks of sickness are recorded by Wesley in his *Journal* and Diary. Many of these attacks were serious. These facts are significant for students of Wesley's philosophy. He had a gospel for man's body. It should be added that Wesley's wit, good humour and hilarity, on occasion, delighted all who met him. Only lately has much been said of these attractive aspects. For long the many instances of his playful good humour and wit were little used, lest his reputation for saintliness might suffer. So thought Thomas Walsh, the illustrious Hebrew scholar and evangelist in Ireland, who rebuked Wesley on this account. As a fact, by his unruffled temper and gladness, Wesley reflected and commended ' the glorious good news of the happy God.' " His abounding charity is well known. He begged of the rich, that he might give to the deserving poor. In this way and by many personal economies he was able to distribute £30,000 to the needy. His courteous pity enhanced his gifts. One of the most affecting sights of the closing years of the eighteenth century is that of Wesley, then eighty-two years of age, tramping the streets of London for five days in January 1785, while they were ankle-deep in snow, collecting £200 with which to provide clothes for the poor.

48 WESLEY, PHILOSOPHER AND FOUNDER

He had no children, but he loved children and young people greatly. This is often overlooked. The severity of his century and of his early arrangements for children, as at his Kingswood school, was replaced in his later life by exquisite tenderness, and, on occasion, by playfulness with children. He was remarkably skilful and tactful in his management of men. He was not always as successful in his relations with women, to whom he uniformly displayed courtesy and Christian chivalry. He sometimes lacked discretion and occasionally was duped. His letters to Lady Maxwell and the Countess of Huntingdon were models in their kind. So are those to Miss Ritchie, to whom he commended as example William Law's ideal lady, ' Miranda.' In 1768 Wesley accepted appointment, along with two other clergymen, Venn and Berridge, as a chaplain to the Countess Dowager of Buchan. It is probable that the poet Cowper met Wesley. His comprehensive tribute, given in his poem, ' Conversation,' is too little known.* Wesley, he says, was :

>   A veteran warrior in the Christian field,
>   Who never saw the sword he could not wield ;
>   Grave without dullness, learnéd without pride,
>   Exact, though not precise, though meek, keen-eyed.
>   Who, when occasion justified its use,
>   Had wit as bright as ready to produce ;
>   Could fetch from records of an earlier age,
>   Or from philosophy's enlightened page,
>   His rich materials, and regale your ear
>   With strains it was a privilege to hear.

Only Dr. Johnson compares with Wesley in universality of appeal in that century. His only complaint against Wesley was that the Methodist could not give him enough of his engaging company and

* Applied to Wesley (Coke and Moore's *Life*) eight years before Cowper's death.

conversation. 'The dog enchants you, but he always has an appointment and must leave,' said Johnson; 'I could talk all night with him.'

Wesley was a magnetic, compelling personality. Leadership was his by nature and was naturally ceded to him by most people. His brothers and sisters turned to him for guidance or deliverance, although he was almost the youngest in a large family. Charles puts us upon a secret when he writes of a time when John 'was casting his spell over me.' As I have shown elsewhere,* strong-willed men, different in disposition as bluff Captain Webb the Bristol soldier, John Nelson the Yorkshire stonemason, and Alexander Mather the London baker, looked on Wesley with something akin to awe, and followed him with a dog-like devotion. The explanation of all this is at once simple and profound. Wesley was an exceptional human personality, directed by a sincere purpose and empowered by the Holy Spirit. His one aim constantly, at least after 1738, was the service of God in the service of mankind. Had any purpose less worthy been his, other ways to place and power, easier and more direct, were open to him. It is in vain that any one seeks to account for Wesley's influence as due to his vanity or ambition. One comes upon the repetition nowadays of such grave misrepresentations and exploded accusations, and worse, with astonishment. The late Rev. S. Baring-Gould, in his work issued in 1920, entitled *The Evangelical Revival*, is guilty of lapses from good taste, and of misstatements and insinuations which are unpardonable. The facts which suffer gravely at his hands are abundant, and were easily available. He seemed to be totally ignorant of

* See the introductions to chaps. v. and viii., *Letters of John Wesley* (1915).

D

50 WESLEY, PHILOSOPHER AND FOUNDER

the correspondence between Bishop Gibson and Bishop Secker with Wesley, and the effects produced by Wesley's explanations. Baring-Gould's commendations of Wesley must be appraised accordingly." The explanations given by Wesley of what he was and what he sought to do are those which we have given above, and which are stated more fully in later pages.

A Student's Tribute

As a student of Wesley and his work during many years, the writer ventures to pay his humble tribute to his human hero, and to offer thanks to God for the reception of spiritual and mental stimulus, sustainment in service, and hours of recreative pleasure by contact with Wesley's records. Every year adds meaning to some words written ten years ago. ' As one among the thousands of preachers who serve the commonwealth of Methodism in its several branches in many lands and carry on the work of its human founder, Wesley, I was drawn into wondering admiration of him and his work, and began to feel the spell and stimulus of his character. Since then, helped by many whom I hold in grateful remembrance, I have learned to think of him, not as he is often regarded and misrepresented—as an autocrat, immaculate, a plaster saint, and almost infallible —but far otherwise : as a young, growing man, struggling, sinning, sorrowing, praying, moving upward and onward by divine help ; as in his later days mounting to self-mastery and shining serenity ; as high and lifted up, a genius and a dedicated spirit, but also as glad and humorous, a creature not too bright and good to be followed afar off, in so far as he followed Christ, by the humblest. His strong, gravely-beautiful face looks down upon me in many forms from my study walls, and he seems to sing his living and dying faith, mingled of humility and confidence :

> I the chief of sinners am,
> But Jesus died for me ;

and anon to utter one of his golden counsels : " Never be unemployed ; never be triflingly employed ; never while away time." ' *

(ii.) Wesley's Qualifications, Equipment, and Methods as Philosopher

It is important to establish the claim of Wesley as a philosopher of Christian Experience. He held that Christian philosophy, whatever may be thought of the pagan, could not be more properly defined than in Plato's words. It is θεραπεία ψυχῆς, ' the only true method of healing a distempered soul (*Works*, ix. 194). Granted that Wesley's knowledge of God in Christ was exceptional in quality and range, was he able to appreciate and state its worth and implications ? As a modern pioneer in the use of the Baconian method of induction in spiritual affairs, he collated many instances of Christian experience. What equipment had he for making generalizations, and what were the methods employed by him ? Here we suggest answers to these pertinent questions.

His Critical Temper

Wesley's qualifications in this regard were natural, acquired, and experiential. He was

* From the Preface, *Letters of John Wesley* (1915). The reader is invited to look at the portrait of Wesley given as frontispiece of the present work. It is the most graciously   man of all his many portraits.

naturally critical, not to say sceptical. Hence he feared, for himself, the effect of mathematical methods when applied to spiritual facts (*Works*, vi. 128). He was not naturally disputatious, but even as a child he required a reason for everything he did. He liked to accumulate facts and formulate a theory for their explanation. This philosophic temper never ceased in Wesley. Inanimate, sub-human, human, super-human, spiritual, angelic and demoniac phenomena all held him as their student, and this throughout his long life. He was among the first divines to investigate electricity after Franklin's discovery. He was the first to set up centres in London where the poor could test its curative powers without payment. Those who know not Wesley as he really was say that he seldom noticed scenery, and that his ' passion for souls ' excluded every other interest." The fact is that this passion kept alive and employed every faculty in him, and used every item of knowledge he gathered. All was needed, if he was to understand something of God, and help all men. He noticed many landscapes and beautiful gardens, and delighted in hearing oratorios by masters of music. He was no mere iconoclast. ' God deliver us from reforming mobs ! ' he exclaimed, as he paced the ruins of stately Arbroath Abbey. At Edinburgh, and at the Tower of London, Wesley went to see the effects of music upon wild beasts, and at Coolalough he noticed the behaviour of horses under it. At the opening of Bristol fair in 1790, when he was eighty-seven, he preached to his followers upon the counsel, ' Buy the truth and sell it not,' and later went to study the natural history of a ' monster ' on exhibition in the fair, described it carefully, and offered his theory as to its origin. Few writers employ the note of interrogation as frequently as does Wesley. He systematically conducted his conferences and inquiries, and much of his correspondence, by question and answer." 'Confessions of an inquiring spirit,' is a fitting title for many thousands of his pages.

Equipment and Experience

Wesley's natural critical temper was developed and equipped by training and experience as scholar and teacher at Oxford University. His mind became a polished instrument, quick and powerful, sharp as a two-edged sword. His investigations proceeded by negative and positive discrimination. Logic he called ' this honest art,' and thanked God that he was able by it to disentangle falsities and expose sophistries, as in his famous bouts with Bishop Warburton. He thought logic an essential part of clerical training. He drilled many students in it at Oxford, where he was moderator in the disputations (*Works*, x. 353). As shown in the next section, Wesley studied the chief works on ethics and metaphysics. He commended Socrates, that ' Christian before Christ,' for his strong understanding and consummate virtue. Plato was expounded to German students by Wesley. Augustine, Aquinas, Bacon, Grotius, were all used by him. Wesley admired the strong understanding of Hobbes, but detested his materialistic and egoistic theories. Wesley thought Hutcheson's *Synopsis Metaphysicae* ' a masterly thing.' He advised students to use Malebranche's *Recherche de la Vérité* (Search after Truth). He admired greatly, and republished, that ' masterpiece of reason and religion ' by John Norris, an Oxford follower of

Plato and Descartes, entitled *Reflections upon the Conduct of Human Life with Reference to Learning and Knowledge*. Wesley also republished much of the work of John Smith, the Cambridge Platonist, with cordial approval of his declaration that happiness comes from ' a true conjunction of the mind with God in a secret feeling of His goodness and reciprocation of affection to Him.' Every student of philosophy enjoys Wesley's appreciation of the epochal *Essay on the Human Understanding*, by John Locke (*Works*, xiii.). That Wesley differed from Locke on some points, and also from the theory of Bishop Peter Browne, which we notice later, shows that Wesley had the temper common to philosophers. He had his own theory and frankly preferred it. However, he declined to admit that he was dogmatical ; nor was he, except upon the essentials of religion.

A Genius for Religion

The richness, range, and strength of Wesley's religious nature, with the moral, emotional, and spiritual experiences through which he passed, were his highest qualification and equipment as a Christian philosopher. It is strictly true that ' he had a genius for religion.' There was in him in large measure, although an Englishman, that awareness of and susceptibility to spiritual realities, which is characteristic of the Hebrew, as seen in characters of Holy Scripture and elsewhere. His religious intuitions were remarkably alert and vigorous, and recall those of St. John ; while his dialectical skill often reminds one of that of St. Paul. Almost anywhere and at all times, Wesley found it easy to realize the presence of Infinite

LIFE AND QUALIFICATIONS

Holiness and Goodness, and to worship Him. He wrote and sang:

<blockquote>Lo! God is here! Let us adore."</blockquote>

This was a characteristic mood. The movements of his spiritual nature in the presence of God, and the effect of other human spirits upon his own spirit, were matters of the highest and deepest import to him. All were duly recorded. He lived in a world of spiritual concerns. As will be shown, he had remarkable experiences of this kind, his evangelical conversion being among the chief. Happily, he was sane, level-headed, and severely practical. While his essential nature was not of this world of time and sense, he remembered that he was in a world where body, soul, and spirit must each and all take duty.

An Example of his Dialectics

A valuable example of Wesley's ability and method as a philosopher may be noticed here, as it is not closely relevant to the facts of religious experience, referred to later, upon which Wesley based his implications as to the Being and Nature of God. This instance is Wesley's own account of the emotional crisis in his life which occurred at Newcastle-upon-Tyne in 1749. The record is virtually his diary of events in his life for fourteen months, August 1748 to October 1749. It is contained in a manuscript preserved in the British Museum, London." The work of an amanuensis, and written in 1788, while Wesley was still alive, it has corrections and additions in Wesley's handwriting, and is an authentic and valuable human document. It is an account of the courtship of Wesley and Mrs. Grace Murray, a widow lady who was in charge of Wesley's Newcastle centre and hostel for himself and his preachers. This lady seems to have been in every way suitable as a wife for Wesley. His love of her was strong and pure : her love of him was of the same character. Through the intervention of Wesley's brother Charles, Grace Murray was married to John Bennet, one of Wesley's preachers. The importance of the document for our purpose is its proof of Wesley's dialectical skill, and of his fearlessness and fullness as a recorder of emotional and religious experience. Few documents exist of its kind which show equal analytic skill exercised by a mind upon itself. Descartes' *Meditations* afford points of comparison. Wesley deals here with primary emotions, impulses, motives, human frailties, and aspirations towards the ideal. If a man was ever able to take himself to pieces with completeness, while remaining intact as investigator, Wesley here achieves the feat. He is seen as remorselessly analytic, as he pursues cause, desire, reason, and result down all the labyrinthine ways of his own mind. Thirty-two paragraphs are filled with reasons for and against his proposed marriage. He deals similarly with the mind of Grace Murray, as far as her earlier diary, correspondence, and statements to him permitted. More important than the display of Wesley's power as analyst is his power as synthesist. All through this subtle study it is evident that he is in quest of a reason for all events. He is seeking wholeness and unity as the cause and interpretation of his experience. All the events which he chronicles, trifling or momentous, ordinary or tragic, past or expected, are evidently regarded by

LIFE AND QUALIFICATIONS

Wesley as items in a divine design or purpose which embraced his discipline and perfecting. All are seen as controlled and appointed, or at least as permitted, by God, to occur to Wesley and to those who are in harmony with that purpose. At the head of this document stand these words, which confess his submissive faith in Deity: 'What Thou doest I know not now, but I shall know hereafter.' At the close of Wesley's poetic version of these events in thirty-one six-line stanzas, are these lines, which show his philosophy and highest aspiration:

> Beneath Thy chast'ning hand I bow:
> That still I live, to Thee I owe.
>
> Be Thou my never failing Friend,
> And love, O love me to the end.

Students of this document as an instance of Wesley's powers of mind, emotion, conscience, and spirit will endorse Dr. Leger's comment that 'God was the lasting, absorbing passion of Wesley.'

His Documenting

This manuscript calls for another note. It is an example of Wesley as diarist, and especially as recorder of intimate experience, of himself and of others. This is one of some thousands of similar human documents which Wesley prepared, or required others to prepare. 'Writ narrative' is an entry which occurs several times a week in his own daily diary. These narratives by Wesley and others had in many instances every quality of first-hand evidence and testimony. They were written within a short time, often a few hours, of the occurrence of the events recorded, by the chief actors or subjects. They have vividness, with full details as to persons, occasion, time, circumstances, and supposed cause of the experience. Often they throb with actuality, and are as convincing as to their truthfulness as a well-drawn portrait. It should be added that such narratives were frequently read by Wesley to gatherings of people who were able to verify or correct many of the particulars included. 'Society, read narrative' is another frequent diary entry. It means that Wesley read in the presence of his Religious Society of Methodist followers an account of his own experience and that of others, which he had deemed worthy of expanding as a fact for his appeals and his philosophy. Generally, these accounts were printed soon afterwards in his *Journal* and later in his *Arminian Magazine*. From such immediate, tested, and attested facts Wesley drew his inductions and made his implications. With Lord Bacon, he held that men must be drawn away from the acceptance of preconceived notions to particular parts of experience. From these parts, tested and sufficiently numerous, the scientific investigator might pass to general truths. Butler argued from the facts of man's moral nature that the universe is a moral constitution. Wesley built upon the facts of Christian experience a Christian philosophy.

His Method and Hypothesis

This summary of Wesley's qualifications as a Christian philosopher indicates the features of his method, which will hereafter be illustrated. We can also gather from them an indication of the type to which he conforms as a thinker. Wesley's method had these features : observation, investigation, written record, comparison, and induction from experiments. He knew and acted upon Bacon's dictum (*Novum Organum*, Preface) ' not to dispute upon the very point of the possibility of any thing being known, but to put it to the test of experience.' It is admitted that he regulated and used his method upon a master principle or hypothesis; but every investigator is guided, more or less, by some principle or some assumption. This determines the facts to be investigated, and makes others of little or no significance for the investigator. Professor Sorley (*History of English Philosophy*) has shown that Bacon, the father of English experimental philosophy, misunderstood the true nature and function of hypothesis, upon which all scientific advances depend. Every philosophy rests upon certain assumptions. Descartes begins by recognizing the act of thinking—' *Cogito, ergo sum* '; Berkeley must needs accept spirits and ideas as real, although he will not allow that objects of knowledge, or ideas, exist except as they are perceived. Clarke takes it as proved that something exists. Wesley likewise accepted a basal principle in his investigations. True, like Anselm, Wesley never ceased his efforts to find support in knowledge for his faith, and to show that his assumption was not excluded by reason. It seems to the present student that Wesley's working hypothesis may be found in a statement in the remarkable preface which he issued, in 1747, with the first volume of his *Standard Sermons* (*Works*, v., Preface). There Wesley utters this impressive confession : ' I am a spirit come from God, and returning to God.' This simple but profound statement includes his belief as to the origin, nature, consciousness, and conscience of man, and the purpose of his existence. It assumes the existence of God, with His government and purpose. It is at once a metaphysic and an ethic. Here we believe we have the master light of all Wesley's seeing. This principle pilots him on his way and leads him onward in his thought and life. This will be shown later in these pages.*

(iii.) *A Mystical, Social, Inquiring Christian*

Can we discover the type to which Wesley's religious personality and philosophy conformed? The problem of classification in religion has always presented difficulties. The latest endeavour to solve it by Professor W. Adams Brown gathers the many varieties under three types, termed imperialism, individualism, and democracy.[10] It is recognized that these terms are not exclusive, and that an individual, while conforming in the main, and in a crisis, to one or other of these types, may show features which associate him with one or both of the remaining types. As a fact, this was the case with Wesley. In him the rationalist and the mystic, the individualist and the churchman, the soul which bows without question before external authority and is also a critical inquiring spirit, all had place. It was, however, the latter in each of these contrasted pairs which was strongest in him. He was more a mystic, a Christian mystic,[11] than a rationalist; more a churchman than an individualist; and his spirit was rather that of the free inquirer, at least as to all things human and all human aspects of divinity, than that of an acquiescent to human authority. Three of his

* Chapter v.

LIFE AND QUALIFICATIONS 61

characteristic phrases indicate the real Wesley. One of these is the line of a hymn, written by his brother Charles, and often used by both brothers. It links Wesley, and all who can use such words, with the mystical type and with intuitionalism. The line is a series of tremendous affirmations and implications concerning the direct contact of the human spirit and its Creator. The authentic Wesley speaks here:

> My God! I know, I feel Thee mine.⁴⁸

With equal definiteness Wesley indicated himself as a social seeker for truth, as one who felt that his findings must be confirmed by those of others. In his young manhood 'a serious man' bade Wesley remember that he could not serve God alone. He said, 'You must find companions or make them. The Bible knows nothing of solitary religion.' The group mind of the fellowship, the class, the Religious Society, or Church, had more weight with Wesley than his own judgement or that of any individual. The phrase, 'I, John Wesley,' appears in a few legal and other documents; while the name which he accepted for his followers was used by him many times, is still used, and has passed into many languages. It was this: The People called Methodists.⁴⁹ The third of these phrases uttered by Wesley which reveal him and help us to place him is the true philosophical maxim, 'Think and let think.' This demand was addressed to an Anglican bishop when Wesley was eighty-seven years old. And Wesley gave the liberty which he claimed. 'I never undertook to defend every sentence of Mr. Wesley's,' said Joseph Benson, the eminent Methodist preacher, scholar, and biblical commentator; 'he does not expect it or desire it. He wishes me, and every man, to think for himself.' Wesley recognized authority, divine and human. 'Eternal fitness' was an ultimate for him as it was for Samuel Clarke. The Bible, the faith of the universal Christian Church, the State, and the Family were authorities which Wesley recognized and obeyed. But to the end of his days he stood for the duties and rights of the mind and spirit of man, as self-conscious, free, and competent within the limitacions of its nature and of the divine design which it reveals. Dr. T. R. Glover, of Cambridge University, lately paid due tribute to Wesley as Church Founder and Christian Philosopher in placing him among those whom he styled four Intellectuals— St. Paul, Augustine, Luther, Wesley—through whom God ' put a new heart into English Christendom on both sides of the Atlantic ' (*Preaching of Christ*, p. 16).

III

THE LITERARY DOCUMENTS OF WESLEY AND HIS CHRISTIAN EXPERIENCE

THE literary works and publications of Wesley contain the records of his own religious and Christian experience and those of many others. From these he made his implications as to the existence and nature of God. His chief literary works are involved in our statement of his argument from Christian experience and his work as Church Founder. They must therefore be summarized and estimated. This is the more necessary as his literary works are not generally known, with the exception of his *Journal* and the Wesley hymns.

Wesley's literary style is more attractive than that of Bishop Butler. Now the style is the man. Clearness, strength, and flexibility are features of Wesley's style. Often it has dignity like that of John Howe or Burke. On occasion there is the solemn pleading pathos of Richard Baxter; sometimes the charm of Addison and the *Spectator* school." Even the satire and sting of Swift are used by Wesley, chiefly in his prefaces. Poetic and other quotations from the classics, ancient and modern, especially the Latin authors, and from Methodist hymns, gleam in his pages." He was an incessant reader. His witty summaries of books and authors show a scholar's catholic appreciation, regulated by a high standard of moral values. His literary model was his namesake in the New Testament : ' I love St. John's style, as well as matter.' He thought that no philosopher, poet, or orator ever chose his words so accurately as St. John. Leslie Stephen was a keen critic of Wesley and differed gravely from his interpretation of Christian experience ; but he admitted that Wesley clothed his thoughts with the plainest language, spoke of what he had seen, never beats the air or slays the dead, or mechanically repeats thrice-told stories, like most of his contemporaries. His arguments represent real thought upon questions of the deepest interest. Wesley's linguistic attainments must not be overlooked. He was skilful in the use of Latin, Greek, Hebrew, and German, and had a working knowledge of French and Spanish.

His Use of Literature

Wesley's philosophic mind and appeal are shown by his unequalled use of literature." He was the first leader of thought to employ the printed page on any such scale for an appeal to man as man. He says he aimed at candid, reasonable men : ' I design plain truth for plain people.' He tested the success of his preachers partly by their use of this mental appeal, and explained a decline of religion among the Methodists in 1768 by their neglect of good literature. In his old age, when the revival of religion had spread throughout the country and into all churches, Wesley related it to the preparatory efforts of the *Spectator*. ' God raised up Mr. Addison and his associates,' said Wesley, ' to lash the prevailing vices . . . and to show the excellence of Christianity and the Christian religion.' Several of Wesley's literary works, which will be often cited here, are now referred to briefly.

(i.) Wesley's 'Journal'

Wesley's *Journal* is an important item, and is widely known. It is indeed a classic in literature of its kind. It covers Wesley's active life from 1735 to 1790. Not to know this work is to be ignorant of one of the chief literary sources for a philosophy of human nature and its implications. Those who know the book best, and similar books, are ready to endorse the judgement of W. Robertson Nicoll: 'There is no book, I humbly think, in all the world, like John Wesley's *Journal*. It has very few companions. Indeed, it stands out solitary in Christian literature—clear, detached, columnar.' It contains many of Wesley's statements of his thoughts, feelings, motives, and decisions as to God and man, and also similar records concerning others. Religious dramas, tragedies and comedies in small, abound in it." Wesley's mind as he recorded these life-stories in his diaries, which he afterwards elaborated for his *Journal*, is evidently wide awake. His critical faculties are evident on almost every page; not less, his shrewd wit and good humour. It is true that he shared the interest of Johnson and other eminent persons of his century in ghost stories. He never disguises his point of view, nor his purpose in writing. He regards the universe as made by God and governed by Him; and men, women, and children as God's offspring, who find the justification of their being in His love, and their

E

well-being in responding to that love; which love is supremely manifested in Jesus Christ, and revealed to them and in them by His Holy Spirit.

(*ii.*) *His ' Appeals '*

The chief single original volume by Wesley, although not the largest by him, contains his *Appeal to Men of Reason and Religion*.⁴⁸ If the portrait of Wesley by John Williams, R.A., painted when Wesley was thirty-eight years of age, shows him as he began his work and bounded onward in his task of changing England, these appeals show his mind in its pristine vigour, his courage and candour, and the pure flame of his moral passion. Not less do they show his yearning pity. The supernatural resources and reliefs which he had found in Jesus Christ by His Spirit he was eager to share with his countrymen, indeed with all mankind. He felt, said, and sang his message, ' O let me commend my Saviour to you '⁴⁹ In his first *Appeal* Wesley quoted from his favourite among the lesser poets, Matthew Prior,* the results of this knowledge and love of God, and this Christian charity, or love, to mankind :

> Soft peace she brings, wherever she arrives,
> She builds our quiet, as she forms our lives;
> Lays the rough paths of peevish nature even,
> And opens in each heart a little heaven.⁵⁰

An impressive feature of this work for our present purpose is Wesley's constant appeal to reason. It would be difficult to find another writer, even in the eighteenth century—that century of reasoning—who more frequently uses this word and its cognates, and who is more prepared to stand

* The poet was a friend of Wesley's brother Samuel.

or fall by the dictates of reason. In Wesley's *Appeal to Men of Reason and Religion* the word is in the title, and the word and what it stands for is on every page. His philosophy is his religion, his religion is his philosophy. Such a statement as the following is not often cited. He asks, ' What do you mean by reason ? I suppose you mean the eternal reason, or nature of things : the nature of God and the nature of man, with the relations necessarily subsisting between them. Why, this is the very religion we preach : a religion evidently founded on, and every way agreeable to eternal reason, to the essential nature of things. Its foundation stands on the nature of God and the nature of man, together with their mutual relations. And it is in every way suitable thereto : to the nature of God, for it begins in knowing Him, and where but in the true knowledge of God can you conceive true religion to begin ? It goes on in loving Him and all mankind. It ends in serving Him, in doing His will.' And by religion, thus consonant with reason, Wesley means essential Christianity. He says so far as a man departs from true, genuine reason, so far he departs from Christianity (*Works*, viii. 12). Therefore Wesley indignantly repelled the charge made against him and his followers by Rutherforth, who said, ' It is a fundamental principle in the Methodist school that all who come into it must renounce their reason.' Wesley wrote thus in rebuttal, ' Sir, are you awake ? Unless you are talking in your sleep, how can you utter so gross an untruth ? It is a fundamental principle with us that to renounce reason is to renounce religion : that religion and reason go hand in hand, and that all irrational religion is false religion ' (*Works*, xiv. 359). Seldom have such statements by Wesley been given due attention. The claim, as here made, is supported by his work as Christian philosopher.

(*iii.*) *Letters to ' John Smith '*

In the same class of literary work as the *Appeals* by Wesley are a series of argumentative letters written by him in the years 1745 to 1748, in reply to ' Mr. John Smith ' (*Works*, xii.).[11] It is known that this is a *nom de plume*. It is believed that the original of it was Thomas Secker (1693–1768), Bishop of Oxford, afterwards Archbishop of Canterbury. The correspondence recalls that of Butler and Clarke ; but in this case it is the senior, Secker (if he it was), who remains anonymous. He had helped his friend, the youthful Butler, to maintain his cover of ' A gentleman in Gloucestershire,' when writing to Clarke. Wesley's letters to ' Mr. John Smith ' are a reasoned exposition of his teaching and his argument from experience, his own and that of others. These, to whom he refers in these letters, numbered more than twelve or thirteen hundred persons, whose evidence he had gathered. ' John Smith ' accused Wesley of ' having arrived, in his own imagination, at a sinless perfection.' Wesley replied, plain and 'home': ' I never told you so: I no more imagine that I have already attained . . . than that I am in the third heavens.'

(*iv.*) *' Rules' for Methodists*

The most significant piece of Wesley literature, in some ways, is the booklet entitled, *The Nature, Design, and General Rules of the United Societies*

LITERARY DOCUMENTS

in London, Bristol, Kingswood, and Newcastle-upon-Tyne (*Works,* viii.). This booklet shows the authentic Wesley—a logical, ethical, metaphysical thinker." He has rediscovered God as motive, author, means, and end of the universe. In this, a mere booklet, he offers a system of thought and conduct and a regimen by which others may enjoy experience similar to his own. He calls the members of the Methodist societies therein described and regulated, ' men having the form, and seeking the power, of godliness,' i.e. god-likeness, a metaphysical concept. He discriminates them by a series of delimitations, and then delineates them in rules which they are able to observe. Methodists ' are those who desire to flee from the wrath to come and to be saved from their sins.' This is to be shown in their conduct: ' first, by doing no harm, by avoiding evil in every kind . . . and secondly, by doing good, by being in every kind merciful after their power ; as they have opportunity, doing good of every possible sort, and, as far as is possible, to all men.' This service is made possible by denying themselves, by ' taking up their cross daily,' and enduring ' the reproach of Christ,' constrained thereto by the master motive, ' for the Lord's sake.' This statement of the Christian Negative and the Christian Positive, as shown by the Rev. Henry Carter in his valuable study *The Methodist*, is followed by another showing the Christian Dynamic. An outline is given of the means by which the human spirit can come into relation with God, or rather, by which the human spirit can become aware of God and of His action upon it, so that it may be prompted to react towards God. The power to achieve god-likeness comes, Wesley teaches, by attending upon all the ordinances of God, the public worship, Bible reading and exposition, the Sacrament of the Lord's Supper, family and private prayer, searching the Scriptures, and fasting or abstinence. Wesley added two highly significant statements to these *Rules*. He claimed that they are taught in ' the written word ' of God, which is ' the only rule, and the sufficient rule, both of our faith and practice ' ; and ' that the Holy Spirit writes them on every truly awakened heart.' Clearly, the claims of reason are here recognized. Appeal is made alike to mind, conscience, emotion, and will. It should be noticed also that in these *Rules* Wesley revived and restated Christian fellowship, a notable feature of the primitive Christian Church delineated in the New Testament. He grouped his followers in small bands and classes, and into a society in each place or district, and all into the United Societies which he superintended. This was the eighteenth-century anticipation of the power and function of the group mind, or the method of thinking together.

(v.) *Hymnology*

The poetry and hymnology of Wesley are of almost first-rate importance, and must be used in any study of his contribution to Christian Thought. They are here frequently quoted. Too little has been made of Wesley's hymnology as a means of estimating his contribution to philosophy. The poetical works of himself and his brother Charles fill thirteen volumes. They first appeared in fifty-four volumes and booklets, from 1737 to 1790. Charles Wesley's poems and hymns may be generally regarded as giving the teaching of his brother

John as well of his own, except in a few expressions, chiefly sacramentarian in character. While Charles Wesley had a larger lyrical gift,'' Wesley's taste was more severe and classical. He required hymns to be ' poetical, rational, and scriptural.' His own translations are numerous and of high worth. The life, power, and beauty of the original are retained, and are enriched by the purity, strength, and elegance of Wesley's English diction. He had exceptional skill in tracing and conveying Christian thought and poetic feeling. He could interpret the speech of the heart, which is the same in all languages, and give it utterance in his own language. Herbert, Addison, Dryden, Watts, and other English hymn-writers and poets, were freely used by Wesley, with some of their peers in the Latin, German, French, and Spanish languages. These serve the English-speaking world through him.''

Wesley plainly declared his purpose as philosopher-divine in his large use of hymnology. In the preface to his standard hymn-book, which appeared in 1780, he said that it contained ' a declaration of the heights and depths of religion, speculative and practical,' that is, metaphysical and ethical. He claimed that no word was used in the book but in a fixed and determinate sense. The experience of real Christians was used, and the book is, in effect, so he said, ' a little body of experimental and practical divinity.' The judgement of James Martineau, a thinker of a different type from that of Wesley and of a century later, is that of many competent judges concerning this work. He said, ' after the Scriptures, the Wesley *Hymn-Book* appears to me the grandest instrument of popular religious culture that Christendom has ever produced.'

The experimental, more strictly the experiential, character of the Wesley poetry in general, and the standard hymns in particular, is specially noteworthy in estimating Wesley as the philosopher of Christian experience. Many of the hymns given to Christendom by Wesley and his brother Charles are autobiographic in occasion and content. The stages of their Christian and philosophical development can be traced in their hymns. That they thus exposed themselves in the service of the human race showed rare courage and a high sense of moral vocation. It was perhaps the happiest stroke of their genius. No religious leaders obeyed so fully the apostolic injunction to teach and train one another with the music of psalms, with hymns and songs of the spiritual life." They supplied their followers with hymns for almost every moral and spiritual occasion and condition. These hymns have thus an evidential value. Quotations from them frequently occur in the autobiographies, biographies, and narratives of moral and spiritual experience on which Wesley based his inductive philosophy.

(*vi.*) *His ' Standard Sermons ' and ' Notes on the New Testament '*

Forty-four Sermons by Wesley, contained in the first four volumes of his Sermons issued by him in 1787-8, together with his *Explanatory Notes upon the New Testament*, were regarded by him, and accepted by his preachers, as a summary of his teaching, both metaphysical and ethical. Wesley was not a systematic theologian or philosopher, so far as his published works are concerned ; nor was Butler. Like Butler, however, Wesley had a system of

Thought. In both these divines, faith was supported by understanding. As Butler gave us his philosophy of religion in outline in his fifteen *Sermons*, so Wesley's philosophy may, in general, be gathered from his *Standard Sermons* and *Notes* with the works above referred to. Butler's *Analogy* filled in the outline and elaborated the teaching of his *Sermons*. Likewise, Wesley's teaching in his *Standard Sermons* must be interpreted in the light of his later discourses, deliverances, and experience, as tested by the experience of others." Wesley's published discourses number one hundred and forty-one. In his *Standard Sermons* he said that he avoided ' all nice and philosophical speculations.' Elsewhere he did not avoid these. The limitations, powers, and claims of the human mind, and its quest for truth of all kinds, have seldom been stated better than by Wesley in his discourses entitled ' The Imperfections of Human Knowledge,' and ' The Case of Reason calmly considered.' In the last-named discourse Wesley takes Butler's words, and rebukes those who imagine that reason is of no use in religion, and who despise and vilify reason. Another feature of Wesley's *Sermons* balances his zeal for knowledge. It has been pointed out that thirty-two of the forty-four *Standard Sermons* deal with ethics, i.e. religion in conduct. Wesley held that the vision of God is followed by the service of man.

Wesley's *Explanatory Notes upon the New Testament* was a considerable contribution to English biblical scholarship in the eighteenth century. Many of Wesley's translations and corrections anticipated those of the Revised Version (1881)." Charles Wesley assisted his brother in the work, which was destined to be of wide and continuous service to many students of the New Testament. It is indispensable to all who would appraise Wesley's contribution to thought. In his corrections of the Greek text, as well as for much of his comment, Wesley used the work of Bengelius, *Gnomon Novi Testamenti*. He used also the works of Heylyn, Guyse, and Doddridge. He designed this work chiefly for plain, unlettered men, who understand only their mother tongue, who yet reverence and love God's Word and have a desire to save their souls. Wesley's declaration that 'the Scripture of the Old and New Testament is a most solid and precious system of divine truth' must be received as his steadfast belief. His recognition of some of the principles of textual criticism and a reasonable higher criticism must also be remembered. He was not a worshipper of the Bible as a book. It was no fetish to him, nor regarded by him with the awe of superstition; but as a library containing the supreme divine revelation, which should be loved and studied with filial reverence, and with eagerness to understand and obey its commands. When he arranged the Book of Psalms for use in worship he exercised his critical faculty upon the Old Testament Scriptures. He left out many Psalms, and many parts of others, 'as being highly improper for the mouths of a Christian congregation' (*Works*, xiv. 317). In neither of these authoritative works (*Sermons* and *Notes*), nor indeed in any of his works, did Wesley claim absolute authority or finality for his teachings. He is always a learner and philosopher: 'Whereinsoever I have mistaken, my mind is open to conviction. I sincerely desire to be better informed. I say to God and man, "What I know not, teach Thou me"' (*Notes on the New Testament*, Preface).

(vii.) 'Wesley's Philosophy'

This necessary statement of the literary work of Wesley may be closed with a notice of his chief publication in philosophy. Many short statements on this subject appear in his works. The work now cited shows his deep interest in natural theology and the creative processes used by God. It also shows Wesley's use of the theory of knowledge propounded by Bishop Peter Browne. *Wesley's Philosophy* is the short title borne by five volumes entitled, *A Survey of the Wisdom of God in the Creation; or, a Compendium of Natural Philosophy*. It has five parts, which treat in succession of man, brutes, plants; the earth, water, fire, air, and meteors; the system of the world; heavenly bodies; and the properties and causes of natural bodies. To this last part are added an abridgement of Bonnet's *Contemplation of Nature*, referred to by T. H. Huxley, and an extract from a work by Deutens, entitled *Inquiry into the Origin of the Discoveries attributed to the Moderns*. The chief contents of the first two volumes of the *Philosophy* were translated by Wesley from the Latin text of J. F. Buddœus, a Jena professor of philosophy; but Wesley altered every chapter, almost every section, by retrenchment or enlargement, and inclusion of much information gathered from Ray, Derham, and Nieuwentyt, and from Oliver Goldsmith's *History of the Earth and Animated Nature* (1770). The work thus grew from two to three and finally to five volumes. The important introduction to this work, and the conclusion, are wholly by Wesley. Although the *Philosophy* is largely a compilation by him from the works of others, it must be taken as generally containing his teaching.

He read the first edition of two volumes with his London preachers as their tutor in 1764. The gradual growth of the work during fourteen years, and its composite form, resulted in some variation in several statements in it. Wesley has counsels for readers who think all such studies vain, and for others who are unduly absorbed by them. This *Philosophy* was an entirely worthy effort for its purpose, and a significant issue, and companion, of Wesley's evangelistic work. It was among the earliest attempts to provide a popular compendium of philosophy in England. This work was eagerly welcomed. It was printed in its final form of five volumes in 1777. Of this, Wesley issued four editions. Its first edition in 1763 anticipated the *Natural Theology* of Paley by nearly forty years, and Oliver Goldsmith's work, *History of the Earth and Animated Nature*, by seven years. Paley would have delighted in Bonnet's and Wesley's pages, although no reference by him to them has been traced.

Charles de Bonnet (1720–93) of Geneva, was a famous naturalist, strongly opposed to Voltaire and Rousseau. From Bonnet's works, in the fourth volume of Wesley's *Philosophy*, there is a remarkable anticipation of a modern scientific theory. In Chapters II. to IV. Wesley gives Bonnet's theory of the gradual progressive development of nature by God, especially in the organic and human forms. Wesley shows himself to be a modern thinker. He popularized an anticipation of the theory of evolution, destined to be associated in the nineteenth century with the names of Darwin and Wallace. Using Bonnet's scientific investigations, Wesley states his views. His words, translating those of Bonnet, must be given. ' All is metamorphosis in the physical world. Forms are continually changing. The quantity of matter alone is invariable. The same substance passes successively into the three kingdoms. The same composition becomes by turn a mineral, plant, insect, reptile, fish, bird, quadruped, man. The organized machines are the principal agents of these transformations. . . . Inorganized beings answer to organized as to their centre. The latter are designed for each other. Plants are allied to plants. Animals and plants are linked together by their mutual services' (*Wesley's Philosophy*, iv. 129, 130). Again, Wesley says, 'There are no sudden changes in nature; all is gradual and elegantly varied. There is no being which has not either above or beneath it some that resemble it in certain characters, and differ from it in others. . . . From a plant to man . . . the transition from one species to another is almost insensible. The polypus links the vegetable to the animal. The flying squirrel unites the birds to the quadruped. The ape bears affinity to the quadruped and the man. . . . By what degrees does nature raise herself up to man ? How will she rectify this head that is always inclined to the earth ? How change these paws into flexible arms ? What method will she make use of to transform these crooked feet into supple and skilful hands ? . . . The ape is this rough draft of man ; an imperfect representation which nevertheless bears a resemblance to him, and is the last creature that serves to display the admirable progression of the works of God ! . . . There is a prodigious number of continued links between the most perfect man and the ape' (*Wesley's Philosophy*, iv. 58, 73, 102, 109)."

It should be remembered that Bonnet and

Wesley left their readers in no doubt that they regard this system of development as a mere *process* used by God. The process was not regarded by them as the *cause* of life. Wesley says, ' What is nature itself but the art of God, or God's method of acting ? True philosophy ascribes all to God.' And again Wesley says he published his abridgement of Bonnet's *Contemplation of Nature* so that ' the adorable Wisdom and Goodness of the great Author of Nature ' might be placed in the strongest light (*Ibid.*, iv. 60). Wesley regarded each human being, and every human being, as a creation by God. The Cause, the first, instrumental, efficient and final Cause is God, according to the teaching of these Christian philosophers. They say that ' Between the lowest and highest degrees of corporeal and spiritual perfection there is an almost infinite number of intermediate degrees. The result of these degrees composes the *universal chain*. This unites all beings, connects all worlds, comprehends all the spheres. One Sole Being is out of this chain, and that is He that made it ' (*Ibid.*, 72). Bonnet and Wesley anticipated Paley in regarding the created universe as a temple, with man, the sum of creation, bending there in grateful adoration of his Maker, God. ' Man alone soars to *God*, the *Principle*, and, prostrate at the foot of the throne of the Almighty, adores with the profoundest veneration, and with the most lively gratitude, the Ineffable Goodness that created him ' (*Wesley's Philosophy*, iv. 72, 108).

Wesley's Metaphysics

In the fifth volume of his *Philosophy* Wesley devotes an appendix of fifty pages to mental philosophy : ' I now intend to speak particularly of the Human Understanding, chiefly on the plan of the pious and learned Dr. Peter Browne, late Bishop of Cork, in Ireland.'" Wesley gives the sections which deal with ideas of sensation, the idea of spirits, and the properties of the ideas of sensation ; also the sections on pure intellect and its operations, the kinds of knowledge and evidence, and the improvement of knowledge by divine revelation. Browne differed from Berkeley as to our knowledge of spiritual nature. He differed from Locke too, as to our knowledge of mind. He confines ' idea ' to the images we have of sensible objects : ' The mind has no idea of her own operations.' Body and mind cannot be known in the same way, although our mental operations are connected with physical sensations. Only by analogy can we know mind or spirit, whether the human spirit or the infinite spirit. We can have no idea of a spirit, and we define it by a negative ; i.e. by saying that it is something that is not matter. Hence, Browne says, ' Properly speaking, we have no idea of God. We come to our knowledge of His very existence not from any idea of Him, but from our reasoning upon the works of the visible creation.' Browne distinguishes mathematical from moral certainty. Conclusions from arguments of the former class follow by natural necessity ; consent to them is compelled by the facts. Moral certainty requires the consent of the will to what is received as probably true. Browne elaborated his theory concerning knowledge by analogy, in his later work : *Things Divine and Supernatural conceived by Analogy and Things Natural and Human*. In some of its features Browne's philosophy recalls that of Butler, already noticed. While Butler used analogical reasoning to remove difficulties encountered by theistic belief, he did not assert that our knowledge of spiritual reality was merely by analogy. Nor did Wesley agree with Browne in this. He used Browne's work, *Human Understanding*, when instructing his London preachers in 1756. On most points he said that he preferred this work to that of Locke; but we may be sure that on this crucial question of immediate, though limited, knowledge of God as possible to man, Wesley would contrast his own teaching with that of Browne.

Criticisms of Wesley's compendium of philosophy drew from him a confession of his continued interest in the subject, and of his declining dogmatism. He was seventy years old. Under the *nom de plume* 'Philosophaster,' a writer in the *London Magazine* for 1774 questioned some of Wesley's statements in his *Philosophy*. Wesley admitted that on some of the points raised he was in error. In general, however, he maintained his ground, and he continued to issue this work. 'Permit me, sir,' he wrote to his critic, ' to give you one piece of advice. Be not so *positive*; especially with regard to things which are neither easy nor necessary to be determined. I ground this advice on my own experience. When I was young I was *sure* of everything. In a few years, having been mistaken a thousand times, I was not half so sure of most things as before. At present, I am hardly sure of anything, but what God has revealed to man.' This was Wesley's attitude as philosopher and divine.

It is not without interest that in the same year that Wesley issued his *Philosophy* he issued also an edition of Milton's *Paradise Lost*, abridged, and with notes of explanation. He looked upon poetry as a deeply significant product of the human mind. He wrote of Homer as an amazing genius and frequently quoted from him. He used and annotated fully the works of Shakespeare ;* but he declared that ' impartial judges gave the preference to *Paradise Lost* before all the poems of any age or nation.' All the editions of Wesley's *Philosophy* bear on the title-page the confession of Milton's faith and philosophy :

> These are Thy glorious works, Parent of Good,
> Almighty ! Thine this universal Frame,
> Thus wond'rous fair ! Thyself how wond'rous then !

Wesley added to this Theism teachings which are specifically Christian, as will be shown.

* His copy was burned after his death by one of his preachers, John Pawson, a Methodist of less catholic literary taste than Wesley (*Wesley Studies*, 176), as some others have been since that age.

IV

CHRISTIAN EXPERIENCE AS SEEN IN WESLEY AND OTHER TYPES OF HIS PERIOD AND SINCE

THE indications of Wesley's fitness to note, record, collate, compare, and use the facts of Christian experience, given in previous pages (Chapter II.), are here followed by a summary of his statements of his own religious and Christian experience, by several typal instances which he collected and examined, and by other instances since the eighteenth century. Upon such facts Wesley and Christian philosophers base their implications as to the existence and nature of God.

Typal Christian Experience

It has been given to elect spirits of the human race to regard themselves as men of destiny, as purposed items in the cosmic and moral order of which God is the first and final cause, and to believe that their experience of that order was a finite revelation of it. Their teaching was derived from divine revelation which culminated in Jesus Christ, and authenticated by their experience. It was supported by the appeal to consensus. Theologians and historians cite many such instances. St. Paul is the classic instance for many. He declared

CHRISTIAN EXPERIENCE

that 'God chose to reveal His Son in me in order that I might preach'; and, 'In me Jesus Christ first showed forth all His longsuffering' (Gal. i. 16; 1 Tim. i. 16). In this feature, as in much besides, Wesley resembles St. Paul. He had vivid experience of God in Christ. It was given to him to have experiential knowledge of the action of God in Jesus Christ upon his personality by the Holy Spirit, and of the reaction of his own spirit towards God. These experiences formed the substance of his teaching concerning God and man, when these experiences had been suitably tested. Wesley believed that he had immediate knowledge of spiritual reality. Charles Wesley supplied the words which enshrine this feature of Wesley's contribution to thought. He himself led the testimony which he taught many to utter, as thus:

> What we have felt and seen,
> With confidence we tell,
> And publish to the sons of men
> The signs infallible.
> His love, surpassing far
> The love of all beneath,
> We find within . . .

Wesley's own spiritual experience is therefore of capital importance for us, and must be examined at some length.

It should be noticed here that, with Wesley as guide, we pass to the observation of religious experiences which were, or became, specifically Christian in their character. Wesley was deeply interested in religious experience in general. He collected and collated interesting facts as to the aborigines of North America, and elsewhere, in their early and pre-Christian periods. It is, however, as a Christian philosopher, as the exponent of the implications of Christian experience, that he was distinguished in his century and must always command attention. Here Wesley advances beyond Berkeley, Clarke, and Butler. They were theistic philosophers. To Theism Wesley added the concept that the cause of all things, and their unifying and interpreting principle, is God in Christ, operating by the Spirit or energy of God. Wesley's idealism is that of Berkeley, Christianized. Existence, from which Clarke sought to demonstrate the being and attributes of Deity, is, with Wesley, existence as seen in Jesus Christ. Human nature as designed by God, which is therefore a revelation of Him, and which Butler sought to interpret, is considered by Wesley in its Christian experience as renewed or quickened by the Spirit of God. Wesley examined his own experiences, and those of others, as believers in and imitators of Jesus Christ. From these, Wesley traced certain implications as to the existence and nature of God, the ultimate Reality.

(*i.*) *Wesley*

Wesley's experience is a classical example of its kind. There was nothing magical in it. It was orderly and, in the best sense, natural; while as to its cause, it was supernatural. It was caused by God. Like the experience of God in Christ given to St. Paul on the way to Damascus, which St. Paul believed to be an experience of the immediate action of God upon him, Wesley's transforming experience, known as his evangelical conversion, was prepared for both negatively and positively. The psychologist finds ample material for an explanation of the occurrence, except its cause: that belongs to metaphysics. Negatively, Wesley

CHRISTIAN EXPERIENCE 85

had been prepared by disappointing experience in his moral and spiritual life extending over thirteen years (1725-38).[10] Positively, he had learned from books, chiefly the New Testament, and from several living persons, that an experience of God in Christ by the Divine Spirit is open to man as man, and was actually enjoyed by some. It was most worthy of the divine purpose, and much to be desired by man. This condition of the inner nature Wesley describes in a hymn-line as that in which

> Fear, and sin, and grief expire,
> Cast out by perfect love.

Stages of his Spiritual Experience

The stages by which Wesley's experience reached this ideal are recorded by him in his diaries. They are summarized in his singularly lucid and coherent account entitled, 'A Plain Account of Christian Perfection, as believed and taught by the Reverend Mr. John Wesley from the year 1725 to the year 1777' (*Works*, xi. 366).[11] The year 1725 marked a well-defined stage in his life. A year earlier he had attained manhood. The chief religious influence in his life up to this time had been his love of and deference to his mother. Susanna Wesley was a woman of exceptional gifts of mind and heart. She retained her influence over Wesley until her death in 1742. The title often given to her, 'The Mother of Methodism,' indicates her character and power. Wesley has described his religious state anterior to this notable year, 1725. He says that, while he still said his prayers in public and private, he 'had not all this while so much as a notion of inward holiness: nay, went on habitually, and for the most part very contentedly, in some or other known sin.' The influence of his mother upon him was now supplemented by that of 'a religious friend'—probably Miss Betty or Miss Sarah Kirkham of Stanton Rectory—and by religious books." Bishop Jeremy Taylor's work, *Rules and Exercises of Holy Living and Dying*, came into his hands (1725). Wesley says, ' Instantly I resolved to dedicate all my life to God, all my thoughts and words and actions.' He now began to record his religious experiences and vows. One page in this first Oxford Diary may be cited as a specimen of many contained in it, and in his diaries, until May 24, 1738. It is for a day in December 1725, and contains an affecting chronicle of his failure to keep the vow above recorded, although it had been renewed again and again." These confessions are accompanied by prayers to God for pardon and help, and by a new resolution.

Dec. 1, 1725.
Breach of vows : hence careless of fixing days of mortification, &c.
Pride of my parts or holiness : greedy of praise : peevishness : idleness.
Intemperance in sleep : sins of thoughts : hence useless or sinful anger.
Breach of promise : dissimulation : lying : rash censures : contemning others : disrespect of governors : desire to seem better than I am.—K. ε. [Κύριε ἐλέησον—Lord, have mercy !]
RESOLUTION : To fast, &c., every Wednesday in a month.—K. β. [Κύριε βοήθει—Lord, help !]

This transcript, from an intimate human document by Wesley, demands two remarks. The moral failures here recorded must be judged in the light of the high ideal which Wesley had set up in the vows prompted by his reading of the Scriptures and Bishop Taylor, as stated above. Some would say it was an inaccessible height which he there proposed to reach. The further remark is that this diary entry is confirmed by his general statement quoted above, by the confession of a habit of sin stated in his letter to his mother (*Letters*, 45) and by other authentic statements from Wesley concerning this stage of his religious development. It is impossible to miss the contrast which this page presents to thousands of pages which record his thoughts, emotions, and doings after the religious crisis of 1738. His later methodical habits of devotion, his humility, his strict limitation of sleep, untiring industry, punctiliousness in keeping his promises and speaking what he called 'the naked truth,' his deference to the humblest exponent and representative of truth—all these shine out upon the background of breach of vows, pride, indulgence in sleep, lying, and disrespect of authority, revealed by Wesley's confession given above. Nor was this contrast contrived as an argument or illustration. The document showing Wesley's early condition was not composed upon the serene heights which he afterwards reached. This poignant record was made at the time of the experience to which it refers. An adequate and efficient cause for the change in him, from this plight to the triumphs which he afterwards records at their time, must be discovered.

Other features of this preparatory stage of his personality and effort can only be briefly noticed. The year above referred to (1725) was that of his ordination at Oxford as deacon. Three years later he was ordained as priest. These events were occasions for vigorous self-examination and high resolve. Another influential event was Wesley's attachment to and leadership of the Holy Club, or the Methodists, at Oxford (1729). This experience contributed the idea of corporate fellowship to his development. It was probably as influential as any in his mental and spiritual growth and altruistic service. Such pooling of thought and spiritual experience—for comparison, confirmation, or correction—issuing in united endeavour for self-development and the service of others, Wesley continued henceforth to use. He offered it to the world in his teaching concerning the Holy Spirit and in the *Rules for the United Societies*, as already shown.

The period (1735-7) spent by Wesley as an English clergyman among the colonists, and also as missionary to the natives in Georgia, New England, served to convince him more deeply, if possible, than the experience of these preparatory years that there must be more in the Christian religion than he had hitherto known. Of this, positive confirmation reached him by his contact with Christian people from Moravia."[4] Several of these were his fellow-voyagers to Georgia. Their buoyant confidence in God, even when the ship was in the teeth of a gale, and all were faced with death, their humility, fellowship, industry, and radiant steady good humour, showed him what he lacked and also the possibility of possessing it. These impressions were deepened by further intercourse with them in London on his return from Georgia. In particular, he met Peter Böhler on February 7, 1738, 'a day much to be remembered,' and so marked by Wesley in his diary. Böhler, with Martin Luther, whose teaching was received by Wesley a little later, must be regarded as the chief human means which conveyed divine quickening and knowledge to Wesley at this stage.

William Law (1686-1761) and his works must be named among these preparations for Wesley's

CHRISTIAN EXPERIENCE

classic experience. Law was one of the brightest intellects of his century. He combined acuteness, learning, piety, and charm. His Christian character drew from the alien hand of Edward Gibbon, the historian, a tribute which has been styled a monument more lasting than brass : ' In our family, William Law left the reputation of a worthy and pious man, who believed all that he professed, and practised all that he enjoined.' To Wesley, Law had been as an oracle ; but early in 1738 Wesley had become dissatisfied with his previous clerical teachers, including Law. At this period Wesley was truly what the Moravians at Marienborn styled him later, *homo perturbatus* (a man distracted). He wrote two sharp letters to Law, accusing him of inefficiency as his spiritual guide. Law's reply, mingled of biting satire and humility, shows him the better Christian at this stage.[13] Wesley later showed his indebtedness to Law, and his fundamental agreement with him, by continuous use and circulation of several of Law's earlier literary works. Beginning in 1744, Wesley printed nineteen editions of Law's *Serious Call to a Devout and Holy Life*. These copies were all given away. In Wesley's opinion, only *The Christian's Pattern*, by à Kempis, equalled this work by Law. He also printed large portions of Law's treatise, *Christian Perfection*. But he rejected the confusing mysticisms of Behmen, under whose influence Law passed in his later life.[14]

Here, then, is Wesley within a few days of a transforming and empowering spiritual experience. Our analysis shows him to be egoistic, rather hard, somewhat censorious, fluctuating, gravely defective in moral character and achievement. We need not accept his harshest judgements of himself. He was careful to correct these, in footnotes to his narratives issued subsequently to these events. But the above generalizations on his state must stand. His governing conception of his duty at this stage was that of saving his own soul. This led him to reject, in terms far too dictatorial, his aged father's proposal that he would succeed him as rector at Epworth, and maintain the needy family there. He had the same selfish motive as a missionary (*Journal*, i. 422 ; *Works*, xi. 379). Emotionally, he was continually tossed to and fro between moroseness and levity. He lacked the spontaneity, fixity of purpose, gladness, poise, and reposefulness which are the notes of the Christian life revealed in the New Testament.

His Transforming Experience in 1738

The transforming and empowering experience of which Wesley was the subject on May 24, 1738, and from which issued the man and his work as known to the world, is now to be narrated. The chief facts of Wesley's great day are familiar (*Journal*, i. 465). He was then within a month of his thirty-fifth birthday. It is said that St. Paul was thirty-one when similarly transformed. A clergyman of the English Church, Wesley had arrived in London from Georgia on February 1. Wesley's shorthand diary, with the record of his doings hour by hour, breaks off within a month of his great day, and is not resumed until a year afterwards. Happily, within fifteen days of this transforming event, Wesley wrote a full account of it. This he afterwards read to his clever, saintly mother.

Wesley began this day very early. The May morning light of five o'clock fell on his opened Greek

New Testament. This gave him words prophetic of the wondrous life which was to be his before the day closed. 'There are given unto us,' he read, 'exceeding great and precious promises, even that ye should be partakers of the divine nature.' Another scripture on which his eye lighted helped this eager seeker. Just as he was leaving his lodging for the busy city street he read again. 'Thou art not far from the Kingdom of God,' said the open page. Indeed he was not. In the afternoon a friend asked Wesley to attend service in St. Paul's Cathedral. The anthem there had a message for him. It is good to notice the place of scripture, poetry, music, and choral singing in this day of Wesley's spiritual quickening. William Croft's music interpreted the ancient cry of the psalmist, lifted it to God again as if it were that of Wesley, and then assured him of happiness nigh at hand. 'Out of the deep,' sighed Wesley in that plaintive anthem, 'have I cried unto Thee, O Lord : Lord, hear my voice.' Then the music, brightened and heartened in tone, bade Wesley hope in God. 'O Israel,' sang the melody, 'trust in the Lord, for with the Lord there is mercy, and with Him is plenteous redemption. And He shall deliver Israel from all his sins.'*

This night the promise made to the ear was kept to the hope of this inquiring spirit, still wrestling to know the nature and the name of God and the conscious joy of pardon. Wesley had been introduced to one of several Religious Societies which existed in London, in which earnest Christian

* Mr. J. T. Lightwood states that this service was at three o'clock; that Dr. Croft was the composer of the music of the anthem; Dr. Maurice Greene, the organist then; and the organ, 'a noble instrument built by the celebrated Father Smith' (*The Magazine of the Wesleyan Methodist Church*, 1926, p. 61).

people met frequently to hear the Scriptures, to unite in prayer and in planning works of mercy for the poor and neglected. Wesley now went to such a society. It seems likely that this was one of several societies formed by James Hutton, a London bookseller. One of these met regularly, in 1737-8, in a building in Nettleton Court, which was then entered from the east side of Aldersgate Street. Wesley names the street only. It should be remembered that Wesley was at this time the guest of Hutton. It is a fair inference—but it is nothing more—that it was he who overcame Wesley's unwillingness to go to a society meeting on this evening, and that it was to Hutton's society he went, which met in Nettleton Court, off Aldersgate Street." None but Wesley's words may tell the story of that hour, wonderful as it was for himself and the world. He says: ' In the evening I went very unwillingly to a society in Aldersgate Street, where one was reading Luther's *Preface to the Epistle to the Romans*. About a quarter before nine, while he was describing the change which God works in the heart through faith in Christ, I felt my heart strangely warmed." I felt I did trust in Christ, Christ alone for salvation; and an assurance was given me that He had taken away *my* sins, even *mine*, and saved *me* from the law of sin and death. I began to pray with all my might for those who had in a more especial manner despitefully used me and persecuted me. I then testified openly to all there what I now first felt in my heart.'

The teachings of Martin Luther, which gave new life to the Christian Church in Europe in the sixteenth century, were here used to quicken the quickener of England in the eighteenth century.

Almost certainly we now know the very words which thrilled Wesley that May evening. They were read, most likely, by one William Holland, and from the Latin version of Luther's *Preface* or *Prologue to St. Paul's Epistle to the Romans*. Students handle a copy of this translation in the British Museum Library, London, with more than antiquarian interest. William Holland was a master painter who resided in Basinghall Street, near the meeting-room in Aldersgate Street. A week before—that is, on May 17—Holland had himself found Christ as Saviour while Charles Wesley read to him from another work written by Luther. This was his *Commentary on the Epistle to the Galatians*. In turn, Holland now read similar words in the hearing of Charles Wesley's older and greater brother, John. Holland has told us that at his first hearing of Luther's messages, a week earlier, he had himself been spiritually quickened. He says: 'I almost thought I saw our Saviour. . . . When I afterwards went into the street, I could scarcely feel the ground I trod upon.' His voice would quiver with emotion as he read these words to the listening group and to Wesley: 'Faith, through the merit of Christ, obtaineth the Holy Spirit, which Spirit doth exhilarate us, doth excite and inflame our heart, that it may do those things willingly, of love, which the Law commandeth. . . . This so bold an assurance of the mercy and favour of God doth make our hearts merry, glad, and light; doth also erect, raise, and even ravish us with most sweet motions and affections towards God.' It was this description of the 'change which God works in the heart through faith in Christ' which, said Wesley, 'strangely warmed' his heart and moved him to complete

repose upon Christ as his personal Saviour." The
ethical change wrought in Wesley is also significant.
He says that, immediately upon his spiritual
quickening, he began to pray for his enemies. He
had such, and bitter they were at that time. He
had lately escaped their wicked machinations in
Savannah and Georgia. They had followed him,
and were now plotting his ruin in England. The
moral quality of this emotional crisis in Wesley
will be further referred to later. Almost immediately
Wesley's emotions again found lyrical and musical
expression. As was to be the case wondrously in
after years, his brother Charles was now his helper.
Towards ten that evening a troop of friends went
with Wesley from the society meeting-room to
Charles Wesley's lodging in Little Britain, near
by. Wesley there declared, 'I believe,' and all
joined in singing a hymn. Was this the lyric
commencing, 'Where shall my wondering soul
begin?' Charles Wesley had composed this on the
previous day, to commemorate his own spiritual
change.

The capital quality and importance of this whole
experience in his spiritual life was at once evident
to Wesley. In later life he modified some of the
hard things he had written against himself before
this transforming experience, and his experience
after it was not uniformly happy or victorious
(*Journal*, ii. 89). But he never withdrew this
shining record, or lowered his estimate of that hour
when he felt the Spirit of the Highest. He could
not be confounded, nor did he doubt; still less did
he deny the spiritual reality and significance of
that event. Twenty-eight months after it he gave
the story of it to his followers and the world in his
famous *Journal* (1740). More than fifty years of

Wesley's life and almost incredible labours found their inspiration and driving-power in that conscious contact with God, which was maintained, although not always as vividly. It was an experience unequalled by any hitherto known by Wesley. The narrative of it ranks with the *Confessions of St. Augustine* in the authentic literature of the human spirit and of Christianity. Impartial judges have recognized its significance and importance. ' The humble meeting in Aldersgate Street, London,' says Lecky, the historian of the eighteenth century, referring to the event, ' forms an epoch in English history.' It led to that religious revolution in England which is ' of greater historic importance than all the splendid victories by land and sea won under Pitt.' That ' revolution ' and all such results of Wesley's character and work are closely linked with the spiritual event here recorded. It was the first of these remarkable incursions of divine life and power into Wesley's personality. Tides of divine, redemptive energy now came into him and flowed through him; and this in manner and measure as in only a few of our race. Wesley stands in a direct line of world teachers and transmitters of Christianity. Luther, St. Augustine, and St. Paul link him and his message with Jesus Christ.

Preparations for this Experience

It is important to recognize, what has not, I think, been previously observed, that Wesley was specially prepared for the greatest hour of his life and one of the greatest ever known to a human spirit. Immediately before that hour he worshipped

God under very helpful conditions. Attendance at the afternoon service in St. Paul's Cathedral, London, preceded the transforming experience of God in Christ granted to Wesley in the evening of the day. Only a few hours came between this and that. That came to him in the midst of commonplace surroundings. A plain meeting-room, where a few were gathered together in the name of Jesus, with Him in the midst, was the scene. A layman was leading the worshippers and earnest students there. Wesley says that he went very unwillingly. Only mystics would find aids in the bare simplicity of the service; unadorned, adorned the most for them. And this fact is, for all time, of profound significance. Here we see the spirituality of religion and the independence of essential Christianity of elaborate ceremonial and human aids to worship. Nothing could well be simpler, or more devoid of the sensuous and ornate, than the occasion of Wesley's evangelical conversion. Clearly God is found by any one anywhere if he worships in spirit and in reality. But it is here submitted that this hour in Wesley's life is not to be separated arbitrarily from his training and previous experience, nor from the helpfulness of the stately worship in which he joined in the afternoon of his great day. He was a clergyman. He knew the spell which surroundings and aids lay upon the human spirit."
On this high day of his life he used ways of approach to God which had often helped him at Epworth and Oxford, and which this day prepared him for recognizing the strange movement upon and within his spirit as the action of God, in manner and measure hitherto unknown by him. That service in St. Paul's, it appears to the present student, stirred in Wesley's deeper self that Promethean

heat which answered the warming love of God, of which he heard William Holland read that night in the meeting-room. Otherwise, why did Wesley note in his account of this day the impressive features of the service in St. Paul's? Wren's masterpiece of Renaissance architecture, with domes and circles suggesting that which has neither beginning nor end, was all about him. He heard exquisite music, heard the anthem clear, and ' the pealing organ blow to the full-voiced quire below.' He sang and prayed in words hallowed by use and wont in the storied past. Beauty of shape, colour, and sound ministered to his wakeful, wistful spirit. It is a mistake to suppose, as some have said, that Wesley was insensible to these influences. His *Journal* has many descriptions of scenery and noble buildings, and of beautiful forms and sounds. He delighted in good music and singing."[1] 'While the organist was playing a voluntary I found an uncommon blessing,' he says in 1751 (*Journal*, iii. 520). It cannot therefore be doubted that Wesley's nature was prepared and enriched by orderly, devout, beautiful worship, as he moved towards the moment when he saw God in Christ as never before, and felt that he was made a new man in Him. The unnamed friend who asked Wesley to go to a cathedral service that day linked him thereby with the holiness of beauty, as, later, in the simpler gathering he was to be claimed by the beauty of holiness. Next day he went to the afternoon service at St. Paul's again; and again the anthem had special meaning for him. He says, ' I could taste the good word of God in the anthem, which began, " My song shall be always of the loving-kindness of the Lord." '

That the remarkable event of Wesley's evangelical

G

conversion was unnoticed by public chroniclers at the time of its occurrence says nothing against its historicity or value. Afterwards, Wesley and the Methodists were often referred to by them. *The Gentleman's Magazine* noted frivolities and trivialities of the period, and gave particulars of Wesley's unhappy marriage-union thirteen years later; but it did not spare a line for this event of far greater importance. Such neglect is the way of our blind world. Wesley's conversion shares this ignorant silence with some capital occurrences of all time. The birth and death of our Lord Jesus Christ are not named in the *Acta Diurna*, the daily news-letter or gazette of ancient Rome and the Roman Empire. And neither that medium nor the chronicles of his literary contemporaries name St. Paul, although he was creating epistolary literature now read by millions who have never heard of these early news-letters.

Confirmatory Experience

Although this was the most momentous experience of God in Christ and the renewing Spirit granted to Wesley, it was by no means solitary. Students are referred for confirmation of this statement to several outstanding events in the fifty succeeding years of Wesley's physical, mental, and spiritual development and extraordinary work. A great hour in his life was that in Bristol in 1741. He wrote of it thus : ' The words which God enabled me to speak (so I must express myself still, for I dare not ascribe them to my own wisdom) were as a hammer and a flame.' " In the same city, in 1788, his chapel in the Horsefair was crowded by slave-owners and shippers, who imported and sold African negroes there for the West Indies. There was a panic in the chapel. The benches were broken in pieces, and 'the terror and confusion were inexpressible.' In six minutes Wesley controlled the mob of his critics and opponents, and he says, 'All being calm, I went on.' Triumphs of his self-control and energy, due to divine power, as he believed, were as great at his home town, Epworth, in June 1742 (*Journal*, iii. 18). On thousands of occasions, under all sorts of conditions, often in peril, sometimes even to life itself, while he prosecuted his evangelizing and reforming campaign—' contesting the three kingdoms in the cause of Jesus Christ '—he seemed invincible. Of one such occasion he says, ' In the midst of the mob, I called for a chair; the winds were hushed, and all was calm and still; my heart was filled with love, my eyes with tears, and my mouth with arguments. They were amazed. They were ashamed. They were melted down. They devoured every word.' His triumph over the Wednesbury mobs in 1743 is invaluable evidence (*Journal*, iii. 98–103). Different, but not less significant, was Wesley's experience upon what was to him an ideal day. ' I felt such an awe and tender sense of the presence of God as greatly confirmed me therein: God was before me all the day long. I sought and found Him in every place; and could truly say, when I lay down at night, " Now I have lived a day " ' (*Journal*, iii. 157).

The divine power, here seen working through Wesley upon others, is evidently not less remarkable and suggestive than when operating in Wesley himself. As an agent he is a new man compared with what he was before his spiritual quickening and enrichment. Two of his testimonies may gather up his general experience and spiritual condition. He declared forty years subsequently to that event that he had never once suffered from depression or lowness of spirits."ⁱ He was, indeed, as gay a pilgrim as ever trod the King's highway of the holy Cross. Another testimony concerning his general spiritual experience comes from the midst of his married life, in which he was 'wedded to misery.' His ignorant, jealous, and suspicious wife was unable to shake his faith in the divine purpose of good to all creatures. 'By the grace of God,' he wrote to her, 'I never fret. I see God sitting upon His throne and ruling all things well' (*Letters of John Wesley*, 329).

These testimonies are true to the facts of Wesley's life and character. They are attested by many witnesses. It is not claimed that Wesley was a paragon of all the virtues and graces. 'I tell you flat,' he wrote to a critic of his teaching on Christian perfection of spirit and character, 'I have not attained the character I draw' (*Letters*, 122). But it is claimed, and it is generally admitted, that Wesley achieved and maintained the moral ideal in a large measure. His spiritual experience rose and fell. It was not mechanically uniform. It never fell below a high level, and it was steadily and habitually fruitful in ethical results. His character and service constitute notable items in the series of facts from which an induction can be drawn as to the reality and character of the Cause of them. It was permitted to him to have in himself and in his experience many proofs of the direct action of God upon the human spirit, and of the reaction of that spirit towards God.

Sacred Fire: Wesley's Scriptural Metaphor for Christian Experience

Before we consider other typical instances of Christian experience, it is worth while to notice the metaphor of the divine life used by Wesley. In that transforming experience, his evangelical conversion (*vide supra*, p. 92), he said that he felt his heart 'strangely warmed.' As we shall show, fire was his favourite metaphor to represent his Christian experience. The ardent Christian life and service of his followers has expressed itself similarly, and has been recognized in the same terms.* A 'warm-hearted Methodist' is a familiar characterization. 'There are twelve of you,' said Wesley to the Methodists of Carlisle; 'and all professing to have your hearts on fire with the love of God. If you are faithful, you are enough to set this city on fire.' †

Why was it that the natural element heat supplied Wesley with his favourite metaphor? Why did he not use light, or wind, or water? Readers of Jeremy Taylor's works notice his frequent use of running water as a metaphor and symbol of spiritual life and movement. It was Taylor's counsel which prompted Wesley to begin his incomparable *Journal*. But it was not from Jeremy Taylor that he borrowed the forms of thought which he used to express his deepest feeling on that historic day, or whenever his personality utters itself most characteristically. The phrase was of his own

---

* A President of the Wesleyan Methodist Conference (Rev. J. Alfred Sharp, D.D.) had for the subject of his inaugural address, 1921, 'The Religion of the Warm Heart.'

† Quoted as heard by the grandfather of Rev. John Telford, B.A. (*Sayings and Portraits of Wesley*, Preface).

careful choice. It was in terms of 'the sacred fire,'*
and he found it in the Bible.

Wesley seems to have been fascinated by natural fire. Who is not? Doubtless it made its first appeal to him by the many references to it in the Greek and Latin classics. Any direct allusions of his to Prometheus are not recalled; but many times in his writings, prose and poetic, he seems to have the Greek culture-hero in mind. Wesley was among the earliest students of the epochal works of Bishop Berkeley, the myriad-minded philosopher of Idealism, in the first part of the eighteenth century. As we have shown (*vide supra*, p. 24), fire fascinated him also. He wrote of it as the vital spirit in nature, and the ultimate natural cause of all phenomena. In his work entitled *Siris* Berkeley traces all things by a chain of causes up to God as the first and final Cause of Spirit, invisible, intangible, imponderable, but real. He created, says Berkeley, 'the Ether or pure invisible Fire, the most subtle and elastic of all bodies, which seems to pervade and expand itself throughout the whole universe.' This elemental fire engaged much of Wesley's thought and writing in his remarkable work in five volumes, *A Compendium of Natural Philosophy*, a survey of God's works.

It was easy for Wesley to pass from the consideration of natural fire to its moral analogues—holy love, enthusiasm, and zeal. His frequent use of fire, natural and spiritual, is remarkable. It animates the whole body of his writings, and, like a living thing, shines, burns, and runs among the else cold, dead words. As all revelation culminates in our Lord and Saviour Jesus Christ, the use of this

* Several of these paragraphs appeared in the *Methodist Times*, 1923, in 'Meditation for Wesley's Day, the Anniversary of his Conversion.'

CHRISTIAN EXPERIENCE 103

idea by our Lord is most profound and significant. By it He indicates the purpose of the Incarnation: 'I am come,' He said, 'to throw fire upon the earth.' On this passage Wesley comments: 'To spread the fire of heavenly love over all the earth.' Fire, like water and wind, is an emblem of the Holy Spirit—God in action in the world of humanity, the Spirit of Life in Christ Jesus, who enters the spirit of man and makes a human personality into a temple of the living God. Fire, like life, is hidden, communicable and communicating, comforting, purifying, and enduring. It is very mysterious, and is dependent for its manifestation and growth in time and space upon the supply of material by which it can live and act.

Wesley seems to have had such thoughts concerning it. For fifty years he wrote about it, sang about it, prayed for this true Promethean fire, this life of God in the spirit of man, and taught others to sing and pray for it. Among the earliest poems of his brother Charles is one of sixty-four lines entitled 'Zeal.' Concerning this divine quality the poet writes:

> Where shall we find its high abode?
> To heaven the sacred ray aspires,
> With ardent love embraces GOD,
> Parent and Object of its fires.
>
> There its peculiar influence known
> In breasts seraphic learns to glow;
> Yet, darted from the eternal throne,
> It sheds a cheering light below.
>
> Through earth diffused, the active flame
> Intensely for God's glory burns;
> And, always mindful whence it came,
> To heaven in every wish returns.

John Wesley gave this poem to the world in the first volume of two volumes of poetry and hymns which he published as *Hymns and Sacred Poems*, 1739. This was the year after his evangelical conversion, with its mystical, transforming experience of God in Christ by the Holy Spirit, when his heart was 'strangely warmed.' Two years after that event, when Wesley and Methodism as the world knows them began to be, Wesley published another similar poem by his brother Charles (*Hymns and Sacred Poems*, 1740). It bears the suggestive title, 'Against Hope, believing in Hope.' It opens with a line which contains in fewest words the most momentous affirmations ever made, even by the Wesleys :

> My God, I know, I feel Thee mine.

In the seventh verse Wesley's 'fire philosophy' and evangelical doctrine leap out. They glow through three verses, which millions of Methodists have sung and prayed since that far distant day.

> O that in me the sacred fire
>   Might now begin to glow,
> Burn up the dross of base desire,
>   And make the mountains flow !
>
> O that it now from heaven might fall,
>   And all my sins consume !
> Come, Holy Ghost, for Thee I call,
>   Spirit of burning, come !
>
> Refining fire, go through my heart,
>   Illuminate my soul ;
> Scatter Thy life through every part,
>   And sanctify the whole.

This was Wesley's song and prayer for himself as he went up and down England for half a century with his new, transforming, communicable experience of God. He was 'setting others also on fire' for God, and for the saving of men, according to Augustine's word, which Dr. T. R. Glover has given to the world afresh—*sed ex amante alio accenditur alius,* ' one loving spirit sets another on fire.'

When Wesley was seventy-eight years of age he told Samuel Bradburn, during one of their Yorkshire journeys, in 1781, that his ' experience ' could always be found in these two verses :

> O Thou who camest from above
>   The pure celestial fire to impart,
> Kindle a flame of sacred love
>   On the mean altar of my heart !
>
> There let it for Thy glory burn
>   With inextinguishable blaze ;
> And trembling to its source return,
>   In humble prayer and fervent praise.

Here is the aged Wesley still guarding the sacred fire. It is the sacred fire of love to God and man, coming from God to the human spirit and continually returning to Him in prayer, praise, and acts of faith and love. This was the burning moral passion of Wesley. One of his preachers once asked Wesley to ' give his experience.' ' You often ask us about our experience, Mr. Wesley ; we would like to learn of yours.' He replied, ' Very well, I will tell you.' Thereupon he repeated this verse :

> Jesus, confirm my heart's desire
>   To work, and speak, and think for Thee ;
> Still let me guard the holy fire,
>   And still stir up Thy gift in me.*

This classic testimony in hymn form has these three stanzas and the following :

> Ready for all Thy perfect will,
>   My acts of faith and love repeat,
> Till death Thy endless mercies seal,
>   And make my sacrifice complete.

* Narrated by J. G. Stevenson, *Methodist Hymn-Book,* 229.

106 WESLEY, PHILOSOPHER AND FOUNDER

In choosing and using these stanzas, Wesley showed not only his convictions, but also that bright wit which Cowper noticed in him. These sixteen lines are all compact of Wesley's theology and philosophy, and his characteristic terms and taste. This hymn-poem, as a whole, is worthy of Addison, whose writings Wesley admired. It has unity of thought and metaphor. Its allusions to a temple and divine worship, institutions which are found in every age and place, have that note of universality which Wesley sounded as Christian thinker. Like most of the Wesley hymn-poems, this is written round a passage from Holy Scripture. This reflects Wesley's acceptance of a divine revelation made by God to man, which culminated in Jesus Christ, the eternal Word. The words used as motto and theme here are from Lev. vi. 13, 'The fire shall ever be burning upon the altar.' This biblical instruction to the priest of ancient Israel is used by Wesley concerning the prayers and praises of every Christian in his worship of God. Wesley used this hymn-prayer, and taught other sincere seekers to use it, and similar words, in their direct approach to God and Jesus Christ. The temple here alluded to is the human personality; the altar is its centre or self.

As a poetic counterpart of Wesley's Christian philosophy, this hymn-poem would not befit him unless it referred to the ethical results of the Christian's mystical experience. The 'heart's desire' which here mounts by faith to God in Christ, descends to 'work, and speak, and think' for Him in deeds of week-day holiness and acts of love to man. The only limit to these actions is the 'perfect will' and purpose of God for man, as seen in Jesus Christ. The whole being is to be like His, a sacrifice, completed in death.

(ii.) Other Eighteenth-Century Types of Christian Experience

The classic and commanding facts of Wesley's Christian experience had thousands of companion instances, known to him and tested by him, and by others, in the eighteenth century. Here we briefly recount typal instances. The illustrious familiar cases of Charles Wesley, George Whitefield, and John Fletcher may be omitted here, since each was, in several features, like that of Wesley; although each yields its own distinctive note in the common Christian evidence and implication. Nor do we give the familiar case of John Nelson, Wesley's famous lay coadjutor. We select for notice here four distinct types. Except that they all enjoyed a Christian experience which was fundamentally like that of Wesley, they were in almost every feature contrasted with him: i.e. in disposition, quality, training, character, manner of life, and locality of service. All of these persons were well known, ' living letters read and known ' by many. Moreover, their lives entered into the life of their locality and nation. The public archives supply evidence as to their character and service. Similarly the phrase, ' suffered under Pontius Pilate' points to the historicity of Jesus Christ. In each case, original documentary and literary evidence is available for examination.

Asbury

Francis Asbury (1745–1816) was the chief human agent in the moral revolution which accompanied the political revolution in America in the eighteenth century."⁴ These, together, changed the British colonies of New England into the United States. Asbury followed Methodist pioneers from Ireland, and, almost singly, laid the foundations of what is now the largest Christian Protestant community there. Curnock, an expert English student of Asbury, endorses the estimate pronounced by Americans : ' Asbury in labours, suffering, spiritual force, intensity and persistency of purpose, and absolute selflessness, rivalled, if he did not outrival, Wesley.' Dr. E. S. Tipple, the latest biographer of Asbury, has likened this Francis to St. Francis of Assisi. As St. Francis took Poverty for his bride, so Francis Asbury espoused the Road. This was the lady of his chaste love. It was not given to him to know the love of sister or wife. He made another choice. His mystic marriage vow was this, to which he was true until his death : ' I hope I shall travel as long as I live ; travelling is my health, life, and all, for soul and body.' His American itinerations covered two hundred and seventy thousand miles during forty-five years. Nor was this due to his love of wandering. Divine pity, and love of the man who lived by the side of the road and the trail in the wilderness, prompted this dedication and sustained this devotion. Asbury believed himself called by God to this ministry. As a youth he worked at his father's forge at Handsworth, near Birmingham, in the midlands of England. In 1762 Wesley appointed him to be a Methodist preacher. Asbury was inwardly moved to accept this. His fifty-five years of itineration and preaching hold a record unparalleled in Christian history. He was particularly drawn to America as his sphere, and Wesley judged that there was a divine call to this for Asbury. The wilderness of the New World became his circuit, on foot and on horseback. Amidst wild nature, with its almost unbroken strength and beauty; amongst scattered, daring, desperate, needy peoples, and untamed native tribes, went Asbury. Privation, hardships, and perils of all kinds were endured voluntarily and with good humour. This prophet, shepherd, and evangelist of the long road was a pioneer of law, order, and civilization, a teacher of the humanities, and of the worth of man as man. He was a Christian democrat. Chiefly, he was a herald of the redeeming Cross of Jesus Christ.

A study of Asbury's *Journal*[15] and of confirmatory documents, discovers several features in him of evidential value as to the action of God in Christ upon the human spirit and its reaction towards God in Christ. The chief of these is Asbury's steady awareness of the Presence of God. This Presence was at once his court of reference and of judgement, and also his source of inspiration. He was a lone man for very much of his working life, or in conditions in which human counsel, support, or control were very slight. He practised the presence of God as truly as Brother Lawrence. Here are Asbury's testimonies—almost the latest extracts in his *Journal* : ' My consolations are great. I live in God from moment to moment.' Again he says, ' From my stand in the woods I spoke . . . I felt that the word was given me.' In this connexion it is significant of Asbury's spiritual and mental quality that he continually read the Hebrew Bible and the Greek and Latin Testaments; and that Freeborn Garrettson declared that Asbury prayed the most of any man he knew.

Asbury's relation to God produced independence and strength of character. Upon the outbreak of the War of Independence, the English clergy returned home to England. Wesley, a loyalist, summoned his preachers home also. Asbury declined to obey, as he had an intense conviction that he was needed in America. He carried his life in his hand for some years, as he had not taken the State oath. When Washington became President of the United States, Asbury led the Methodists in their congratulations to him. Although appointed by Wesley as Superintendent of Methodism in America, along with Thomas Coke, Asbury declined to accept the office unless he was chosen by a conference of the preachers whom he was to lead. So appointed, he used the title 'Bishop' despite Wesley's protest, because he thought it was warranted by a presbyterial episcopacy. This policy he held to be scriptural, suitable to the conditions of the work he was called to do, and conducive to orderliness.

The fearlessness and moral courage of Asbury also indicate his reliance upon divine resources. Fearing God, he feared no man, nor Nature in her wildest scenes or moods. Hence, at least in part, came his physical endurance. All his life Asbury was an invalid. He was an old worn-out man at fifty years of age. Often he had to be lifted off his horse during his terrible journeyings. Asbury was a martyr for God as well as a prophet of God.

His sense of God's presence and care made him completely unselfish. His allowance as bishop was sixty-four dollars (£12 10s.) a year. He helped his poorer assistants by money, sometimes obtained by selling his few spare possessions. He helped his aged parents in England lovingly and by self-sacrifice. 'I study daily what I can do without,' was his filial resolve.

Brackenbury

Robert Carr Brackenbury (1752–1818) of Raithby Hall, Lincolnshire, contrasts at many surface points with Asbury and Wesley.¹⁴ In substance, his Christian experience was as theirs. He was of historic British family, a wealthy landowner, a minor poet, and a thoughtful prose author. Educated at Cambridge, he passed without any emotional crisis into conscious fellowship with God. His mind was of the reflective, philosophic order. His religious experience began with introspective tendencies, prompted by contact with Platonic thought at his university. Friendship with Wesley and his followers prepared him for duty as a Methodist itinerant preacher, which he discharged during forty years. This work began with the consciousness of 'a divine influence infused into his mind and heart, carrying with it a tide of heavenly love.' Such experience enabled him to overcome his natural diffidence. It also prompted fellowship with any who shared the same experience, notwithstanding difference in social status or acquirements. Wesley noticed Brackenbury's happy attitude towards his tenants in their united worship of God. He and they saw that 'Love, like death, makes all distinctions void.'

Silas Told

A schoolmaster and prison chaplain in London, Silas Told (1711–83) presents another type of Christian experience. His autobiography is a human document of first-rate importance, comparable with Defoe's works.¹⁵ It has indisputable historic and evidential value. Told believed himself to be the subject of divine interpositions during his life as a sailor and a rebel against God and man. He received a divine impression through a sermon of Wesley's in 1740, ' at the close of which,' Told says, ' however strange it may appear, a still, small voice entered my heart, with these words : " This is the truth."' The extraordinary labours and triumphs of Told afterwards in London prisons, among criminals and persons who were condemned to death, indicate his reliance upon superhuman sanctions and resources. Wesley (*Journal*, vi. 221) declared that no man had been so useful in that melancholy office for a hundred years. God had given Told peculiar talents for it, and he had amazing success therein. The greatest part of those whom he attended died in peace, and many of them in triumph of faith. Turnkeys, sheriffs, hangmen, and malefactors alike confessed him to be their helper. Sometimes Newgate had forty prisoners under sentence of death at one time. Told allowed himself to be locked in a filthy cell with each prisoner in turn. He pleaded their cause with man and with God. When the fatal hour came he accompanied them to the place of execution. All this work was done, during thirty years, for no reward except approval by God and by a renewed Christian conscience. Told shares the imperishable fame of John Howard as a prison reformer and friend of humanity.

Lady Maxwell

The last eighteenth-century type to be noticed here is Lady Maxwell (1742–1810).[18] Notwithstanding the restraints imposed by her social status, by the Calvinism of Scotland—the country of her birth and residence—and also by ' that strange reserve which so prevails in North Britain,' as Wesley noted, she dared to 'speak the naked sentiments of her heart.' As thus : 'I have dwelt in the secret place of the Most High, and abode under the shadow of the Almighty. My fellowship with Deity hath been particularly near, solemn and sweet, more so than words can express, with increasing power to realize the divine Presence, to be all attention to an in-dwelling, in-speaking God. I have also been enabled to get through much business.' This was her experience in 1775 and later. Lady Maxwell was only slowly brought to this realization of Deity. Wesley's letters guided her mind through fear of God to this love of God in Christ and this mystic fellowship with God. Southey, who was not a sentimentalist, and admired Butler rather than Wesley, said that the diary of Lady Maxwell 'showed more of high enthusiastic devotion, unmingled and undebased, than is found in any other composition of the kind.' The ethical counterpart of this Christian experience is notable. For fifty years Lady Maxwell was known in Edinburgh for her philanthropy. During this period eight hundred children passed through the schools which she provided, and many poor youths obtained university training. Embarrassed tradespeople, with the sick and poor, shared in her generous help, which her tactful courteousness enhanced in value.

Wesley's Collections of Christian Experience

As stated above, Wesley systematically collected facts of spiritual and Christian experience. The life-stories of his preachers, the men who assisted him in his evangelistic and social work in the

British Isles and other countries, Wesley regarded as of high value. These furnished cogent and abundant evidence of the truth of his teaching, and facts for his inductive argument for the existence and nature of God. Each of such helpers was requested to furnish Wesley with such an account. He urged his request until it was complied with. 'You do not send me your journal yet,' he wrote to Freeborn Garrettson, a wealthy New England slave-holder who voluntarily manumitted his slaves, and was a Methodist itinerant preacher. Dislike of self-advertisement, and seemly reticence as to the intimacies of the spiritual life, must give way, so Wesley claimed, in order that divine truth might be manifested, illustrated, and enforced by these written testimonies. For such purposes he freely used these documents. 'I have long resisted your importunate desire to give you an account of my experience,' Valton wrote to Wesley, in sending his autobiography."

Besides these extended documents, Wesley required his preachers also to send him a circumstantial account of 'every remarkable conversion and every remarkable death' which occurred within the circle of their labours. This method of accumulating and publishing facts of Christian experience was steadily practised by Wesley from 1738 until his death in 1791. He published biographies of his coadjutors, Whitefield and Fletcher, in sermon or volume. Shorter biographies appeared in the *Arminian Magazine* and in his *Journal*." Hence, as Mr. Augustine Birrell says, the *Journal* ' quivers with life and is crammed full of character.' If many of the persons thus referred to were quite ordinary, and never heard of half a mile away from home, it does not follow that their testimony and evidence is worthless and negligible. They are in a great cloud of witnesses to certain facts, common to the experience of all of them, and of Christian people of all ages. These testimonies taken collectively are weighty, and of high moral and spiritual value. In each case the statement is based upon an autobiography, or personal testimony. The facts were tested, and the narrators were trustworthy. Wesley often commended the records for perusal. 'I earnestly desire that all our preachers should seriously consider the preceding *Account*,' Wesley wrote at the end of the life-story and experience of Alexander Mather (*Arminian Magazine*, 1780). Wesley prefixed a note of modification of his own religious views caused by his study of another record of experience, that of Thomas Firmin. 'I was exceedingly struck at reading the following Life; having long settled it in my mind that the entertaining wrong notions against the Trinity was inconsistent with real piety. But I cannot argue against matter of fact. I dare not deny that Mr. Firmin was a pious man, although his notions of the Trinity were quite erroneous' (*Arminian Magazine*, 1786).

Features of this Evidence

In closing this chapter concerning Christian experience, as seen in Wesley and others of his period, we notice some features. The facts collected are very numerous; they are varied and include all types of character and all classes, and degrees in the intensity of the experience; the instances are generally given in detail; they were supported by credible evidence in their period, and can still be investigated and verified. Wesley stated that his teaching that a man can know, and fear, and love God, was supported by the experience of twenty thousand persons. Such facts he offered as his ' living arguments.'[11]

(*iii.*) *Later Typal Instances of Christian Experience*

In essence, Christian experience is the same in all generations. To the foregoing remarkable instances of Wesley and others in the eighteenth century, we now add several typal instances of such experience since that period. The basis of our argument will be thereby extended to our own age, and the implications to be drawn later from the experience of Wesley will be confirmed. As in the former instances, we give only such a statement of facts as will associate these typal lives with our argument. The authentic records, named in the additional notes and literary authorities, and in the Appendix of this volume, must be regarded as an integral part of our argument. A principle of selection in these instances is that adequate information concerning them is available, and is sufficient for every test. The doings of these persons entered into national and civic records. ' These things were not done in a corner.'

Gladstone

William Ewart Gladstone (1809–98),[12] whose life and activity were as representative of the nineteenth century in Britain as Wesley's of the eighteenth, had a vital and vitalizing experience of God in Christ. Gladstone was versatile beyond his peers. He was four times British Prime Minister—a unique record. As statesman he added two million voters to the electorate and secured or inspired beneficent enactments more in number and richer in quality than any modern statesman. His ungovernable thirst for knowledge of all kinds led him to remove all taxes upon knowledge, to open universities to all applicants irrespective of creedal tests, and to offer opportunity to the poorest. He was himself a distinguished classical and modern scholar. His studies of Homer and Bishop Butler are of permanent worth. As a church historian, theologian, and lay ecclesiastic, Gladstone ranked with Döllinger and Lord Acton. All this was summed up and surpassed in the encomium by Salisbury, then Prime Minister, on Gladstone's death. He styled him a 'great Christian man.' His Christian faith animated and empowered Gladstone all through his prolonged illustrious career. Dean Church noted that he had the habit of going direct from communion with God to the discharge of great duties of State. Morley knew Gladstone closely for many years. He affirmed that 'the thought with which Gladstone rose in the morning and went to rest at night was of the universe as a sublime moral theatre . . . to exhibit sovereign purpose for good' (*Recollections*, ii. 94). As a fact, Gladstone's 'thought' went deeper and higher. For him, that 'sovereign purpose' was not an abstraction nor an impersonal force, however good. In his view, phenomena, history, power, and beneficent purpose were manifestations of an infinite Person—God in Christ, who operated by the Holy Spirit. He assured W. T. Stead that living faith in a personal God was the mainstay of civilization : ' I do not hold with " streams of tendency." After sixty years of public life, I hold more strongly than ever to the conviction, deepened and strengthened by long experience, of the reality, and the nearness, and the personality of God.' Gladstone knew experientially that vital union with God which he expounded in his interpretation of Bishop Butler (*Butler's Writings with Subsidiary Studies*, vol. iii.). Hence his famous definition of Christianity as 'the presentation to us, not of abstract dogmas for acceptance, but of a living and a Divine Person, to whom we are united by a divine incorporation. It is the reunion to God of a nature severed from God by sin; and the process is one, not of teaching lessons, but of imparting a new life, with its ordained equipment of gifts and powers' (*Nineteenth Century*, 1888, 'Robert Elsmere'). The life, work, and character of Gladstone are to be regarded as evidence of such action of God, and of human reaction towards God. Gladstone's secretary and intimate friend, G. W. E. Russell, says, 'We see Gladstone in the higher part of his nature fixed and immovable, living in intimate and conscious relation with unseen realities. His inner life was lived unbrokenly with God.' A characteristic note of Gladstone's apprehension of God was humility and a deep sense of his own imperfection. When he was dying, he told Mrs. Benson, wife of Archbishop Benson, that 'nobody needs your prayers more than the poor sinner who is here before you.'

Westcott

Brooke Foss Westcott (1825–1901), a New Testament scholar, philosopher-divine, Anglican bishop, and social reformer, cherished humbly but intensely the conviction of his personal relationship to God in Christ, the supreme manifestation of Deity." This conscious experience animated

his unequalled scholarship. By this, in co-operation
with such friends as Lightfoot, Hort, Moulton,
and others, Westcott gave afresh to Christendom
the New Testament of our Lord and Saviour
Jesus Christ. To Westcott the universe was
a revelation of God : ' We may truly feel that
God not only transcends, but is immanent, and
makes Himself known through all that we come
to know of the world. The Divine light is seen
in and through and not around the objects of sense '
(*Incarnation and Common Life*, 428). Westcott
had a mystic sense of the presence of God ; but
his mysticism, as W. R. Nicoll said, was not suffered
to take the place of science (*Princes of the Church*,
144). Indeed, it was his love of facts and scientific
induction therefrom which sustained his teaching
concerning the Incarnation. He held that that
was the supreme Fact for the mind and heart of
man. God in Christ was his philosophy. This
eternal Fact, realized in time, showed ' that unity,
to which physics and history point, is not to be
found only in a dispersive connexion of multitu-
dinous parts, but is summed up finally in One who
is God ' (*Christus Consummator*, 158). With that
One Westcott believed that he was in conscious
relation. He declared that we do not lose the
sense of the vastness of the divine life in our glad
consciousness of its immediate power (*op. cit.*, 14).
He believed that he shared the divine life, which
he reverently expounded : ' *This is the life eternal
that they may know*—know, such is the force of the
word with a knowledge widening from how to know
under the discipline of experience and opportunity
—*Thee, the only true God, and Him* whom Thou
didst send, even Jesus Christ ' (*op. cit.*, 84). This
experiential knowledge of God in Christ bore fruit

in Westcott's efforts to shape common human life according to life as revealed in the Incarnation. A notable instance was his success in settling the great coal strike in Durham in 1892. Since Deity became incarnate by Jesus Christ, Nature is sacramental; 'this fleshly robe the Lord hath worn.'

William Booth

William Booth (1829–1912) and the work of the Salvation Army, of which organization he was the human founder and first 'General,' afford impressive evidence of divine activity.¹⁴ Booth was an eccentric as to church order and method, but his aims and achievements were unselfish and beneficent. Many results answered every germane test as to their genuineness and moral value, and excited the thankful wonder of all concerned for the highest welfare of the human race. From a different standpoint and by another method than those of Bishop Butler, Booth showed the origin, authority, and possibilities of man's moral nature as designed by God. In the century when some held that the worth and implications of conscience had been invalidated by Darwin's theory of evolution, Booth demonstrated that the spiritual nature of man is a part of human experience. In nearly every climate and among nearly every people, the most civilized and the most savage, he appealed to the moral nature of man, and by the power of his plea transformed the worst of men, even the lowest and most debased, into good citizens capable of extreme self-sacrifice. In Booth's *Life*, and in narratives based on instances of his redemptive service,¹⁵ Mr. Harold Begbie offers unimpeachable evidence that men and women, radically bad, radically evil, a

burden to the State, a scandal to civilization, and
a disgrace to humanity, became honest, industrious,
kind, and happy under the influence of the Christian
religion directed upon them by Booth. It was also
claimed by Begbie for Booth that he did more than
any other man, in the latter half of the nineteenth
century, towards the creation of the Social
Conscience which later made possible the League
of Nations (*Life*, ii. 437 *et seq.*). The personality
and influence of Booth surprised himself and the
world. Compared with Wesley, he showed no
promise. Advantages of birth, breeding, ability, or
training, or of position, money, or influence, he
lacked. Such as he had as a Methodist minister,
he resigned." He stood, in 1865, a solitary, poor
man on desolate Mile End Waste in the East End
of London. He became the central human hope
of millions, and the adviser of monarchs and princes
and the learned. Since Simon Peter, the Galilean
fisherman who uttered the central truth on which
Christianity was built, no more unlikely agent of
a world-wide Christian organization appears in
history. If it be said that occasion offered the
opportunity, it remains to be shown *why* Booth
took it by the hand, and *how* he was able to do so
(*Life*, i. 255). He never doubted, and never allowed
any one, neither millionaire, nor scholar, nor church
leader, to doubt that what he was, and what he
did, was the direct result of the action of God upon
him and through him. His journals and letters
show this (*Life*, ii. 176). William James found
that, while churches may live upon tradition, church
founders owed their power originally to the fact of
their direct personal communion with the divine
(*Varieties of Religious Experience*, 30). No Hebrew
prophet nor Christian apostle was more sure that

he had seen, heard, and felt the power of God than was Booth (*Life*, i. 255 *et seq.*). If his testimony is denied, the results of his experience of the Divine are very difficult to explain.

Cadbury

George Cadbury (1839–1922) was different, in almost every surface feature, from any typal character already considered. He owed almost nothing to ceremony, symbol, or tradition. These meant much to Gladstone and, in some form, to Booth. Ardent and boisterous expressions of religious feeling such as constantly broke from Booth were repugnant to Cadbury. His religious persuasion was that of the Society of Friends, whose tenets are covered by von Hügel's description of Mysticism—an endeavour to find God at first hand, experimentally in the soul herself, independently of all historical and philosophical presuppositions (*Life of George Cadbury*, 5).'' During many hours and the highest moments of consciousness Cadbury obeyed the divine command, ' Be still and know that I am God.' He gained the treble reward—knowledge of himself, others, and God. Alone under the stars, or on a hill overlooking a wide landscape, nature was to Cadbury the handmaiden of the spiritual (*Life*, 254). The voice of the Lord God was heard in the garden in the cool of the evening and this son of Adam was not afraid. He listened, he felt, and received the impress of Reality, as did Wordsworth in his poem ' Expostulation and Reply ' :

> Not less I deem that there are powers,
> Which of themselves our minds impress,
> And we can feed these souls of ours
> In a wise passiveness.

The divine will became often crystal clear to him. The Inner Light showed him the right one among perplexing ways, since the spirit of a man is the candle of the Lord. To Cadbury, God was the one Reality which made life intelligible. As to the nature of God, his mind was unquestioning and incurious, says Mr. A. G. Gardiner. He was as sure of God as of the sun shining at midday (*Life*, 299). The result in Cadbury and his conduct, of this awareness of God and of His action upon him, was exceptional in quality, power, and range. His character was one of unwavering rectitude and a high measure of goodness. Calumny assailed him in vain. He confronted the forces of evil. His was not that ' fugitive and cloistered virtue, unexercised and unbreathed,' which Milton declined to praise, ' that never sallies out and sees her adversary.' He fought unweariedly in the cause of God and humanity, and was nobly tolerant of methods other than his own. With life-long personal effort to uplift individuals, he combined persistent and novel plans for helping communities. The physical, mental, and spiritual planes were all claimed. On the first, he promoted the reconciliation of God and man through the spiritualizing of the material conditions (*Life*, 301). He taught and sedulously practised the principle that a man is a steward of all his possessions. He does not own them, he owes them. He planned and built a garden city for industrial workers, the first of its kind, and the seed of many. He loved the gaiety of open-air activity. At Selly Oak, Birmingham, he established five colleges, a university in small, and stimulated the love of the mind for God and its employment in social service. Christian worship with the use of music and song he enjoyed, and enjoined upon

124 WESLEY, PHILOSOPHER AND FOUNDER

others. This and other developments showed his wish to break through Quaker tradition, where necessary. He strove to unite the churches in a common witness. The sincerity, unselfish and modest service of this Quaker Christian drew from Newman, a Roman Catholic cardinal, his blessing and an admission which broke through the limits of his dogma. 'Mr. Cadbury,' said Newman, 'God will find some way of saving you.'

Whyte

As the words Reason and Love are most frequent among these used by Wesley, the words Evangelical and Experimental were shining favourites with Alexander Whyte (1836–1921). These factual terms were central in his understanding, conscience, and character. He was 'an experiencing Christian,' as thinker, preacher, and writer.[11] A typal man of his generation, he had markedly the note of catholicity. He was a minister of the Presbyterian Free Church in Scotland and Principal of New College; while he had for his human hero the greatest of the Puritan divines and the 'Atlas of Independency,' Thomas Goodwin, and Cardinal Newman as a friend. Whyte published selections from Newman's works, with an 'appreciation.' Similar discriminating and illuminating studies were of Santa Teresa the Spanish Superior, Jacob Behmen the German mystic, Bishop Andrews, Samuel Rutherford, Thomas Shepherd the New England Puritan, William Guthrie, James Fraser the laird of Brea, Sir Thomas Browne of the *Religio Medici*, William Law, Bishop Butler, and Wesley. Whyte was eclectic in spiritual appreciation. He was at once remarkably fervent and tolerant. His

CHRISTIAN EXPERIENCE 125

definition of 'catholic' was his own portrait : 'The true " catholic," as his name implies, is the well-read, the open-minded, the hospitable-hearted, the spiritually-exercised Evangelical, as he is called. He is of no sect. He is of no school. He is of no occasion. He comes of no movement. He belongs to all sects, and all sects belong to him' (*Thirteen Appreciations*, 314).

These features make Whyte's investigations and experience of high value. Biography and the auto-biographic element in literature enthralled him. He gathered from the flower-fields of the soul of all ages and lands. Personality, as of Plato, Homer, Cicero, and Plutarch, he drew into mystic fellow-ship with Dante, Shakespeare, Milton, Knox, Bunyan, Baxter, Wesley, Cowper, and Spurgeon. And it is not too much to say that these masters were recalled by Whyte's skill in analysis, inter-pretation, and use of the imagination. His know-ledge of the experience of these elect spirits, and of many lesser, indeed quite ordinary, individuals, with the Supreme Experience of Jesus Christ, was unique. He spoke and wrote of them with a rare accent, often in language of mystic power and beauty, supplied by his singularly original person-ality. He minted the coin he uttered.

Whyte said that 'theology was to Luther an experimental discipline.' Even so, Whyte believed that it pleased God to reveal Himself in him, Alexander Whyte. What he thus learned he taught, subject to confirmation, correction, and enlarge-ment by the revelation in Holy Scripture, and chiefly by 'the walk, conversation, and character of Jesus Christ our Lord.' A volume with that title was the finest flower of Whyte's genius. It is an imperishable literary offering upon the altar of the Supreme Experience, by a quick, amply-furnished, imaginative mind, and a heart blood-tinctured of a veined humanity. Whyte experienced God. Even so, as Whyte reverently stated, ' Jesus Christ verified divine truth in Himself for thirty experimental years,' as the incarnate Son of God.

The authentic Whyte appeared in many statements like this one in his *Life* (p. 316) : ' My name is Alexander Whyte, and I can put my name in that verse alongside the name of the dying thief and William Cowper.' That poet wrote of the experience of the pardoning love of God, realized by faith in Christ's death, as by the penitent robber crucified with Jesus. Whyte said,

> And there have I, as vile as he,
> Washed all my sins away.

The devotional verses beginning ' Rock of Ages,' and ' Just as I am,' were Whyte's favourite hymn-prayers, frequently used, and often expounded in terms showing appropriating and daring Christian faith, accompanied by deep emotion. Awe and reverence chastened every word used by Whyte concerning Deity ; utter humility, every word concerning himself. Whyte's best-loved phrase, descriptive of the relationship of God and himself, was from Samuel Rutherford's experience, in Mrs. Cousin's words :

> With mercy and with judgement
> My web of time He wove.

By the printed page, Whyte's Edinburgh pulpit and class-desk extended their range throughout the English-speaking world. Millions were awed and inspired by his statements of his experiential knowledge of God. Like Wesley, he delighted in making gifts of books, including his own works.* Whyte enjoined upon ministers to keep that incomparable storehouse of Christian experience, Wesley's *Journal*, ' always lying open beside your study Bible ' (*Appreciations*, 380).

A Summary

Such typal lives as are here noted, from Wesley to Whyte, seem to us irrefragable proofs that there is some One to whom we can give no name but that of God. Otherwise, whence came these personalities, and myriads of others of which they are types ? If it is said that they are exceptions, it seems to us that inferences from them are as reasonable as from remarkable lives of any other class. The contention of von Hügel seems unanswerable : ' It is impossible to see why Plato, Aristotle, Leibniz and Kant, and why again Pheidias and Michael Angelo, Raphael and Rembrandt, Bach and Beethoven, Homer and Shakespeare, are to be held in deepest gratitude as revealers respectively of various kinds of reality and truth, if Amos and Isaiah, Paul, Augustine and Aquinas, Francis of Assisi and Joan of Arc are to be treated as pure illusionists, in precisely what constitutes their specific greatness.' **

The cumulative effect of Christian experience such as that of Wesley, of those here referred to, and of Christians generally, is to give certitude of the reality of God as convincing as anything of which man can have knowledge. Dr. J. R. Illingworth, in his Bampton Lectures, *Personality, Human and*

---

* The arrival of twenty of these volumes, and letters from Whyte, are inspiring memories.

Divine (Lect. v.), claims that 'all who admit the probability, or even the possibility, of a personal God, must be arrested by the spectacle of "this great cloud of witnesses," claiming to have known Him as a person is known. The fact attested is an interior certainty of personal intercourse with God, and, as such, is quite distinct from any consequence or doctrine in whose favour it may subsequently be used—a purely personal fact. The persons who attest it are a minority of religious people, and not therefore to be confused with those who merely believe in its possibility without professing its experience. But though a relative minority, they are strictly "a multitude whom no man can number," competent, capable, sane, of no type or temperament, as old as history, as numerous as ever in the world to-day.'

V

WESLEY'S IMPLICATIONS OF CHRISTIAN EXPERIENCE

THE broad, common fact of Christian experience cannot be denied. However explained, it *is*. The records of Wesley and other typal men considered above show conclusively that they had what they regarded as experiential knowledge of God in Christ by the Holy Spirit. It is now to be shown that Wesley as a Christian philosopher used such facts to imply the existence and nature of God. He represents those who declare that they know God, love God, and obey God, because of His action upon them, and, through them as agents, upon others. These invincible convictions are validated by appropriate effects in their character and conduct. They love and serve their brother whom they see because, although no man hath seen God at any time, they know God in the same way as one human spirit knows another human spirit. Now, if they know, love, and obey God, God exists for them as the Object of knowledge, love, and obedience. These divine effects in them and through them predicate God as the only adequate Cause, and His character as indicated by the kind of results of His action upon them, in them, and through them. Such experience gives to Christian thinkers an interpretation of the universe. All they know or discover is unified in God in Christ. Their philosophy is Christo-centric. It was given to Wesley to trace these implications from Christian experience afresh and with singular impressiveness. His findings are, in their essential features, those which are yielded by Christian experience in every age, and land, and by all kinds of persons. They are therefore of abiding significance.

(*i.*) *The Implications of Christian Experience as shown by Wesley*

In tracing the implications which Wesley drew from facts of Christian experience, we recall and employ an hypothesis which, as suggested, was used by him for his induction. As stated on page 59, this was expressed in his remarkable dictum, 'I am a spirit come from God, and returning to God' (*Works*, v., Preface). This pregnant saying ranks with some others which reveal the authentic Wesley, e.g. 'I look upon all the world as my parish,' and 'we think and let think.' Wesley's genius is in this as in these. When he uttered this, he gave it every sign of importance and authority. It occurs in his most characteristic short piece of writing, the Preface to his *Standard Sermons*. He prefixed it to this statement of 'the essentials of true religion,' uttered for 'the bulk of mankind.' He summoned 'candid, reasonable men' to see 'the inmost thoughts of my heart.' He trusts that 'whereinsoever I have mistaken, my mind is open to conviction.' Such is the setting of this imperishable summary of Wesley's Christian philosophy: 'I am a spirit come from God, and returning to God.' The assumptions in such a statement are those common to thinkers who, like Wesley, receive

CHRISTIAN EXPERIENCE

the teachings contained in the Christian Scriptures. The moral and spiritual intuitions of these Scripture teachings—at least such of them as relate to the life of man upon earth—Wesley held were verifiable by Christian experience. The facts of that experience become the rational basis of faith. Anselm found in ontological reasoning support for his faith; Wesley argued from the facts of Christian experience. As a philosopher, he analysed and synthesized the contents of his consciousness and that of Christian persons, together with its results in character and conduct.

That God is

The existence of God, the ultimate Reality, is implied by Wesley from the fact of personal supernatural action upon his spirit. He affirms his personality, ' I am a spirit,' and from this he infers the Divine Personality. ' Whoever is able to say to himself, I am, will never know rest until he can turn to God and say, Thou art, and then, laying his hand in the Great Father's hand, venture to say, We are ' (Maclaren, *Expositions*, Luke xx. 24). Wesley declared that he was aware of this relationship. He believed that the supreme objective Reality, God, was subjectively experienced by him. He describes the life of God in the soul of one who believes in Him thus : ' God's breathing into the soul, and the soul's breathing back what it first receives from God; a continual action of God upon the soul, and a reaction of the soul upon God, in unceasing love, praise, and prayer ' (*Works*, v. 232, 296).[10] Of such immediate personal action Wesley had himself experience; so had thousands of persons whom he knew. ' I felt my heart strangely warmed,' he wrote of his own transforming experience described in the last chapter. By statements received into his mind, which were read in his hearing on that memorable evening, Wesley held that there was an action by God the Holy Spirit upon his (Wesley's) inner nature, his self. Then and often, by what he thought and felt, he was aware of the action of another Spirit upon his own, a Spirit superior to his own. He had what is called by psychologists the feeling of 'otherness.' That such experience in one's personality is caused by the action of another is inferred from the knowledge that it is not produceable at will, and by the fact that its effects are not always such as the subject may desire. Therefore it is not due to auto-suggestion. As Dean Inge says, nothing could be more devastating to the mystic than to be persuaded that his own mind is the creator of the vision of Truth, Goodness, and Beauty which draws him upward. . . . The Spirit . . . is quite independent of himself (*Relativity, Logic, and Mysticism**). Wesley passed through thirteen weary years of longing for such action upon his mind, conscience, emotions, and will, as he at length experienced in 1738. Nor was this 'otherness' a singular or exceptional feature in his Christian experience, or that of other persons. He carefully noted the frequent occurrence of such action, with this feature in it, upon his own personality. He taught others to do the same. He and they believed that God was the Person who thus acted upon them. Professor C. C. J. Webb defines the term Personality of God as that relation in which the religious man knows himself to stand, as experienced in prayer, worship and song. Religious experience becomes illusory if the

* Aristotelian Society, *Supplementary Volume iii.*, 182.

personality of God be denied. Many facts of this experience have been noticed in our previous pages.

Wesley indicated one class of the facts of such divine action upon him by the use of the note of exclamation (!) in his shorthand diaries and his sermon register (*Journal*, vi. 379 *et seq*., viii. 28, 161, 169 *et seq*.). On one occasion this sign in the diary is expanded in the *Journal* into the phrase ' enlargement of spirit.' That is, he was aware of some power other than that which he controlled, which filled him as the wind fills the sails of a ship. Wesley uses this cryptic sign in such a manner as clearly shows that he intended to indicate by it thankful wonder at divine action. It occurs in his private diaries when he records his use of prayer, the reading of Holy Scripture, religious fellowship, or the Holy Communion, or when he preached. Wesley's diaries show many occasions on which he had this experience of action by another and infinitely superior Mind and Person upon and in him. Sometimes weeks and months pass without the use of this sign. He knew, what was stated long afterwards by Matthew Arnold, that

> We cannot kindle when we will,
> The fire which in the heart resides,
> The spirit bloweth and is still,
> In mystery our soul abides.

As is found by all philosophers, Wesley admits that there is something which cannot be accounted for in terms of human thought in these facts of spiritual experience. There is an ' unexplained residuum ' as to their cause, time, and manner. He covered this by the word ' strangely '—' I felt my heart strangely warmed,' when writing of his crowning experience. Why this event occurred to him at that time, in that manner, he could not explain. Who can explain everything about anything? Nevertheless, here was the event, the spiritual effect of which he was aware: 'I felt.' Now every effect requires a cause.

That the cause of this effect, and of all such experiences, was superhuman, Wesley inferred from the power of which he and those affected were aware in the action upon them. These incursions, uprisings, and stirrings of physical, mental, moral, and spiritual power indicated their origin as not only from Another than the self who was the subject of them, but as from a Source more than human. No mere natural explanation as to the cause of this sense of power experienced was adequate to the facts. Francis Bacon reckoned martyrdoms among miracles because they seem to exceed the strength of human nature."[11] Wesley's experiences, and his collections of such facts, showed that men and women were enabled to become, to endure, to think, to speak, and do that which, without this enabling, was impossible to them. St. Paul declared concerning himself that 'In Him who strengthens me, I am able for anything.'

The moral and spiritual quality of such a superhuman Cause was inferred by Wesley from the kind of experience and its results in conduct. 'I am a spirit come from God,' i.e. from personified Goodness, Wesley affirmed. He believed that Infinite Beneficence or Love was the cause of his being and of his experience, and of other facts of Christian experience. Even before his own transforming experience, the logic of facts compelled him to make this implication. He offered this evidence to his brother Samuel, scholarly and sceptical as he was, who doubted the validity of such inferences and the facts on which they were based. 'You deny that God does now work these effects; at least, that He works them in such a manner. I affirm both, because I have heard these facts with my ears and seen them with my eyes. I have seen (as far as it can be seen) many persons changed in a moment, from the spirit of horror, fear, and despair, to the spirit of hope, joy, peace; and from sinful desires, till then reigning over them, to a pure desire of doing the will of God.' The whole tenor of their life was changed—' till then, many ways wicked; from that time, holy, just, and good' (*Letters of John Wesley*, 58).

Here, then, were facts of religious experience: the impact of another mind, consciously felt by its recipient; the sense of superhuman, indeed of seemingly infinite, power; and a moral quality and a tendency to goodness, mercy, and truth consciously recognized. Now, according to the familiar Cartesian formula, the cause must contain formally and efficiently at least as much as the effect. Whatever other philosophers might conclude, Wesley found himself compelled to conclude that these effects predicated God, the ultimate Reality, as their Cause. They came from God, the source of his own spirit as he declared in his hypothesis. The Fact of God, His existence, was verified by such experience of God's action. For himself, and for many in his age and since, Wesley expressed this philosophy in poetic form, and sang it with devout thankfulness. He entitled the verses, 'Gratitude for our Conversion' (*Poetical Works*, i. 176). He described God's action upon the human spirit, and its reaction towards God. The mind was convinced as to the Fact of God by experience of God, thus:

> I thank Thee, uncreated Sun,
>   That Thy bright beams on me have shined;
> I thank Thee, who hast overthrown
>   My foes, and healed my wounded mind;
> I thank Thee, whose enlivening voice
>   Bids my freed heart in Thee rejoice.

In this testimony, as in much besides, Wesley was restating the evidence afforded by devout spirits throughout the ages. We noticed that of Anselm and of Descartes. It was the experience of Johann Scheffler (1624–77),[11] which Wesley translated in the above lines. This was also the experience and testimony of St. Augustine (354–430). Scheffler found that experience so like his own that he embodied it in this hymn. In this translation Wesley in turn made it his own. Afterwards he taught thousands to use these words to utter their testimony as to the Fact of God. In his adoration of God, Augustine had said: 'Too late have I loved Thee, Beauty so old and yet so new, too late I loved Thee! . . . Thou wert with me, but I was not with Thee. Things held me far from Thee, which, unless they had their being in Thee, had no being. Thou didst call, and cry aloud, and break through my deafness. Thou didst blaze forth, and shine and scatter my blindness. Thou didst touch me, and I burned for Thy peace.' This was his experience of God. Its essential features are common to that of millions of Christians, as they were of Wesley.

God in Christ

The philosophy of Wesley is specifically Christian. Like that of St. Paul, his mysticism centred in Christ (Deissmann, *St. Paul*, 132). Wesley offered an interpretation of the universe which is not that of Deism, nor that of Theism, but that which is implicit in the Christian religion (*Farther Appeal*, ii. 69–78). That is to say, Wesley held that Christ is the eternal Truth for the mind, as He is eternal Goodness for the affections, and eternal moral Beauty for the conscience of man. In his exposition of the Prologue of St. John's Gospel, Wesley states ' that Jesus Christ is *the Word* whom the Father begot or spoke, from eternity ; by whom the Father speaking maketh all things ; who speaketh the Father to us.' The universe is intelligible, and Christ is the Word by which its meaning is communicated. He is the Revealer of the eternal, incomprehensible, invisible Reality. Wesley showed that the facts of experience of Christian persons implied that it was God in Christ who acted upon them : ' We love . . . because He loved (i.e. God loved) us first.' On this passage (1 John iv. 19), which is of profound significance in philosophy as well as in divinity, Wesley says, ' This is the sum of all religion, the genuine model of Christianity. None can say more : why should any one say less, or less intelligibly ? ' Not less emphatic is Wesley's endorsement of the further declaration of St. John, thus : ' We know (i.e. we have fundamental, experiential knowledge, γινώσκομεν) that the Son of God has come, and has given us insight to know Him who is the Real God ; and we are in Him who is real, even in His Son Jesus Christ. This is the real God, this is life eternal ' (1 John v. 20).

This fundamental knowledge is confirmed by Christian experience—experience of God in Christ. From it the existence and character of God can be implied, as by Wesley from his own experience and that of many. God has done in them and for them what Jesus Christ did for men while He was upon earth. He had given pardon, peace, and power. They were reconciled to God and brought into harmony with the divine purpose of the universe. The statement of St. Paul as to his own experience was theirs : ' It pleased God to reveal His Son in me ' (Gal. i. 15, 16). This anticipated the language of modern psychology. Wesley regarded such experience as the heart of the Christian life, as ' scriptural Christianity.' " In so doing he made a notable contribution to thought in his century and for all time. Here he passed beyond the evidences and proofs offered by Berkeley and Clarke and Butler. He showed common human nature as indwelt by Christ. Such persons have, said Wesley, a divine ἔλεγχος *evidence* or *conviction* of the love of God the Father, through the Son of His love ; the peace of God ruling in his heart, a peace which, passing all understanding, πάντα νοῦν, all barely rational conception, kept his heart and mind from all doubt and fear, through the knowledge of Him in whom he had believed (*Works*, v. 39). In a word, the Christian has experience of God as holy, infinite Love. This was the experience of God in Christ, this was the indisputable evidence that God is, and that He is infinite Goodness, which burst into the rapturous songs of the Wesleys and their followers : "

> O for a thousand tongues to sing
> My great Redeemer's praise,
> The glories of my God and King,
> The triumphs of His grace !
>
> Jesus ! the Name that charms our fears,
> That bids our sorrows cease ;
> 'Tis music in the sinner's ears,
> 'Tis life, and health, and peace.
>
> He breaks the power of cancelled sin,
> He sets the prisoner free.

This concept of God as infinite, holy Love, supremely manifested in Jesus Christ, and applied to a human personality by the Holy Spirit, who is God in action, explains the experience of God which Wesley used in his argument that man knows God and loves God, because God loves man. Dr. F. B. Jevons has shown that it is by love manifested that a human personality can know another personality and can be known by another. Otherwise one is inaccessible to the other. Love, shown in words and actions, is the way of understanding, and becomes a bond between persons. It is impossible to speak of inaccessibility where love exists (*Personality*, 150-5). Jesus Christ as the supreme manifestation of the love of God enters into man's personality. The human will responds to that manifestation; and by responsive love man comes to know God and enters into union with Him. St. John declares that we know, we have believed, the love God has for us. God is Love, and he who remains in love remains in God, and God remains in him. This was the core of Wesley's philosophy. Christian experience had amplified and confirmed the philosophical concept of the love of God which he formed in his young manhood and stated in his brilliant disputations for the master's degree at Oxford University. His three lectures had this as their climax. One of these was on natural philosophy, *De Anima Brutorum;* a second, on moral philosophy, *De Julio Cesare;* the third on religion, *De Amore Dei.*

God as Father

Christian experience yielded to Wesley confirmation of the Christian teaching that God as infinite

Love is the Father. This is His eternal relation to Jesus Christ, who is called His Son, according to the Christian Scriptures. A similar, though lower, relationship towards God is open to the human spirit. Jesus taught His followers to think of, to pray to, and make filial claims upon, the Heavenly Father; while St. Paul wrote of the Father from whom every family in heaven and on earth derives its name and nature. 'Father' as a descriptive name for the origin and cause of things is used in many religions. It is, however, agreed by students of comparative religion that this relationship, experienced uniquely by Jesus Christ, taught by Him and by St. John and St. Paul, and experienced by them and by Christians generally, has immeasurably greater meaning than mere creational paternity. God in His fatherly relation was the supreme fact of the universe in the experience and teaching of Jesus Christ." He taught men to call God 'Father.' This use of the name had the correlation of filial duty to God and the brotherhood of mankind. Jesus Christ also taught that divine paternity and sonship are, in essence, community of mind, character, and purpose. The children of God are those who are like God. He spoke of persons who 'belong to your father the devil, and you want to do what your father desires.' Wesley maintained this distinction. He held that, through experiential knowledge of God in Christ, the human spirit may become partaker of the divine nature, and be in communion with Him. He dwells in God and God in him. Christian experience, Wesley held, implied this knowledge of God as Father (*Standard Sermons*, i. 298). This was a notable restatement of vital truth, alike for theology and Christian philosophy. It had long been neglected, and with heavy loss. Few human beings would be likely to *love* God as He was set forth in the discourses of Clarke and Berkeley, and other eighteenth-century divines. The later writings of William Law were an exception in this respect. Generally the monarchic character of Deity was enforced. God was thought of as almighty power and elective will, as in the teaching of Calvin." It was given to Wesley to restate New Testament teaching as to the Fatherhood of God. He taught men to cherish the feeling of awe as they thought of Deity, and fear was retained as a motive in conduct; but it was the awe and fear of a child for a beloved father, the fear of grieving one who loves and is loved. Nevertheless, there was nothing fond or fondling in this concept of God as Father of all and, as in the deepest sense, the Father of His renewed children. Wesley's concept united the holy majesty of God with His tender love, as thus:

> O God, of good the unfathomed sea!
> Terrible majesty is Thine!
> Who then can that vast love express
> Which bows Thee down to me?

In Christian experience this infinite Love was realized as that of a father to his child. They who had this experience addressed God thus, 'My Father, my God.' The action of God in Christ by His Spirit towards them caused their reaction towards God as His children. They humbly sought to obey the scriptural injunction: 'Copy God as His beloved children, and lead lives of love, just as Christ loved you and gave Himself up for you.' These ethical results, which faintly resembled those exhibited in perfection in Jesus Christ, were evidence that God the Father existed, and that they had knowledge of Him. The practical working-out of this philosophy by Wesley and his followers revived New Testament ideas and terms. The Christian community was regarded as an enlarged family. 'The brethren,' 'brother,' and 'sister,' are names which appear frequently in Wesley's documents and letters, as they did in those of St. Paul and St. John. For Wesley, the doctrine of the Fatherhood of God was the foundation of Christian theology and the culmination of philosophy. From it issues the noblest ideal for Christian sociology—mankind as the family of God upon earth.

As God the Holy Spirit

From facts of Christian experience Wesley implied the spiritual nature of Deity and the Person and work of the Spirit of God. Here his philosophy coincides in part with that of Berkeley, who held that ultimate Reality is Mind or Spirit: 'God is Pure Spirit, that Governing Spirit whose Will constitutes the laws of nature' (*Works*, i. 274). God is Spirit, Jesus Christ taught. Wesley constantly used this and other Scripture phrases, e.g. the Spirit of God, the Spirit of Christ, the Holy Spirit. In the light of Christian experience, Wesley refers to himself as a *spirit* come from God. He thought of himself as a spirit having and using a mind and a body. From this fact Wesley inferred that the essential nature of God, the Cause, is Spirit. From his spiritual Christian experience, confirmed by that of many others, he drew inferences which, he believed, confirmed Scripture teaching as to the Person and work of the Holy Spirit. The importance of this contribution to thought is only now being appreciated. Wesley was almost alone in England—certainly he was a pioneer in his period—in these investigations and implications (*Standard Sermons*, ii. 341). A contemporary philosopher-divine, Jonathan Edwards (1703–58), rendered much service in America by his masterly philosophy of the religious revival there, which centred in Northampton, New England. This, he claimed, was a work of the Spirit of God. In England Bishop Warburton held a very different view of Wesley's teaching as to the Holy Spirit and His work then proceeding in the Evangelical Revival. Warburton stated in precise terms that the direct personal influence of the Holy Spirit is limited to the Apostolic age. Aside from the teaching of Wesley and his followers, one searches the discourses of British divines and thinkers of that century almost in vain for references to this subject. It is regarded now as worthy of the fullest and closest exploration."

The Holy Spirit, Wesley taught, is the Comforter or Strengthener, other than God and Jesus Christ and yet one with them, whom Jesus promised to send in His fullness to take His place, as Comrade and Helper of His disciples on earth. The Holy Spirit is God in action in the world of men. From Him comes divine energy. He creates, unites the obedient into fellowship with God and His children, and enlightens, assures, enlivens, empowers, and guides them. Wesley claimed that he had himself such experience of these personal activities of the Spirit of God, and that he knew many others in like case. They were aware of the action of Another Spirit upon their spirit. They received help that does not originate in man; nor is it planted in man, like a seed, and left for him to develop and increase by his own efforts. The Spirit enters and dwells in the human spirit, as St. Paul taught

(1 Cor. iii. 16). Hence the prayer which Wesley used and taught many to pray in song :

> O come and dwell in me,
> Spirit of power within !
> And bring the glorious liberty
> From sorrow, fear, and sin.

The personal action of the Holy Spirit upon the human spirit was specially traced by Wesley in his characteristic teachings concerning assurance and sanctification. He claimed that it is the Holy Spirit, as God in action, who convinces the human spirit of its sinfulness, and assures it of its personal part in the universal divine revelation and work of Jesus Christ as Saviour. The Holy Spirit is also the Agent by which man is drawn towards the measure of development which belongs to the fullness of Christ, instead of remaining immature. Leaving the latter teaching, the former is now noticed. The work of the Holy Spirit as to the fact, resources, and obligations of the paternal relation of God to the human spirit—' adoption '—and the filial relation to God—' sonship '—referred to above, were the subject of careful exposition by Wesley (*Standard Sermons*, x., xlv). He taught that ' the testimony or witness of the Spirit is an inward impression on the soul, whereby the Spirit of God directly witnesses to my spirit that I am a child of God ; that Jesus Christ hath loved me, and given Himself for me.' The Holy Spirit is the Person testifying to a person (the human spirit) as to the above facts. Wesley reaffirmed this teaching, and in the same terms, after twenty years' further experience and investigation. He claimed that it was confirmed by the experience of many, not of two or three, not of a few, but of a great multitude. He adds, appealing to his hearers and readers, it is confirmed by *your* experience and *mine*. ' The Spirit bore witness to my spirit that I was a child of God, gave me an evidence hereof ; and I immediately cried, " Abba, Father ! " ' Such experience gave to those who were the subjects of it absolute certainty concerning God :

> His pardoning voice I hear ;
> He owns me for His child,
> I can no longer fear.

The mark of all full spiritual experience, as Clutton-Brock said, whether it be of beauty or of righteousness or of truth, is always certainty (*The Spirit*, 294).

Another action of God in Christ by the Holy Spirit, observed by Wesley in the facts of Christian experience, was the creation of a new fellowship and unity among those in whom He dwelt. He found such a distinct fellowship among New Testament Christians. It was reproduced in the deep mystic fellowship and oneness which the Christian enjoyed with all persons of any and of every Christian name and rank who had received the Spirit of Christ, the Holy Spirit. Professor H. J. Knowling and Professor Anderson Scott have called attention to the significance of the new Christian fellowship, ἡ κοινωνία, which emerged by the action of the Holy Spirit at Pentecost, following the disappearance of the physical form of Jesus Christ from the earth. There was a new inward oneness of His followers ; they were characterized by 'togetherness,' coming together and acting as one ; they had a social meal together, and shared one loaf as a symbol of their unity ; and they had the same intuition of truth (*The Spirit*, 132). All these features Wesley noted, and endeavoured to reproduce among his followers.

Before his spiritual quickening he knew several Religious Societies which existed in London, Bristol, and elsewhere. A society was a group of earnest Christians who met regularly for prayer, Bible study, and religious fellowship, in addition to attendance at the customary church services. Each society had an enrolled membership. It became an entity and a fellowship. Such societies Wesley and his followers formed wherever they could.[18] All of them, as formed by the Wesleys, were connected as the 'United Societies' of Methodist people. For use by the local church or society, Wesley followed the Moravians and revived the ἀγάπη, or love-feast of the New Testament age. At this Wesley instructed the Methodists to use small cakes and water in token of their fellowship. The meal was followed by a narration of the facts of Christian experience and hymn-singing. In the creation and work of this local and connexional fellowship Wesley saw the action of the Holy Spirit. Its features recalled the promises of Jesus Christ concerning the work of His Spirit, and their fulfilment in New Testament times. The Wesley hymnology has new, deep notes and special terms on this subject. Those who used it besought the Father, Son, and Spirit to unite them, by the Spirit, and in the Spirit. They longed for the harmony of pure love to God in Christ and to one another by the one Spirit, which should issue in united testimony and endeavour.

> Each to each our tempers suit,
> Heart to heart as lute to lute.
> Join our new-born spirits, join,
> Each to each, and all to Thine.
>
> Move and actuate and guide;
> Divers gifts to each divide;
> Use the grace on each bestowed,
> Tempered by the art of God.[19]

The manner of this action of God by the Holy Spirit upon the individual human spirit, and in the fellowship of such kindred spirits, Wesley did not profess to explain. He stood for no one way by which the Holy Spirit produced this inward condition. He said, ' The Spirit so works upon the soul by His immediate influence, and by a strong though inexplicable operation, that the stormy wind and troubled waves subside, and there is a sweet calm ' (*Works*, xiv. 360). Wesley declared that the demand for a minute philosophical account of the manner and of the *criteria*, or intrinsic marks, by which this voice of God the Holy Spirit is known cannot be met in the case of such as have no experience of the divine action upon themselves. Spiritual things are spiritually discerned. Professor C. C. J. Webb compares the understanding of such spiritual experience, only possible for those who share it, with that of the effects of music— ' thrilling,' ' penetrating,' ' moving,' &c. If we ask how musical instruments can do this, the answer is, he says, in the way in which all who are musical know that they do (*Problems on the Relation of God and Man*, 251).

We may anticipate a later section, and notice here an obvious criticism upon such experience. It is that the human spirit may be deceived as to the source, character, and content of such testimony. Some exaltation of one's own spirit, desire, or auto-suggestion, may be the source ; and the character and content may be self-determined : as is sometimes said, ' We hear what we wish to hear.' Even so, the exaltation, the wish, and its rise and form, all remain unaccounted for. Moreover, delusions cannot destroy facts supported by many testimonies, as are these facts of Christian experience

Wesley's intimate knowledge of himself, and of many others, with his collections of spiritual experiences, made him well aware of all such possible delusions. Following the teaching of Scripture, he insisted that the immediate action and testimony of the Holy Spirit to the human spirit should be confirmed by the evidence and testimony of one's own spirit (*Standard Sermons*, i. 221). This last is one's consciousness that he knows himself to be possessed of the spiritual and ethical marks which are observed in one who is assured by the Holy Spirit of his membership in the family of God. The outward proof that an expert has correctly named the nature of a tree is that it bears the fruit of that nature. The chief fruits of the Holy Spirit's testimony and action on man's spiritual nature are love, joy, and peace, with the power for congruous conduct in love of others, joy-giving, and peace-making. These were the very signs and tokens which Wesley observed in the conduct and character of many who averred that they had the mystic inner testimony uttered by the Holy Spirit. That testimony was confirmed by this testimony of a good conscience in them. By observation of themselves, their inner and outer life, they knew themselves to be humble followers of the supreme embodiment of Truth, Goodness, and Beauty—Jesus Christ. This two-fold testimony was found to be the source of abounding joyfulness. It was the assurance of personal participation in the life and love of God. Wesley bursts into eight eloquent repetitions of the words ' I rejoice,' as he considers this spiritual and mystical, but not mythical nor fanciful, experience. He claimed that this teaching was just as ' new as Christianity,' and as old

(*Standard Sermons*, i. 233). He stated that his father, the Rev. Samuel Wesley, Rector of Epworth, among many others, had experiential knowledge of it. During his long last illness he often declared this to Wesley : ' The inward witness, son, the inward witness, that is the proof, the strongest proof of Christianity.'

Implication of Divine Purpose

These implications of Christian experience as to the existence and nature of God as ultimate Reality obviously include infinite knowledge and power, with order and moral purpose as governing ideas. In the classic phrase which, as we have indicated, may be taken to be the hypothesis upon which Wesley worked in gathering the facts of Christian experience, there is a statement of moral purpose : ' I am a spirit come from God, and returning to God.' Wesley found in himself and his experience, and in that of others, evidence of sublime, beneficent design and intention. We have shown that he thus regarded the varied events of his life. In general there was sequence, coherence, and moral value, he argued, in the events of human existence. By His Spirit, God had taught Wesley, so he believed, the truth which Jesus Christ stated concerning the meaning of His own earthly existence : From the Father I came, and I entered into the world ; again I leave the world and I go to the Father ; the Father who sent Me, He it was who ordered Me what to say and what to speak. And I know His orders mean eternal life (John xvi. 28, xii. 49, 50). Wesley's dictum echoes that of Jesus Christ. Jesus Christ, Man, was also a spirit come from God and returning to God. Wesley's

Journal, and the facts which he collected, give the impression of an underlying, controlling moral purpose in human life. This purpose is educative, disciplinary, and preparatory. Like as the seasons march in order serviceable for man, Wesley believed that all events are parts of an infinitely wise, loving, holy purpose, resembled by that of a father for his child. The human spirit is thus prepared, as Wesley believed, for co-operative service with God upon earth, prepared to return to God, who gave it life here, and prepared for eternal bliss and service after death. This infinite, eternal purpose of God was most evident to Wesley in the experience of Christians. These he knew as those who are described by St. Paul—those who were consciously and strenuously working at their salvation with reverence and trembling, since they believed it is God who in His good will enables them to will this and to achieve it.[100] It was this conviction which stirred Wesley to write in condemnation of the closing lines of Pope's elegant piece, ' Verses to the Memory of an Unfortunate Lady.' Pope says:

> Life's idle business at one gasp be o'er,
> The Muse forgot, and thou beloved no more!

' " Idle business," indeed ! ' says Wesley ; ' if we had no better business than this, it is pity that ever we were born ! But was this all the business of his life ? Did God raise him from the dust of the earth, and breathe into him a living soul, for no other business than to court a mistress, and to make verses ? O what a view is here given of an immortal spirit, that came forth from God, and is going back to God ! ' (*Works*, xiii. 386).

Students of Wesley's life who do not grasp his philosophy have written of him as living and acting in an atmosphere of miracle and divine interpositions. Interruptions of Nature and the usual order appear to occur for him, and for others of whom he tells. To Wesley these were not interruptions; rather they were manifestations of the supreme order and of the Orderer and Purposer, from whom the human spirit came, to whom life, in the Christian, was a continuous return in happy, trustful obedience and co-operation, and to whom the spirit was destined to return after its life upon earth. Particular providences were not regarded by Wesley as arranged for him as an individual, but for him as a child of God and a fellow worker with Him, whose Providence is over all His creations to accomplish His world purpose. Wesley's friend, Dr. John Byrom, composed verse-settings of these beliefs (*Miscellaneous Poems*). Wesley admired these, and passed them on to others (*Letters*, 368). They conveyed his thoughts as to the purposes of God for man upon earth, and after death.

> With peaceful mind thy race of duty run;
> God nothing does, or suffers to be done,
> But what thou wouldst thyself, if thou couldst see
> Through all events of things as well as He.
>
> Faith, Hope, and Love were questioned what they thought
> Of future glory, which Religion taught:
> Now Faith *believed* it, firmly, to be true,
> And Hope expected so to find it too;
> Love answered, smiling with a conscious glow,
> 'Believe! Expect! I *know* it to be so.'

A Summary

The several implications shown by Wesley in the facts of Christian experience, and stated in this section, may now be gathered together. He conceived ultimate Reality as infinite, personal, fatherly holy Love; as supremely manifested in Jesus Christ, and operant in the world of men by the Holy Spirit. These implications are, in general, confirmed by the experience of Christians in all ages.

(*ii.*) *Confirmation of these Implications by the Nature of Man*

Speculative philosophy, said Wesley, ascends from man to God; practical philosophy descends from God to man (*Philosophy*, i. 14). The implications which Wesley as philosopher-divine traced in the facts of Christian experience concerning the existence and nature of God, the ultimate Reality, were confirmed, Wesley held, by their congruity with the nature of man, with his needs, and with his highest ideals. A philosophy of the universe, if based upon Christian experience, appeared to Wesley to offer a rational explanation of man and satisfaction to his needs and stimulus to his aspirations. Berkeley's idealistic philosophy had similar commendation. His concept that God is omnipotent Goodness, Power, and Intelligence attracted many inquirers by the fact that the universe becomes intelligible on that assumption. Our 'cosmic experiences' approve the venture of our faith. All reasonable human intercourse with the phenomena presented in the universe is found to need the support of intellectual and moral faith. Conversely, naturalism, materialism, and mechanism leave most men dissatisfied. They are therefore unable to accept either of them as an explanation of world phenomena. The philosophy based on Christian experience, however, can appeal to pragmatic sanctions. It fits man and works well. The Christian is the highest type of man. The type shows what he is, or may become, upon this workable philosophy. Justin Martyr found Christianity to be the only philosophy that is sure; and for this, with other reasons, that it is suited to man's needs.

They offer an Explanation of the Nature of Man

The hypothesis of Wesley's inductive philosophy —' I am a spirit come from God, and returning to God '—indicates his teaching on the origin and nature of man. He regarded the spirit as the chief part of man, his innermost nature. This teaching is significant. God is Spirit, as we have seen, and God in action is called the Holy Spirit. In his fullest exposition [101] Wesley regarded man's nature as tripartite (*Works*, xi. 447). Man consists of body, soul, or mind, and spirit. This scriptural teaching Wesley used and enforced, especially in his findings and implications as to Christian experience. He distinguished these parts in man's nature without dividing it or impairing its unity. His evangel was for the whole man. The spirit, he said, is ' the highest principle in man, the immortal spirit made in the image of God, endued (as all spirits are, so far as we can conceive) with self-motion, understanding, will, and liberty. The soul seems to be the immediate clothing of the spirit.' This agrees with some modern psychologists who regard the soul as the intermediate element in the nature of man; the body being the lowest, the spirit the highest, of the three parts. Wesley regarded the last-named, the spirit, as the special organ of God-consciousness in man, and its function as spiritual-mindedness.[102] He practised and enjoined upon others the duty of complete, daily renewed, dedication of the whole being to God.

> My spirit, soul, and flesh receive,
> A holy, living sacrifice;
> Thou hast my spirit, there display
> Thy glory to the perfect day.

Man's nature, as thus found in Christian experience, indicates its origin. Humanity, especially Christian humanity, offers indications of its source. The life of God is in man. He bears the image of God. Wesley here agrees with Butler as to the nature of man as designed by God. Every man has religious experience. This reaches its highest form in Christian experience. Wesley declared that ' no man living is entirely destitute of what is vulgarly called natural conscience.' But this is not natural; it is more properly called preventing grace : i.e. the grace which comes before conscious love of God. 'Every man has a greater or less measure of this, which waiteth not for the call of man. There is no man that is in a mere state of nature; there is no man, unless he has quenched the Spirit, that is wholly void of the grace of God' (*Works*, vi. 512). With the help of a scholarly and saintly clergyman, John Fletcher, Wesley resisted and rejected the teaching of Calvinists that 'a natural man is as dead as a stone.' With equal vigour, Wesley asserted that 'no infant ever was, or ever will be, sent to hell for the guilt of Adam's sin ' (*Works*, xii. 437). Without using the term psychology, Wesley expounded mental philosophy. He held that, while the moral and spiritual change wrought in man by God in Christ through the Holy Spirit, whether wrought suddenly or gradually, made no organic alteration in him, it completely rearranged the functions of his nature. He became a new man practically. There is, said St. Paul, a new creation whenever a man comes to be in Christ (2 Cor. v. 17). In this event, conscience is relieved of its burden of guilt, increased in its sensitiveness and power, and closely associated with an infallible standard, supplied by Holy Scripture as interpreted by and in Jesus Christ who is the Word of God. The mind is attracted to love and learn the Mind of God in Christ, revealed by the Holy Spirit. The emotions are centralized in that of love, and this love is moved by Infinite Love. 'For Christ's sake' becomes the master motive both of self-development and service of others. The will, being delivered from slavery to evil habit and tendency, becomes free. It is empowered by conviction of truth and by purified desire. Wesley's concept of God as acting directly upon the human spirit and causing its reaction towards God recognized the human will and its real, though necessarily limited, freedom. Rashdall styled Wesley a Libertarian because of this teaching. Wesley revolted from Calvinism not only because of its view of God with ruthless decrees as to man's 'election,' but because that teaching degraded the nature of man. He rejected Fatalism and Mechanism as falsified by human experience and destructive of morality. He said, 'I cannot believe the noblest creature in the visible world to be only a fine piece of clockwork' (*Thoughts upon Necessity*). The recoverability and salvability of man were features of Wesley's working philosophy. He sang this evangel, and inspired all who would help him to sing it :

> Come, all the world ; come, sinner, thou
> All things in Christ are ready now.

The suitability to mankind of a philosophy which included such an invitation is manifest. It interpreted man to himself. As it quickened conscience it quickened consciousness. By knowledge of God a man was brought to know himself. He learned that he was of God, from God, and for God. The cosmic and moral order which he found in phenomena and himself, unifying knowledge and indicating God as first and final Cause, explained his own being also, as in Wesley's dictum, ' I am a spirit come from God, and returning to God.' In the concept of God as Father, manifested in Jesus Christ and working by the Holy Spirit, man finds that he is dear to God ; can be conformed to His image ; may share His spiritual, holy nature ; and can achieve the divine purpose and co-operate with God therein, ' a worker with God ' (2 Cor. vi. 1).

They satisfy the Needs of Man

The conception of Deity implied from the facts of Christian experience offers satisfaction to the needs of man. That conception is thereby confirmed as true. Besides a sense of obligation, man has an ineradicable sense of dependence. He is a needy creature, as to his body, mind, and spirit. Often he is tired and worn, and quivers with pain. He finds himself ignorant, and therefore disquieted and fearful. He is often mistaken and defective. He needs must love the highest when he sees it ; but often he appears to be blind to beauty in her loveliest forms. He knows himself to be morally impotent and offensive. ' I know the good, but I do the bad,' said Ovid, voicing the confession of mankind, even of elect spirits like St. Paul (Rom. vii. 15–25). And each human spirit knows himself to be a solitary, who nevertheless longs for fellowship and to be understood by love which evokes and responds to his love.

These common human needs Wesley felt intensely. If the outlines of Wesley's life and work given above are read again, it will be realized that his experience was singularly varied and inclusive. Poverty, the burden of debt, physical ailments, sufferings and perils, emotional crises, poignant grief, domestic misery, misunderstanding and desertion by quondam friends and lovers—all these he knew experientially. Intense thirst for knowledge kept him searching for the fountains of truth or singing his pæan to ' Primeval Beauty.'[103] Hunger and thirst after righteousness, the most ancient pangs of the human spirit, he knew. His quest for the assurance of divine pardon, for peace, poise, self-control, moral power and joy, drove him for long years over land and sea. ' I know their sorrows,' he could say, as he looked at the poor and the rich, at prisoner and monarch, at the tempted and the tried. Neither so-called noble savagery, nor contented ignorance, nor affected gaiety deceived him. He knew well that often a crown is better to look at than to wear.[104] Experience, observation, and tested knowledge convinced him that nothing but infinite Pity is sufficient for the infinite pathos of man's life and needs.

It says much that a man so various as Wesley, with an eager, disciplined mind, a nature formed for friendship and love, and a genius for religion and practical helpfulness, found a working philosophy in the implications which he traced from Christian experience. These afforded him an interpretation of existence adequate for immediate needs, with a promise of increasing understanding in the afterwards of earthly life and beyond it; and also the solace and stimulus of infinite Love as ordering, permitting, or conducting every event of existence for the perfecting of the individual and all who linked themselves with the moral purpose of the universe. As the sympathetic student turns the closely-written, cryptic pages of Wesley's diaries, and even those of his versatile *Journal*, he fancies he hears Wesley singing to his needy self the faith which his brother had expressed, and which thousands shared with them :

> Peace, doubting heart! my God's I am:
> Who formed me man, forbids my fear;
> The Lord hath called me by my name;
> The Lord protects, for ever near;
> His blood for me did once atone,
> And still He loves and guards His own.

The closing couplet of that verse includes a feature in Wesley's concept of God as Infinite Love which met a deep need, felt by him and by many. It is an allusion to the scriptural doctrine of the death of Jesus Christ for the sins of the human race. Whatever theories are held in regard to the purpose and meaning of the death of Jesus Christ, it must be linked with religious sacrifices and the sufferings of the innocent in all ages and lands. The fact of it exhibits, as does nothing else, the crime and sin of man against Infinite Love. It shows also the manifestation of that Love, which reaches its culmination and makes its redeeming appeal in the sufferings and death of Jesus Christ. Wesley was conscious of his own moral defectiveness and offences. As we have seen, he was fettered in youth and manhood by a clinging habit of sin. He knew that, morally and spiritually, he was not what he was designed to be. He was painfully aware of moral inability. He was granted times of spiritual insight, when he saw God's relation to himself. This was applied, through the common faculty of faith, to a particular object. He saw himself as a sinner, guilty and weak; and God as Saviour in Jesus Christ, and as a Renewer and Strengthener by the Holy Spirit. Here was his deliverance from clinging sin. His will gained freedom and was empowered. Here too was the Divine Comrade who dispelled his loneliness. Wesley found that this teaching was as water to the thirsty, as life to the dying, in thousands of instances. At Epworth, in 1742, where large audiences waited upon his messages, delivered in the open air, Wesley cried out on one occasion, ' Art thou a sinner ? ' A gentleman in the crowd uttered the thoughts of the heart for many. ' Sinner enough,' he replied. And, like many there and elsewhere, he came to know Jesus Christ as Saviour.

Such a conception of God as ultimate Reality, which meets the needs of man as does this offered by Wesley, is entitled to regard on that account. It comes home to men's business and bosoms. As Coleridge said of Holy Scripture, ' It *finds* me.'

They develop Man's Capabilities

The philosophy built up by Wesley from the facts of Christian experience provides for and inspires the fullest development of the capabilities of man. It is in harmony with his highest hopes. Wesley's concept of God as first and final Cause, the heavenly Father, includes union with God in Christ by the Holy Spirit. This union is not absorption. The christianized personality partakes the divine nature, as a branch in the true Vine, and has eternal life and supernatural resources. This was the hope which Wesley set before man. He found it in the New Testament Scriptures. It is realizable through faith. Faith is an attitude of the human mind by which it realizes the invisible, the imponderable, and intangible, and actualizes them in time and space, for divine purposes. It co-operates with the will of God. The prayer of faith, ' Lord, what wilt Thou have me do ? ' is followed by effort to do the will of God.

Wesley was a man filled with hope and faith, as well as love. These were features of his Christian experience. He despaired of no man, not even of himself. Concerning an abject victim of the habit of intemperance he wrote, ' Incite him not to cast away hope. Nothing but his despair of conquering can totally destroy him ' (*Letters*, 256). Of faith, the wonder-working companion of hope, Wesley was the chief herald and champion in his century. His four discourses upon this subject are remarkable for comprehensiveness, clearness, and force. They include the last sermon written by him. To the end of life, his was a peering, wistful, venturing spirit. He held that the spirit of man can leap towards an ideal and be empowered to actualize it in large measure. This is the staggering but unmistakable teaching of Jesus Christ : ' It shall be according to your faith.' Wesley unites metaphysics and ethics in his verse :

> All things are possible to God,
> To Christ, the power of God in man,
> To me, when I am all renewed,
> When I in Christ am formed again.

This most significant Christian phrase, ' in Christ,' occurs one hundred and sixty-four times in St.

Paul's writings (Deissmann, *St. Paul*, 128). What limits can be set to the operations of man in God and indwelt by God? Wesley often used the bold description of faith written by his brother Charles:

> Faith, mighty faith, the promise sees,
> And looks to that alone;
> Laughs at impossibilities,
> And cries, It shall be done!

The ideal which Wesley held before man is thus the very highest conceivable. It is conscious participation in the divine nature, and wholehearted co-operation in its creative and redemptive purposes. In St. Paul's phrase this ideal was thus stated: 'You shall be my sons and daughters, saith the Lord Almighty.' A more inspiring concept is impossible. It is an inexhaustible ideal and an eternal hope. It comes from God through Jesus Christ: 'He said to me, You may be sons of your Father in heaven: you must be perfect, as your heavenly Father is perfect' (Matt. v. 45, 48). This moral idealism is behind Wesley's teaching as to Christian perfection. This, with his doctrine of Assurance and his universal appeal to mankind to believe in God as Infinite Love, are his chief contributions to theology. In its moral aspects he called his idealism Christian Perfection. It coheres with his Christian philosophy and is the ethical counterpart of his metaphysic. By perfection Wesley meant that which is complete in all its parts and performs all its functions. Man is made for growth and development towards God. Accordingly, Wesley rejected the idea of finality, both as to the human discovery of truth and its manifestation in act and character (*Works*, xi., 'Plain Account' and 'Brief Thoughts').[144] His definition of Christian perfection is that it is the humble, gentle, patient love of God and our neighbour, ruling our tempers, words, and actions. This ideal and hope inspire prayer, as thus :

> Turn the full stream of nature's tide ;
> Let all our actions tend
> To Thee our source : Thy love our guide ;
> Thy glory be the end.
> Earth then a scale to heaven shall be ;
> Sense shall point out the road.

Nor was this inspiring ideal of perfection or completeness offered by Wesley to the individual only. He held that humanity also is intended for, and is invited to realize, this divine purpose. In his Oxford University sermon, *Scriptural Christianity*, Wesley offered a draft picture of the earth and mankind when this hope reaches fruition. ' Let us stand a little,' he says, ' and survey this strange sight, *a Christian world* ' (*Standard Sermons*, i. 103). In such a world he saw that subhuman nature flourished under industry and invention. Oppression, extortion, injustice, racial war, were all of them absent. Mercy, kindness, love, and truth were everywhere. Happy are the people, quotes Wesley, that are in such a case. His philosophy had the note of progress—physical, intellectual, moral, spiritual, social, racial, universal progress.

If it be fact that ultimate Reality is infinite Goodness, Truth, and Beauty—or, as Wesley stated in arguing from facts of Christian experience, if the Cause and End of all is Infinite Love as the heavenly Father, manifested in Jesus Christ working by His Holy Spirit always and everywhere—it can be affirmed that these implications commend themselves to the thoughtful mind by their fitness. They afford to man as man, to mankind everywhere, a working explanation of his origin, nature, and destiny; satisfaction for his needs, and a hope and an ideal. The hope and the ideal are indeed,

> Beyond my knowing of them, beautiful,
> Beyond all knowing of them, wonderful—
> Beautiful in the light of holiness.

Nevertheless, man appreciates these as gleams of Infinity and finds them magnetic to himself at his best.

All Christian Experience the same in Essentials

We conclude this statement of the implications and confirmations from Christian experience as to the being and nature of God by recalling a fact noticed at the opening of this chapter. This argument rests upon experience which is common to all Christians everywhere. Wesley and several typal characters were noticed, and his implications in Christian experience were traced. The expert and his experience incites and rewards attention. But this is not essentially different from that of each in his class. The experience of the Christian commonalty supports the inferences drawn from that of their leaders. The experience of all shows how truly congruous with man's nature and its needs and possibilities is this belief concerning God and His action upon man. All Christians, the expert and the tyro, are really one. They differ in attainment, sectional name, creedal expression, and form of service; they are one in their worship of God in Christ by the Holy Spirit, as infinite Goodness, Truth, and Beauty. All realize that it is their privilege to know God by faith, to love Him, and to imitate Him in character and conduct. The humblest, most imperfect, sincere Christian has, in a measure, his realization of God in Christ which is enjoyed in fullness by all the saints. Of the saints, Dean Inge says that it will be found that these 'men of acknowledged and pre-eminent saintliness agree very closely in what they tell us about God. They tell us that they have arrived gradually at an unshakable conviction, not based on inference, but on immediate experience, that God is a Spirit with whom the human spirit can hold intercourse; that in Him meet all that they can imagine of goodness, truth, and beauty; that they can see His footprints everywhere in Nature, and feel His presence within them as the very life of their life, so that in proportion as they come to themselves they come to Him. They tell us that what separates us from Him and from happiness is, first, self-seeking in all its forms; and, secondly, sensuality in all its forms; that these are the ways of darkness and of death, which hide us from the face of God; while the path of the just is like a shining light, which shineth more and more unto the perfect day. As they have toiled up the narrow way the Spirit has spoken to them of Christ, and has enlightened the eyes of their understandings, till they have at least *begun* to know the love of Christ, which passeth knowledge, and to be filled with all the fullness of God' (*Christian Mysticism*, 325). These marks had Wesley's experience of God: these truths he told men concerning God.

VI

CRITICISM OF THE PHILOSOPHY OF CHRISTIAN EXPERIENCE

WESLEY's philosophy, as based on Christian experience, shares the criticism directed against all Christian experience and argument therefrom. In addition, there are criticisms which are directed against Wesley's presentation of this statement. Three objections are here noticed: that such philosophy can only claim limited acceptance; that it is based chiefly upon facts of emotional experience; and that the experience used is self-caused. Reference is also made to special features in Wesley's presentation.

(i.) *That it is limited in its Appeal*

Christian experience is as rock beneath the feet of those who have it. It is also the ground of their most cogent appeal to others. They have the certitude of the man in the gospel story, whom Jesus Christ cured of his blindness; and, like him, they become missionaries for their Healer. This man said, ' One thing I do know, that once I was blind, now I see. Do you want to be His disciples?' [100] Here is shown at once the strength and weakness of this argument. Its force is limited to those who have shared the experience. To them it is almost everything; to others it matters little. At least, so it is sometimes contended. In the present case it is *Christian* experience which is considered. This, by its nature, is limited to Christians. Only they can use it, or feel its full force.

The limitation contained in the statement, ' I know this because I have experience of it,' applies to knowledge of every kind so obtained. Nevertheless, such knowledge is accepted as real if it complies with proper tests. For instance, it has been said that only he who has felt the pangs of hunger can properly pronounce that word, i.e. he cannot know what he speaks of unless he has personal experience of hunger. Nevertheless, the word hunger is used to describe a fact by those who avoid personal knowledge of its content. We feel the force of an argument based upon the experience of intense hunger, although we have not shared the experience. The cogency of such an argument is due to two features in it. The experience on which it is based has been shared by many besides the one who argues from it; and it is open to any to test his argument by enduring similar experience. These two features give real and wide cogency to the argument from Christian experience. Those who have had an experience of God in Christ by the Holy Spirit are truly ' a multitude whom no man can number.' They include all types, ranks, classes, and races, and these in all stages of development. Differing in nearly every other feature, in this they agree absolutely: they know God by experience. By the Holy Spirit's action upon them they are sure of God in Christ, or they are not sure of anything. The subjective experience of God guarantees the experient's explanation because, and in so far as, the explanation is supported by common experience. It is sober truth to say that there is not, nor can there be, any fact of experience, apart from self-consciousness, of which so many are sure as of this—that God is. Whether man knows it by intuition or infers it is not material. The ineradicable religious instinct of mankind as recorded in history, is proof that God is the great Fact for man. The Christian religion is at once the deepest satisfaction and the strongest reinforcement of that instinct. In a sense Christian experience is a development of religious experience, which is universal. Moreover, it is open to all to test it experientially, each for himself. There is nothing occult nor selective in Christianity. Its mysteries are open to all; any one may be of its elect.

Certainly this was Wesley's interpretation. He held the philosophic clue of the maze—that the universal is the true. His practical Christian philosophy has been summed up in five universals: that every one needs divine spiritual quickening and energy; that every one can receive it; that every one can thereby achieve Christian completeness; that every one may be conscious of receiving it; and that every one should testify of it in fellowship and service. He systematically and steadily excluded the evidence of the peculiar, the eccentric, and the fanatical. Like all investigators, he records such instances of experience. He knew well the small appeal which they make to reason, and that the exception proves the rule. It was, however, from the normal and the common that he made his induction. The testimony of 'feelings' of the individual were tested by him by their conformity to type. The Archetype and Ideal is the mind of Christ, the Son of Humanity. Wesley grouped his followers in bands, classes, societies (churches), and conferences. He submitted his 'experience,' and required them to submit theirs, to be tested by the corporate mind. He stood for the *communis consensus fidelium*, the verdict of the community of the faithful. As always when it renews its life, Christianity as interpreted by Wesley was intensely missionary. The argument from Christian experience is widely based, and all may test it. In this way its appeal becomes practically unlimited, and all who are willing to do so can become aware of its power. That it imposes conditions for this is referred to later.

The criticism that the argument from Christian experience is limited in its force is sometimes stated in another way. If this experience is produced by the work of the Holy Spirit, the Spirit of Christ, and of God, bringing Jesus Christ into the individual human spirit and also into communities, the argument must be limited to those who know of Jesus Christ. Two-thirds of the human race are at present under the disability of ignorance of Him. Admitted that the number grows less in each succeeding generation, it is still very large. The argument from Christian experience can neither help these nor appeal to them, at least in its direct form. This criticism is true in part. Because of its truth, Christians feel themselves under deep and continuous obligation to obey the missionary impulse and communicate to others the good news of the love of God in Christ; to explain to all the purpose of the religious instinct with its satisfaction in, and development by, Christian experience. St. Paul did this. 'Men of Athens,' he said, 'you are a most religious people. I proclaim to you what you worship in your ignorance.' Wesley, and

CRITICISM OF EXPERIENCE 169

many of those upon whose Christian experience he based his philosophical implications, discharged this obligation, as we have shown. It must not, however, be overlooked that the appeal and action of God in Christ by the Holy Spirit preceded, went beyond, and is continued beyond, the knowledge of Christ imparted by the New Testament records. Jesus Christ did not limit His appeal to those who knew Him in His earthly life, nor do Christian apologists. In expounding the prologue of St. John's Gospel, Westcott says that the Word, before the Incarnation, was the one source of the many divine words; and Christ, the Word Incarnate, is Himself the Gospel. The true Light which lighteth every man was ever coming through the ages, and was universal while personal. Faith and goodness may be unconscious of their relation to the historical Jesus Christ; but they are spiritually and vitally connected with Him in God by the Holy Spirit, through His activity in each man and every man.[1] Conscience in man is related to the conscience of Jesus Christ, in whom it testified that He did always the things that pleased God. God is immanent and transcendent. Of this eternal truth the Incarnation is the supreme manifestation in time and space. Jesus Christ therefore recognized the attitude of the human spirit towards truth and goodness as shown towards Himself. He declared Himself to be the Light of the World, and that Abraham the patriarch rejoiced in mystic fellowship with Him, Jesus Christ. He stated also that in the Last Judgement He will regard helpfulness to men, shown by those who had no conscious knowledge of Himself, as shown to Himself. That they had the experience of the action of God in Christ by His Spirit is attested by their deeds. They acted as Jesus Christ would have acted : ' I tell you truly, in so far as you did it to one of these brothers of Mine, even to the least of them, you did it to Me ' (Matt. xxv. 40). The essential Christ, the Christ of history, and the Christ of Christian experience, is the same God in Christ acting by the Holy Spirit, everywhere, always. This teaching was repeated by Wesley in effect. He was a catholic theologian by religious conviction, as well as by his philosophical tendencies. He believed that the Roman Emperor Marcus Aurelius, ' a strange heathen,' would, with Old Testament saints, enter the heavenly Kingdom of God. ' I have no authority,' he wrote in 1790, ' from the Word of God to sentence all the heathen and Mohammedan world to damnation. It is far better to leave them to Him that made them, and who is the Father of the spirits of all flesh. . . . I believe the merciful God regards the lives and tempers of men far more than their ideas ' (*Works*, vii. 353).[1**] ' Rest not,' he pleads, in his noble sermon entitled ' The General Deliverance,' ' until you enjoy the privilege of humanity, the knowledge and love of God.' In Wesley's view, the essential Christian experience is the same always, everywhere, and in all ; or, it is possible to all.

It is admitted that there are two conditions which limit the enjoyment of Christian experience, and thereby, the full effect of the argument based upon it. There is a price to be paid for this inestimable possession. The conditions are these : absolute sincerity in the search for truth and earnest endeavour to act in obedience to it. No one can understand a person unless sincerely he wishes to do so. Obedience is the organ of knowledge. Any one who chooses to do the will of God can have real, though limited, knowledge of God. Isaiah declared this of God, 'Thou meetest him that rejoiceth and worketh righteousness, those that remember Thee in Thy ways.' This teaching has been described as 'a great staircase with three flights in it, and at the top, God's Face.' Moral harmony of a human will with the divine will bring knowledge; sympathy with it brings understanding of it; right-doing brings man face to face with God, who is the Righteous One, and whose Spirit prompts and sustains every effort made towards the moral ideal. This is the regimen for those who would have experience of God in Christ by the Holy Spirit.'" Nor is this knowledge singular in imposing a regimen upon those who would have it. Knowledge of every kind has conditions which must be met before it is attained. Darwin told an inquirer that the secret of discovery is 'Meditation, meditation.'

Did Wesley demand special features in Christian experience, and thereby limit the range and usefulness of the argument he based upon it? That he did this is one of several misrepresentations concerning him and his teaching. It was repelled by him, but it still lingers. Baring-Gould repeated it, and other errors, in his unworthy work already referred to, *The Evangelical Revival*. It is said that Wesley required an emotional crisis as evidence of action by the Holy Spirit upon the human spirit and its reaction towards God; that conversion, or any spiritual experience, must be instantaneous; and that every one who is in Christ is conscious of the fact, by the testimony of the Holy Spirit given along with the testimony of his own spirit thereto. Not one of these statements represents Wesley's mature teaching or practice. Wesley's critics are often strangely ignorant that they are repeating mis-statements made in Wesley's day, which have been refuted again and again. Examples of such errors are found in Bishop Gibson's charge to his clergy in 1747. Wesley's Letter to him supplied the corrections (*Works*, viii. 481). These are often ignored, with other refutations. The types of Christian experience summarized above, e.g. Brackenbury and Lady Maxwell, besides Wesley's many explicit statements, show that some of his chief workers passed through no emotional crisis. Like every decision, religious decision is instantaneous. It is a knife's edge; but, says Wesley, ' I believe a gradual work both precedes and follows that instant. Be this given in an instant, or by degrees, hold it fast: Christ is yours ' (*Letters*, 394).

Even such philosphers as William James misrepresented Wesley on this matter. Methodists, he said, demand a spiritual crisis, and he quoted Wesley's summary of many cases which met this demand : ' sanctification is commonly, if not always, an instantaneous work.' This statement, however, does not make instantaneousness a test of the genuineness of Christian experience. Wesley there refers to one kind of it only. He invites his readers, following immediately upon this quotation used by James, to leave undecided the question whether this work is wrought instantaneously or gradually (*Works*, vi. 491). Nor did Wesley require that every one should possess conscious knowledge, or ' feeling,' of the action of God in Christ by the Holy Spirit. He desired all to seek, and he taught that all may obtain this assurance, and thereby an increase of their peace, joy, and power ; but he did not make its possession a test. Joseph Benson, the classical tutor at his school at Kingswood,

CRITICISM OF EXPERIENCE

Bristol, had not this happiness, at least for several years; but in his letters to him Wesley did not question the genuineness of his Christian experience and his direct knowledge of God. It was only at the beginning of their work that the Wesleys taught that unless one knows his sins are forgiven, he is under the wrath and curse of God. After fifty years of experience Wesley affirmed that 'the Methodists know better now.' [110]

(ii.) *That Emotion is its Chief Element*

A second criticism offered upon the argument from the facts of Christian experience is that its chief feature is emotion. In any case it is alleged that Wesley relied too largely upon this feature. To this criticism as a whole the reply may be made that, according to modern psychology, man is largely a creature of emotion (*The Spirit*, 85). The motion of the will is dependent upon emotion. The gateway to the Christian life is the emotion of love, says Principal H. Maldwyn Hughes, M.A., D.D. (*Theology of Experience*, 147). The facts of Christian experience show that few persons have full and rich knowledge of God and divine things whose emotional nature is feeble. This must be so if ultimate Reality is holy Love. On the other hand, it is untrue to say that, in Christian emotion, which moves the will, the mind has not its full share in the apprehension of truth. The supreme command as uttered by Jesus Christ includes both, while it shows that love is the central emotion: 'You must love the Lord your God with your whole heart' and 'with your whole mind.' Christian civilization shows that both parts of this command have been obeyed. The Renaissance of

174 WESLEY, PHILOSOPHER AND FOUNDER

Learning and the Reformation of Christianity in the sixteenth century are two aspects of one movement of the Holy Spirit. Protestantism ' sustained the experimental method and sought in nature the mind and will of God.' Apart from the divines referred to in the present study, three leaders of thought in the eighteenth century, Newton, Addison, and Dr. Samuel Johnson all loved God devoutly. In the last century, among a multitude of such persons, eminent alike in thought and Christian faith, Livingstone, Lincoln, Clerk-Maxwell, Kelvin, and Gladstone, may be mentioned. Professor Arthur S. Peake, M.A., D.D., reminds us in his *Christianity, Its Nature and Truth* (p. 294), that ' We do a great injustice to religion when we disparage its emotional quality.' A large, decisive part is played in religion by emotion ; ' and where we are dealing with a God who is conceived not simply as the philosopher thinks of Him, but as the Father of Spirits whose inmost nature is love, the religion can be no other than emotional in character.' [111]

It is true that emotion was appealed to by Wesley, and this largely. It is often evident in the facts of Christian experience which he used in his argument. In this part of its work and testimony Methodism was affected by the wave of emotionalism which passed over Europe in that century, and which in other aspects of it is associated with the teaching of Rousseau and Schleiermacher, to whom we refer later. It is not correct, however, to say as Liddon does in his study, *Some Elements of Religion*, that ' in Wesleyanism and kindred systems, feeling, not knowledge ; feeling, not morality ; feeling, not even conscience, is the test of acceptance of satisfactory religion.' If this has

CRITICISM OF EXPERIENCE 175

ever been true of any considerable number of the followers of Wesley they have been, in so far, false to him. This statement is supported by many facts above cited, e.g. Wesley's large provision of literature and insistence upon its use; his intellectual training of his preachers; his love of philosophy and formulation of it for others. The truth of the matter is that Wesley helped to restore emotion to its due place and function in religion. It has an important place, as is shown by Dr. F. B. Jevons (*History of Religion*, 409) and other philosophers. Religious feeling is the distinguishing part of human nature. As such, Wesley recognized and used it. Nevertheless, he duly recognized all the other faculties. His appeal to man for allegiance to Prince Emmanuel was made to every court in the ' city of Mansoul '; sense-perception, reflection, reason, imagination, emotion, conscience, and will. This John Bunyan showed in his allegories, which are at once emotional and mental masterpieces, unsurpassed in their kind.* That the heart should be recognized seemed strange to many in that cold, hard century. Many in that period feared or despised that which was much needed, moral enthusiasm. Wesley hated false emotion and pseudo-enthusiasm, as much as Butler hated them. He forbade excitement, loud shouting, saying the same words many times, and jumping about in religious gatherings. Physical phenomena, as fainting fits and seizures, occurred under his calm, logical preaching in the earlier years of his ministry. They have often appeared in similar revivals of religion. While Wesley thought that some of these might sometimes be signs of divine or other spiritual

* Cf. *John Bunyan*, by the author of *The Autobiography of Mark Rutherford* (W. H. White).

agency, he did not desire them; certainly he never required them as an indication of the presence and power of God, or of the genuineness of Christian experience. During thirty years of his later work they were seldom seen (*Journal*, iv. 359).

It should be recognized as one of Wesley's contributions to thought and life that he helped to reclaim the noble word enthusiasm. He used it with its highest meaning (*Standard Sermons*, ii. 84). He believed that man can be the dwelling-place of Deity, by the Spirit of God; he can be possessed and used by moral passion, guided by reason and experience. Locke had defined enthusiasm wrongly. 'It is founded,' he said, 'neither on reason nor divine revelation, but rises from the conceits of a warm or overweening imagination.' Wesley argued this matter with Thomas Church, prebendary of St. Paul's Cathedral, 'a gentleman, a scholar, and a Christian.' That clergyman drew a word picture of an enthusiast, according to Locke's definition; but, said Wesley, 'it is no more like me than I am like a centaur' (*Works*, viii. 406). The worth of emotion and enthusiasm is revealed in conduct. Ethical fruitfulness is the test. If the emotions are aroused by God the Spirit, and are used by Him, the result will be goodness or godlikeness. If the Spirit dwelling in a human personality is the Spirit of Jesus, the consequent conduct and character will resemble His. Wesley and those who thought with him accepted this test, as we have shown above.'[11] So do those who claim for emotion its due place in Christian thought. It is ridiculous to require that that must be excluded from the highest sphere of activity which is admired and regarded as necessary in business, politics, and pleasure.

CRITICISM OF EXPERIENCE

(iii.) That Christian Experience is Self-suggested

The criticism offered upon the argument from Christian experience that human experience of God is produced by the Christian who has the experience, may be briefly referred to. An obvious answer to this criticism has been already given (p. 147). If Wesley manufactured his Christian experience, why did he seek it so long in vain ? It is psychologists who urge the objection now before us, under the name Auto-suggestion. They allege that the mind of the Christian creates his experience of what he calls Reality or God, in fulfilment of his own desire for that experience. These critics may be reminded that they are beyond their province in explaining origins and causes. Psychology is strictly concerned with mental states and processes. It should be content to show, as it does, that Christian experience is valid as a state of conscious mind. If, however, some students of the mind allege that awareness of God in Christ in the Christian mind is produced by that mind, i.e. is self-suggested, self-generated, they must be reminded that the problem of who or what is the true First Cause is not solved by their account of it. What, or who, is the cause adequate to generate the Christian mind which, it is alleged, generates this experience of God in Christ ? Effect, cause, process, are not the same. If Wesley had a genius for religion, who created Wesley with that genius ? The answer to such criticism of the argument from Christian experience is like that which explodes the sneer of the cynic about the self-made man. He says, ' The self-made man worships his maker.' But the man who made himself does not exist. We are therefore thrown back upon first principles. Christian experience of

God as the ultimate Reality answers the same tests as to its genuineness as other experience of which the same man or any other man is conscious. If God is not real, there are no realities.¹¹⁹ If the idea of God refers to no objective reality, says Professor Waterhouse, if man's faith is but the echo of his own heart's cry, religion has not been simply an unparalleled blunder, it has been the most piteous tragedy of mankind (*Philosophy of Religious Experience*, 75). We must add that this is emphatically true of the idea of God in Christ. The infinite perfection of it, which man dimly perceives and finds it impossible to describe, indicates its origin as from the infinite Reality, God.

(iv.) *Other Criticisms of Wesley's Statement of the Argument from Experience*

We have here used Wesley's formulation of Christian philosophy based on experience, and we may reply briefly to some other criticisms directed specially against him. Wesley's statement is said by some to lack originality; conversely, he is rejected by others as an innovator. These contrasted criticisms answer each other in part. Wesley did not claim to be a teacher of new doctrines in either theology or philosophy. As already stated, he declared that his teaching was as ' new ' as that of the New Testament, and as old. In the New Testament St. John was his supreme teacher and helper, and among the writings of that apostle the First Epistle was Wesley's favourite. Its philosophy is that of spiritual intuition and Christian experience. Metaphysical knowledge and ethical value are co-ordinated in that small, priceless book. Its key words are ' love,' ' know,' and ' do.' Wesley thought this book ' the deepest part of Holy

CRITICISM OF EXPERIENCE

Scripture.' He expounded the contents four times at intervals of twenty, two, and seven years. He was of the Johannine school of philosopher-divines. Professor Arthur S. Peake has shown how large a part the religious experience of the authors of the books of the Bible played in the creation and form of their writings (*The Bible*, xiv.). Many of Wesley's experiences are like chapters of the *Acts of the Apostles*.

Nor did Wesley claim to be strictly original in his statements or methods. He was a waiter upon Providence. He tried freely the suggestions of others. He adopted statements which accorded with divine revelation, and methods which worked well towards realization of the Christian ideal. It was in method that he introduced several innovations which aroused criticism and opposition. Such were field-preaching, the use of unauthorized forms of religious service in unconsecrated buildings, conducted by persons who had only Wesley's authority. As to his teaching, it cannot be doubted that Wesley rediscovered and restated certain aspects of divine truth, and this with such definiteness and brightness that they appeared to be new. In that cold century, and in such a world as ours, it was natural that his teaching of Christian perfection should arouse criticism, misrepresentation and opposition. Again, to those who had forgotten the New Testament and the experience of the saints, such as St. Bernard of Clairvaux, it seemed a thing incredible that one might know that God had forgiven his sins. Certainly he must not declare such knowledge, if it was his happy possession. For no other 'crime' than that he said that he had this knowledge, Edward Greenfield of St. Just, Cornwall, was adjudged by the magistrates there to be worthy of banishment from his family or of death (Wesley's

Journal, iii. 185). Wesley's contributions to Thought as a Christian philosopher contrasted sharply with the sermons of the period, which appealed almost exclusively to prudential motives. Lecky says they taught little that might not have been taught by the disciples of Socrates or Confucius. In his *English Thought in the Eighteenth Century* Leslie Stephen admits that the exertions of Wesley, and the successes which followed them, are a sufficient proof that they were needed, and could not have been accomplished either by the rationalist or the orthodox. The creed of the one party was negative, that of the other was lifeless.

Wesley claimed that the secret of his success, and that of his followers, was a vital, vitalizing, communicable experience of God in Christ by the Holy Spirit. The features of this experience, apparently unknown to or overlooked by many in his century and restated afresh by Wesley, were these five : that divine holy love is the central emotion of the Christian life ; that this love is stirred within man and, if welcomed, is fully imparted by the action of God in Christ by His Spirit upon the human spirit ; that such experience of God is possible to every one ; that by it the human spirit has assurance, certitude of truth, joy, and peace, with power for sacrificial service ; and is drawn continuously onward towards Christian perfection or completeness. As we have shown, it was from the facts of such experience of God in Christ operating by the Holy Spirit that Wesley drew his implication as to the existence and nature of God. By doing so he formulated a philosophy, an interpretation of the universe, which is confirmed, as to its essential features, by Christian experience in all ages.

VII

THE PHILOSOPHY OF CHRISTIAN EXPERIENCE SINCE WESLEY

In the nineteenth century, following upon that of Wesley, Christian experience, as offering an explanation and interpretation of the universe, deepened, strengthened, and widened its foundations. The number of those who rested their faith upon it and governed their conduct by it was greatly increased. Always useful and popular in its appeal, it was then examined and enforced by the foremost philosophers and divines. Wesley therefore began to secure recognition as a Philosopher of Christian Experience. We have sought in these pages to indicate his importance in this regard. We now notice some representative thinkers since Wesley and their use of Christian experience. Here it is only possible to name a few of these, and by brief summaries to direct attention to their works.

Schleiermacher

It has been shown that Wesley was deeply indebted to Luther, to the German Pietists (chiefly through their hymns which he translated), and to Moravian teachers. It is of interest to notice that, in turn, the philosophy and theology of Wesley may be said to have gained a central place in later thought through the influence of a German theologian and philosopher, Friedrich D. E. Schleiermacher (1768–1834).[114] Like Wesley, he was influenced by Moravianism.

As an exponent of the religious feeling and Christian experience, Schleiermacher interpreted Christian theology in harmony with what he thought are the reasonable convictions of the human mind. He united Idealism and the revelation of God in Christ. He held that the religious feeling is *a priori*, and must be recognized along with the empirical factor in knowledge. The religious feeling developed in Christian experience is the touchstone of reality, according to Schleiermacher. Man knows God in his experience of God. Christ in man, in his consciousness of redemption, authenticates the Scriptures of revelation. Therefore, religion is not the acceptance of a dogmatic faith, nor the practice of religious observances, but a vital experience of God. It is direct contact with God in one's emotional and moral nature, which is deeper than thought. In man, in the deepest self, there is found this feeling. Its note is that of dependence. Schleiermacher held that the common element in all the varied expressions of piety which distinguishes religion from all other feelings—that is to say, the essence of religion—is this : that we are conscious of ourselves as absolutely dependent, or, in other words, in relation to God. The underlying principle in the universe is God. The real and the ideal are one in Him. He is the Cause, and the feeling of dependence relates man, as man, to Him. Knowledge of God and union with God are not primarily or chiefly acts of the human will or of mind, but of feeling. Through meditation and self-contemplation man may become united with the Eternal.

The one mediator to man is Jesus Christ. He redeems and reconciles, and leads to Holiness. Schleiermacher taught, alike from pulpit and philosopher's desk, that the religious experience of the individual must be developed and tested in a Christian community. The private conscience must bow to the claims of Christian tradition. Several points of resemblance, between these views and those of Wesley as expounded above, will be seen.

Like Wesley, Schleiermacher was charged with giving undue emphasis to the subjective and emotional elements in knowledge and religion. He did not follow Wesley in his view that divine revelation culminated in Jesus Christ. Instead, he seems sometimes to make Christian experience the judge of Jesus Christ, as thus : ' Who is Jesus Christ ? The revealer of God, the Saviour. Why ? Christian consciousness declares it. How does Christ reveal God and save men ? Christian consciousness has no answer, and it is unnecessary to raise these questions.' Schleiermacher gave little or no recognition to the Person and work of the Holy Spirit, God in action. Wesley's contribution was notable for the treatment of this Christian truth.

' *The Varieties of Religious Experience* '

In the present century William James, a professor in Harvard University, U.S.A., led the way to the full recognition of the worth and significance of the facts of religious and Christian experience which is now given everywhere. The Gifford Lectures on natural religion delivered by James in Edinburgh in 1901–2, were entitled *The Varieties of Religious Experience : a Study in Human Nature*. This work helped much in the breaking down of the dogmatism of physical scientists which had prevailed since the restatement of the theory of evolution and materialism in the nineteenth century. James made room for the consideration of moral and spiritual phenomena, as human documents. By the method of the questionnaire, used by Dr. E. D. Starbuck and others, and by his own researches in religious biography, James made a considerable collection of facts of religious experience. The range of illustrative instances is very wide, and includes many classical cases, e.g. Augustine, Bunyan, Mohammed, and Joseph Smith the Mormon. Reference is made to Wesley's views; but his own remarkable experience is not used. Prominence is given to that of William ('Billy') Bray, a Bible Christian Methodist, ' an excellent little English evangelist.' Religion is defined by James, for his purpose, ' as the feelings, acts, and experiences of individual men in their solitude, so far as they apprehend themselves to stand in relation to whatever they may consider the divine.' Such a definition permitted the examination of any variety of religion. Experiences of Christians are included; but these are not related to Christ, as in Wesley's implications. With James the characteristic of religion is solemn emotion, which gives the subject an enthusiastic temper, a new range of power, and a new reach of freedom—' with the struggle over, the keynote sounding in our ears, and everlasting possession spread before our eyes.' The life of religion consists of the belief that there is an unseen order, and that our supreme good lies in a harmonious relation thereto. This is the religious attitude of the soul. James found that many persons possess the object of their belief in the form of quasi-sensible realities directly apprehended. One said, 'I could not any more have doubted that God was there, than that I was. Indeed, I felt myself to be, if possible, the less real of the two' (p. 66). Such experiences are not given to all persons; but such as have them probably cannot help regarding them, James admits, as genuine perceptions of truth. Such realizations as these are often associated with a 'conversion' or 'new birth' of the subject.

James gave wide currency to the distinction made by Francis W. Newman between 'the two families of children on earth, the once-born and the twice-born.' The former think of God as the animating Spirit of a beautiful, harmonious world; the latter as a strict Judge and King. Conversion seemed to James to vary in accordance with these conceptions of Deity. Religious conversion is a term used by James as synonymous with regeneration, receiving grace, the experience of religion, or gaining an assurance. Conversion may be a sudden or gradual event, and its types are differentiated by the attitude of the personality. James adopts the distinction of types given by Starbuck—the volitionist type and the type by self-surrender. Psychologically, conversion is due largely, James explained, to the subconscious incubation and maturing of motives, deposited by the experiences of life: 'when ripe, the results hatch out, or burst into flower.' This view of the accumulations and power of the transmarginal or subliminal consciousness of man stands for much in the philosophy of religious experience as formulated in this work. James claims that there is actually and literally more life in our total soul than we are at any time aware of. It is through this wider self that saving experiences come to our conscious self. The subconscious self is the intermediary between nature and the higher region. The further limits of our being plunge into another dimension than the sensible and understandable. There ' we and God have business with each other' (pp. 515–7). Hence the possibility of mystical experience. The four marks of such states of consciousness are ineffability, noetic quality, transciency, and passivity. James claimed that the existence of mystical states absolutely overthrows the pretensions of non-mystical states to be the sole ultimate dictators of what may be believed.

Like Wesley, James insists upon the test of the worth of conversion, whether sudden or gradual, by the fruits of life, i.e. the ethical results. Saintliness is characterized by asceticism, strength of soul, purity, and charity. It is the collective name of the ripe fruits of religion (*Lectures*, xi.–xiii.). A philosophical judgement on essential goodness, however and whenever produced, is this : ' The real witness of the spirit to the second birth is found only in the disposition of the genuine child of God, the permanently patient heart, the love of self eradicated.' This recalls features of Wesley's teaching on Christian perfection, or perfect love ; but it is in contrast with Wesley's teaching of the direct witness of the Holy Spirit. James held that the attempt to demonstrate the truth of the deliverances of direct religious experience is hopeless. Intellectual processes can classify, define, and interpret facts. They cannot produce them. Religion adds the feeling of reality to all accounts and explanations of its facts. The Divine is actually present, is experienced, and between That and ourselves relations of give and take are actual. As we have stated, Wesley showed this relation as divine action and human reaction. Whilst philosophy cannot account for the Cause of the facts of religious experience, it can construct a Science of Religions. James thought that this might eventually command general public adhesion, equal with that given to a physical science.

'*The Religious Consciousness*'

Professor James Bissett Pratt[111] continued the methods of James, and has given the results of a further examination of the facts of religious experience. His work is entitled, *The Religious Consciousness: a Psychological Study.* Here facts of Christian experience are recognized, and as such. The division of their subjects into the large groups, Protestant and Roman Catholic, is noted; also the regimen which is observed where the fuller Christian experience is found. Religion is here distinguished from morality. While every 'religion' is in part morality, religion has the additional feature of belief in some one or some thing. Religion may be studied as giving a philosophy, a study of Reality and an attempt to determine the truth about the Determiner of Destiny; or as an account of the moral and spiritual development of mankind, the history of religion; or as the science of mind, the psychology of religion. The last describes the workings of the mind of men, as far as these are influenced by the concept of the Determiner of Destiny, and investigates the religious consciousness scientifically. However this consciousness is caused, it is a fact for psychology. For, says Professor Pratt, 'when one compares the deeply religious and spiritual person with the best and bravest of those who are not religious, it is found that the former possesses something which the others lack. It is not that he is any better than his non-religious brother, nor more appreciative of beauty and love, nor any braver. It is rather that he has a confidence in the universe and an inner joy, which the other does not know. . . . He is therefore able to shed a kind of peace around him which no mere argument, and no mere animal spirits, and no mere courage can produce.' This religious consciousness is in close relation with man's subconscious life and, in abnormal personalities, with the co-conscious life. A man's religion is not made up of clean-cut, conscious processes; it is closely connected with his whole psycho-physical organism. The fringe region of consciousness, with instincts, habits, slumbering memories there, and his nervous system, largely determine a man's character and affect his religion. Religion goes deep into personality and ' is knit up with all that we are, and all that we hope to be.'

In Professor Pratt's view, the term Conversion may be used in one sense to describe the whole moral and religious process of the adolescent period. The child at birth is a little animal, ruled by natural instincts. There must be a new birth, when the new self emerges to govern natural instincts and impulses. The form and manner of conversion is, Professor Pratt argues, largely determined by preconceptions in the subject of it. Some expect violent affective experiences; others, a long process of moral development. Here is a recurrence to the distinctions noticed above, between ' once-born ' and ' twice-born ' men, and the ' volitional ' and ' self-surrender ' types of conversion. The experience of conversion does not always follow

LATER PHILOSOPHY

conviction of sin : ' it is not sin that troubles them, but misery, and the chief thing that fills their consciousness, and brings about the change, is not a struggle away from sin, but a striving towards something new.' Sudden and remarkable conversions may be explained, psychologically, by the sudden rise of ideas, convictions, and emotions from the subconsciousness into normal consciousness. Theologically, they are explained by the action of God upon the human spirit (pp. 155, 160). Belief in a God and in a future life are the distinctive features of religion. The idea of God as an all-inclusive Absolute is favoured by the rational tendency of the mind ; but there is also a demand that the divine shall be congruous with our moral sense. The idea of God has also, for most men, a pragmatic value. It helps to faith, because it arouses religious emotion and meets a demand of the heart. But this pragmatic element is not the only one. Always there have been men who meant by the term ' God ' more than any idea of God—something genuinely transcendent. In really religious cases, Professor Pratt notes that ' the convert feels the presence of a new friend who loves him and to whom he is endlessly grateful and whom he is coming to love passionately.' In many cases getting converted means ' falling in love with Jesus.' Four types of religious belief may be distinguished : authoritative, based upon the natural credulity of the mind, that is, ' our faith is faith in someone else's faith ' ; reasoned belief, which rises from argumentation, explicit or implicit; emotional, resulting from an emotional experience, usually mystical in character ; and volitional, which results from the will to believe. If all these four sources of belief are used, the highest and healthiest faith in the spiritual world and God will be developed and maintained.

Professor Pratt's teaching is noteworthy for his contention that the structure of the mind requires the use of means to express and cultivate religious life. These are chiefly worship and prayer. Worship is objective and subjective, as the worshipper offers glory to God or seeks spiritual help for himself by worship. Objective worship in its instinctive act of self-abasement is as natural and enduring as man's finitude. The Church should stimulate and direct it. Communion with God, in prayer and private worship, is vital to religion.'[116] This is seen in the facts of Christian experience here collated. While the subject of the existence of God as the object of prayer is here relegated to metaphysics, psychology points out that 'the subjective effects of prayer are almost invariably due, directly or indirectly, to some real faith in the objective relation.' In mystical experience, 'the consciousness of a Beyond,' there is a sense of feeling of a Presence. This is not mere belief in it; nor does it result from sight, hearing, or touch; nor is it reached as a conclusion by thought. It is an immediate and intuitive experience of a being or reality, says Professor Pratt. For the Christian, this is God in Jesus Christ by the Spirit, as taught by Wesley and his school.

The Spirit: the Relation of God and Man.

The philosophy of Christian experience also receives enforcement in a recent work entitled *The Spirit: the Relation of God and Man considered from the Standpoint of recent Philosophy and Science*.[117] In this work, edited by Canon B. H. Streeter,

Christian experience is cogently treated from the standpoint of present-day thought. Professor A. Seth Pringle-Pattison considers the fundamental subject of the immanence and transcendence of Deity. Christian theology affirms that God is both immanent and transcendent, as shown in its doctrine of the Incarnation, God manifest in the flesh. An immanent view of God which equates God and nature is virtually pantheism; and if the concept of God is of a purely transcendent Being, there can be no recognition of His activity as indwelling Spirit. In the human life and death of Jesus, the infinite transcendent Being and Nature of God as self-giving Love is regarded as revealed. The spiritual fact of divine immanence makes possible communion with God. The Spirit is the illuminative presence of God which operates in every soul which He has created. The concept of the Spirit is here regarded as ' the final and complete account of the one God as the Father of spirits, their Creator, Inspirer and Redeemer.'

Miss Dougall here shows that the Spirit of God, God in action, acts always in accord with nature. Whatever is true is God's way of revealing Himself. This is confirmed by the spiritual experience of Christian people. Its facts are explainable by the laws of psychology. What we call natural law is the instrument, tool, and weapon of man; and all life, culminating in man's free spirit with its intelligence, is God's instrument, used by His Spirit. Religious experience is of value, therefore, as an evidence of God's action in the world, and this is through natural processes. Miss Dougall shows that religion, as the fellowship of Spirit with God and men, must have language. Religion must use the language of reason, the terms of mind;

that of art, appealing to feeling, and the sense of beauty; and the language of action—the rite, ceremony, and symbol. The latter is defined as that which manifests to human sense a non-sensuous reality; and the truest symbols for men are those which most naturally manifest the unseen reality, the spiritual.

The problem of the sources of human energy and power is considered by Captain Hadfield, M.B., with suggestions as to its ultimate source, the Spirit of God. Facts of physical, mental, and spiritual life are here investigated to find the psychology of power. It is found that, in part, physical and psychic energy is within the personality; it is natural and also acquired. In part, it comes through heredity. Instinctive power is transmitted from generation to generation. These sources are used by the Spirit of God. There remains, however, in the opinion of several eminent psychologists, another source of power: some impulse that works through us and is not of our own making. Life and power is not so much contained in us; rather, it courses through us. There is cosmic energy, life-force, God, immanent in Nature and especially in man. Here is the dynamic of religion. In its fundamental doctrine of man's love to God, Christianity shows that devotion to a Person is the dynamic of religion, for the altruistic service of man. The promise of Jesus Christ to His followers was, ' Ye shall receive power.' At the epoch of the founding of Christianity, the Spirit of God came as an enhancement of their natural powers, operating in them and through them. That significant experience is considered in this work by Professor C. Anderson Scott, under the title ' What happened at Pentecost ? ' Captain

LATER PHILOSOPHY

Hadfield shows from the experience of applied psychology and psychotherapy, that there are resources of supernatural power open to all persons. These are available through the right use of the instincts, if directed to noble purposes; if, as St. Paul says, we live in the Spirit of God and the Spirit of God dwells in us. Piety is not the only pre-requisite. We must obey the higher laws of Nature. Many modern ineffective persons are not over-worked, but are under-motived. The many points of agreement between this teaching and that of Wesley will occur to the reader. And Wesley's work and character offer abundant illustration of Captain Hadfield's statement (p. 111), 'that there are open to us resources of power available through the right use of our instincts, which, if directed to noble purposes, will free our minds from those worries, anxieties, and marked fatigue, which spoil our lives, and will free us for a life of energy and strength.'

The experience of Christians of the action of God by the Spirit in them, and upon them, shows that the relation is that of personalities to each other. Mr. Emmet likens this to the relation between a musical conductor and the members of his orchestra. His richer personality elicits the subconscious powers of the self of each player. The outside influence of the conductor is a real, necessary factor. This is how God helps man. Jesus Christ has, in infinite measure, this power of empowering men, and of evoking latent capacities. It is felt in personal contact with Him and is received through His Spirit. 'Grace' in man is the result of the contact of man's spirit or personality with the Spirit of God. The 'means of grace' are ways by which that contact is achieved. This contact is a possible experience for all who sincerely seek it. In the last resort, the difference between persons is due to the measure of enhancement of intercourse between the human spirit and God the Spirit. Hence we rightly regard some persons as inspired by God. His Spirit enlivens and enlightens the human spirit. Jesus Christ is the supreme example of this inspiration.

Mr. Clutton-Brock shows that the sense of the beautiful in man gives him experience of spiritual reality. Jesus Christ did not denounce beauty, and the saints of God have caught glimpses of it. Nevertheless, 'it is implied in the Christian faith that we must discipline ourselves to find beauty, if it is not to lead us and lose us in the wilderness.' Self-surrender is the condition of all spiritual experience. We must deny ourselves and follow. When spiritual experience offers itself to us 'we must rid ourselves of all the inhibitions of habit which seem wise to us,' just as the scientist gives up a theory in face of new facts. Such experience gives relief and certitude upon which one can act. Action must follow the vision of God: 'the belief that comes with spiritual experience can only be maintained if it is acted upon.' At its highest, spiritual experience gives man a glimpse, if only a glimpse, of the design of God. Christ shows us what this is. It is His doctrine that we can attain to the same beauty. We can become one with Him; not with natural beauty as in the meaning of the scientist, but with that which is personal in it, seen in spiritual experience. We can become like the lilies of the field as Christ saw them, creatures and children of God.

The climax of man's philosophy is the idea of Christ as the portrait of the invisible God. This statement in this work by Canon Streeter is followed by the suggestion that Christians should think of Christ as the portrait of the Spirit also. Jesus was a constructive revolutionary in His attitude towards the religious ideals and institutions of His time. He was no iconoclast, no lover of destruction for its own sake. He came not to destroy, but to fulfil. The spirit manifested in the life of Christ is the Holy Spirit. This Spirit will guide and empower the followers of Christ to embody His will upon earth. In the constructive thought and creative effort of Christ are seen the characteristic expression of the Spirit of God. The facts of Christian experience of God's Spirit, who is God in action, will continually support belief in the existence of God and give some revelation of His infinite perfections.

'Jesus in the Experience of Men'

Dr. T. R. Glover, of Cambridge University, followed his important work, *The Jesus of History*, by another in which he showed what Jesus Christ has been in the experience of men. Christian experience, that is, the experience which men have had of contact with Jesus and His indwelling by His Spirit since His life on earth, is shown to be of high evidential value. It yields an interpretation of the universe. ' Jesus has reacted on mankind; He has transformed their ideas, blotted out old preconceptions and convictions, and through experience brought men to a new set of principles ' (chap. xiii.). Christian experience verifies the teaching of Jesus concerning God. Jesus has stimulated men to explore God to His depths and heights. The Christian occupation has been with God, following the clue and impulse given by Jesus. There is another side to this. Human experience shows that God is to be apprehended along the line of every human faculty, every sensitiveness. . . . Jesus, besides giving the impulse to explore God, has enlarged human capacity for knowing God (pp. 109, 110). In human experience, Jesus has been ' Alpha and Omega,' beginning and end, origin and culminating purpose (chap. viii.). Men realize that Jesus Christ came in fulfilment of a divine purpose : ' Christ is no chance item in the world's story.' Christian teaching, as seen in the New Testament, states that the universe is infinite, orderly, and thought out by God ; and Christ is suggested as the deepest, the most essential, expression of the very being and mind of God. It is concluded, not unreasonably, that all began with Christ, that Christ is the Alpha. In the experience of men, it is historical fact that ' Jesus has stimulated thought and speculation, and has been again and again the corrective that kept it sane and true ' (pp. 140, 141). So also Jesus in the experience of men has been and is the culmination for their progressive development, the Omega. ' History shows how varied types of nature find themselves in Jesus and grow in Jesus; the artist, the thinker, the popular preacher, the statesman, the linguist, the scholar, the musician have all found freedom in Him,' and husbands and wives, fathers and mothers, have found the like freedom in Him. ' Jesus looked forward and not backward, and in His teaching faithfully interpreted in the light of His mind, there is no hint of fear of progress ' (pp. 143 *et seq*.). Jesus is Alpha and Omega, and is for the Christian the solution of all the mysteries of the world and of human experience. ' He makes all things intelligible; He opens to those who knock. All doors are not yet unlocked, but He has the key.' The Christian experience of Jesus has the promise that His followers shall see the end and this will explain all the doubt and pain of the beginning (pp. 145–7).

Christian experience finds that Jesus is a friend (chap. xi.), says Dr. Glover. The first disciples were chosen ' that they might be with Him ' and share life together. The Jesus of earthly history is found to be the same Friend in human experience since that time. He has still the same aptitude for friendship. The very thought of Him fills the breast with sweetness, as St. Bernard sang; but what is He to those who find Him (*sed quid invenientibus*) to be a Friend? None but they can tell what this is. The friends of Jesus share His ideals, and His interest in other people. They serve them for His sake. Hence the missionary impulse as seen in Christian history, and also the humanizing of life by those devoted to Jesus, those who experience Jesus. ' " I look upon all the world as my parish," said John Wesley, in a sentence memorable in the history of English Christendom. So did unknown men look on the world, remembering a recorded saying of their Friend.' (pp. 192–6). Experience shows that throughout the centuries Jesus has been making the human heart larger, and more human, and more apt to get hold of God and then to want more of Him. In the experience of the Christian, Jesus ' has been, of all beings, the most intelligent of God, the most sympathetic with all God's creatures, the great interpreter, not only of God, but of everything in which God is interested, the bird on the wing, the flower in the field. Where the spirit of the Lord Jesus is there *is* liberty' (p. 258).[116]

These typical studies by philosophers since the period of Wesley confirm the belief that the contribution made by him to the ever-growing knowledge of God by Christian experience is of permanent value and significance.

ILLUSTRATION III

Know All Men by these Presents, that I John Wesley, master of arts, late of Lincoln-College in the University of Oxford, did, on the fifth Day of August in the Year of our Lord one thousand seven hundred and eighty eight, by the Imposition of my hands and Prayer, and in the Fear of God, (being assisted by other ordained Ministers) set apart Robert Gamble for the Office of an Elder in the Church of God: Whom I recommend to all to whom these Presents shall come as a proper Person to administer the holy Sacrament and feed the Church of God. Given under my Hand and Seal, the tenth Day of August, in the Year above written.

John Wesley

A CERTIFICATE OF AN ORDINATION BY JOHN WESLEY, OF A METHODIST PREACHER – ROBERT GAMBLE.

From the Original in the possession of the Methodist Publishing House, London.

ILLUSTRATION IV

Know all men by these presents That we Joseph Coumley and Charles Atmore having been Ordained overseers Elders of the Church of God by the late Rev.d John Wesley and other ordained Ministers died on the nineteenth day of May in the Year of our Lord one thousand seven hundred and ninety two (by the imposition of hands and Prayer ad) in the fear of God set apart Alexander Kilham for the office of an Elder in the Church of God, whom we recommend to all to whom these present shall come as a proper person to administer the holy sacraments and feed the Church of God. Given under our hands and seals the day and year above written.

Jo. Coumley

Charles Atmore

A CERTIFICATE OF ORDINATION OF
ALEXANDER KILHAM, IN 1792,
BY TWO METHODIST MINISTERS WHOM
WESLEY ORDAINED.
From the original in the possession
of the United Methodist Church.

BOOK II

Wesley as a Church Founder

The distinguishing marks of a Methodist are not his opinions of any sort. As to all opinions which do not strike at the root of Christianity, we think and let think.

We do not place the whole of religion . . . either in doing no harm, or in doing good, or in using the ordinances of God. No, not in all of them together; wherein we know by experience a man may labour many years, and at the end have no religion at all, no more than he had at the beginning. Much less in any one of these; or it may be in a scrap of one of them: Like . . . him who dreams he is an honest man, merely because he does not rob or steal. May the Lord God of my fathers preserve me from such a poor, starved religion as this! Were this the mark of a Methodist, I would sooner choose to be a sincere Jew, Turk, or Pagan.

What then is the mark? Who is a Methodist?

A Methodist is one who has 'the love of God shed abroad in his heart by the Holy Ghost given unto him'; one who 'loves the Lord his God with all his heart, and with all his soul, and with all his mind, and with all his strength.' . . . And while he thus always exercises his love to God, by praying without ceasing, rejoicing evermore and in everything giving thanks, this commandment is written in his heart, 'that he that loveth God, love his brother also'. . . . And he accordingly loves his neighbour as himself. . . . His heart is full of love to all mankind, to every child of 'the Father of the spirits of all flesh.'—JOHN WESLEY, *Character of a Methodist*.

The founders of religions and churches, without whom they would not have come into being, have, for the most part, been prophets—that is to say, men of original religious genius; and the same is true to a considerable extent of the organizers and reformers through whom those religions and churches have assumed their present form; but these prophets have themselves sprung from and have exhibited in its most highly developed form the general religious type of their nation or community; and in the creeds and institutions which have taken their rise from their teaching we have a mirror of their activity, so far as it has proved effective in stimulating and raising the level of spiritual life around them and in maintaining it at the height to which it has thus been lifted.—PROFESSOR CLEMENT C. J. WEBB, M.A., *God and Personality*.

WESLEY AS A CHURCH FOUNDER

I

WESLEY'S THOUGHT AS RELATED TO HIS CHURCHMANSHIP

THE conduct and work of John Wesley as the human founder of Methodism issued from his Christian experience. His philosophy was causally related to his Church polity. He shaped an ecclesiastical constitution for 'the people called Methodists' in harmony with his experiential metaphysic. That Methodism has survived from the eighteenth century through the testing years, has become a world-wide community numbering thirty-five millions of adherents, and has every sign of future usefulness, are facts of much significance for the interpreter of Wesley as Thinker and Church Founder. These remarkable facts are important for all the followers of Wesley, of several names in many countries, and, indeed, for all Christian communions. We therefore follow our study of Wesley as Christian Philosopher with this of his work as Church Founder. The same spiritual convictions and principles can be traced in both spheres of his activity.

The Church Polity of Wesley

Wesley was familiar with the Roman Catholic type of episcopacy, with Presbyterianism, and with

Independency, or Congregationalism, besides the episcopacy of the Church of England, under which he was a clergyman. Of these types of Church polity it is evident that Wesley preferred a moderate, presbyterial episcopacy, such as Richard Baxter favoured in the seventeenth century. Wesley did not regard episcopacy as the *esse* of Church government, while it might be, in certain circumstances, of the *bene esse*. Convenient and suitable it might be; essential it was not. When Wesley was at liberty to constitute a new Church in a new country, North America, he framed one which united features of presbyterianism and episcopacy. He replaced the name ' priest ' by that of ' minister,' and the name ' bishop ' by that of ' superintendent.' The church officers named in his famous Letter, reprinted herein (p. 278), in which he outlined a church constitution for the American Methodists, are superintendent, elder, and preacher.* He disliked the term ' bishop.' The episcopal titles do not appear in the several service books which Wesley prepared for use by Methodists in America and elsewhere. Prelacy and monarchic rulership in the Church were abhorrent to Wesley after his evangelical conversion.

A New Testament Churchman

By birth and natural preference Wesley was an aristocrat, a ceremonialist, and a conservative. Taught by experience, he recognized the mystic eminence of all who know God, and listened readily to the humblest member in the one and only spiritual order, the priesthood of believers. He claimed

* President is naturally the name for the one who presides in the highest court of Methodism, the Conference, as Wesley did many times.

THOUGHT AND CHURCHMANSHIP 203

freedom to use or not to use set prayers and the adornments of worship. He became the most daring innovator of his age in matters ecclesiastical. Those who appeared to be called of God, and had the necessary graces and gifts bearing fruit in their labours, he united with himself—an ordained minister—in the priestly functions of intercessory prayer, interpretation and utterance of the Mind of God by His Spirit, and in matters of conduct. Some persons were appointed by him to the prophetic office as evangelists and expositors of the Word, and some of these he ordained to serve as elders in the Church of God. With Wesley, church orders, and even orderliness, were of secondary importance. For himself and for the Methodists the primary consideration was the work of God. 'Church or no church, we must attend to the saving of souls,' he said. Here was his canon and slogan.

Tentative and Experimental Actions

Wesley had no preconceived system of Church government according to which he sought to build Methodism, although his work was coherent and became fairly complete. At his Conference in 1746 he explained alike his acts and his hesitation. He said, 'We desire to follow Providence as it gradually opens.' He knew the season when to take occasion by the hand, and when to reject its offers. Suggestion and necessity were often his guides. 'This is the very thing we have wanted,' he said, as he included small 'classes,' each with a 'leader,' into his system of knowing and teaching Christian truth and enforcing discipline. Nevertheless, the student of the facts of Wesley's work as Church Founder can discern certain governing principles in his activity. These will be traced. Wesley remained a member and clergyman of the Church of England until his death, and wished his followers, the smaller number of whom were in association with that Church, to continue association with it. In effect, Wesley separated himself from the Church of England by violating its rubrics and acting independently of, and as a separatist from, its constituted authorities. He deliberately and frequently claimed powers and exercised functions which appertained to the highest clerical order in the Anglican Church, although he was never more than a presbyter. Through the proper legal process, he arranged for the separate existence of the Church fellowship he established, and this with absolute independence for it of any other ecclesiastical authority. He made it a self-governing, self-perpetuating Church.[119]

The acts of Wesley as Church Founder have been the subject of much questioning by those outside the fold of which Wesley was the chief human shepherd, and by some within. It has been suggested that towards the end of Wesley's life, when some of these decisive actions occurred, his powers were decaying, and he was in the hands of ambitious followers at whose instance Methodism was constituted. It is sufficient to say that the most characteristic features of Methodist church constitution emerged within a few years of Wesley's evangelical conversion, and that Wesley's other activities at the later periods of his life show him to be as dominant and as capable then as earlier.*
The fact is that Wesley was slowly, sometimes reluctantly, compelled to take the steps as Church Founder which we now trace. One followed

* Cf. Appendix, note 132.

another. All were not of equal importance nor in a sequence; but they were generally in one direction and towards a decisive and almost irrevocable result. This was the constitution of a new churchly community.

Wesley's Statements Inconsistent

It is freely admitted that Wesley was not always consistent in his statements when defining his churchmanship or the church polity he constructed for the Methodists. His statements vary to the point of contradiction. The stage of his development and the date of his utterance are of much importance in discovering his teaching. More important are his actions. They speak louder than his words. Indeed, they are decisive. They show him as the founder of a church on New Testament principles, evangelical in its doctrine, evangelistic in presentation and appeal, presbyterian in polity, and quite free from control by the State.

These acts of Wesley must now be noticed, and then their underlying principles. Readers of this second Book are asked to keep in mind the statements herein (Book I.) with regard to Wesley's personality and Christian experience, and his chief thoughts and teachings, as given in his literary documents there summarized. His thought of God and the universe governed his actions as Church leader.

II

WESLEY'S ACTS AS CHURCH FOUNDER

UNTIL his spiritual quickening in 1738, Wesley was a High Churchman. That transforming experience, already examined (Book I., chapter iv.), caused a radical change in his churchmanship. Henceforward he regarded the life of an adult Christian as beginning with an inward experience of God and not at baptism or confirmation, or by formal admission into relationship with a Church. This change of view he clearly stated to ' a serious clergyman ' in 1739 (*Journal*, ii. 274-6), and to his brother, the Rev. Samuel Wesley, M.A. As Miss Wedgwood shrewdly observes, in that change of view the partition line of two great systems is crossed. Wesley's subsequent actions show him as a Church Founder, who was mystical, Protestant and non-sacerdotal, evangelical and evangelistic, and freely progressive. His acts in this kind were repeated, and this attitude was maintained from 1739 until his death in 1791. We note several kinds of activity by Wesley. Each kind showed his resistance of ecclesiastical authority, his virtual separation from the English State Church, and his principles of constructive churchmanship. On the negative side, the fact should be noticed that he never required his followers to conform to the Church of England or to any Church. As early as

1758, when stating reasons against separation from the Church, Wesley desired his preachers to attend the Church services if they had no scruple against them, and only when convenient to them. On the positive side, Wesley slowly constructed another Church communion, with distinctive notes. We refer briefly to each of eight classes of churchly acts by Wesley. He conducted unauthorized and new services; instituted a new fellowship; erected separate buildings for worship; employed laymen as preachers without regular episcopal sanction or ordination; held annual conferences for the definition of doctrine and for the functions of a Church court; executed legal instruments to give continuity to his Church organization; provided a Church constitution with Church services for his followers in America and later in England, and appointed superintendents for these Churches; and he ordained some of his preachers to give the Sacraments. Each of these acts violated episcopal church law and order, as well as that of the State establishment of religion in England. Taken together, they prove indisputably the claims made for Wesley as a Church Founder. It is difficult to see that he could have done more than he did in this way, except to state in plain full terms the indisputable meaning and inevitable results of his actions. Wesley reverted to type in his principles and practice as Church Founder. His paternal grandfather, John Westley,* M.A., a clergyman, was ejected under the Act of Uniformity in 1662, and fined and imprisoned as a Nonconformist. Wesley's maternal grandfather, Dr. Samuel Annesley, a clergyman, was also ejected, and was known as 'the St. Paul of the Nonconformists.' And

* So spelled, until Wesley's father dropped the 't.'

Wesley's mother broke the law and held 'a conventicle,' or irregular religious meeting, attended sometimes by two hundred persons, in order to meet the needs of the Epworth parishioners (Clarke, *Wesley Family*, 330).

(i.) *Wesley Held Unauthorized Religious Services*

In obedience to his new convictions, Wesley preached where and when he willed, without permission of churchly authority. He held no position and had no duties as a clergyman in the diocese of London. Nevertheless, in September of his great year, 1738, he says, 'I began to declare in my own country the glad tidings of salvation, preaching three times, and afterwards expounding the Holy Scriptures to a large company.' In November he preached at Tyburn, to a great crowd gathered at a public execution there. This may have been the first time that Wesley preached in the open air in England. He had done this while serving as a missionary in the colony of Georgia. Such services in England were irregularities. So were several of the sermons he preached in London churches. These disorderly actions and his zealous messages, with their still white heat, alarmed the parochial clergy. One after another they closed their churches against him. Frequently in the latter half of this year Wesley says of the London clergy or of their churches, 'they will bear me there no longer,' or 'here I preached for the last time.' The Bishop of London (Dr. Gibson) left Wesley and his brother Charles in no doubt that they were breaking ecclesiastical law. 'Don't you know,' said the bishop, 'no man can exercise parochial duty in London without my leave?'

A CHURCH FOUNDER'S ACTS 209

Bristol, the metropolis of western England, offered the same alternative to Wesley: either he must stifle his convictions or break church law. His decision was like that in London. On April 2, 1739, when Whitefield had left Bristol, Wesley took up the open-air ministry of that wonderful, irregular evangelist. Wesley felt the importance of this occasion. It was the beginning of his remarkable ministry in Bristol. Distinguishing features of his work as Church Founder emerged there, e.g. small classes, each with a leader, for Christian fellowship and testimony; the office of local preacher; and Methodist finance. Of this historic day Wesley wrote, 'I submitted to be more vile, and proclaimed in the highways the glad tidings of salvation.' Wesley's phrase 'more vile,' may refer to the fact that, the day before, he had attended an open-air service at which Whitefield preached. He thought that was 'vile' and humiliating, as an innovation of ecclesiastical order. 'I could scarce reconcile myself,' he says, 'at first to this strange way of preaching, having been all my life (till very lately), so tenacious of every point relating to decency and order, that I should have thought the saving of souls almost a sin, if it had not been done in a church.' He was, however, relieved and encouraged by his recollection of the fact that Jesus Christ preached in the open air, e.g. the Sermon on the Mount, 'though I suppose,' Wesley adds, 'there were churches at that time also.' On this day Wesley regarded himself as 'more vile,' because, like Whitefield, he preached in the open air.[110]

In Bristol, as in London, the churches were closed against him one by one. A message from those at pretty Pensford is typical. This read, 'Sir,—Our minister having been informed you are beside yourself, does not care you should preach in any of his churches.' The bishop of this diocese, the famous Dr. Joseph Butler, was as clear as Dr. Gibson of London in his condemnation of Wesley's disobedience, as shown on an earlier page.

Wesley afterwards itinerated all over the British Isles and committed similar irregularities. His actions were so regarded, whatever rights his Oxford fellowship gave to him. It is not surprising that magistrates and clergymen tried to hinder his work and that of his followers. The law of the land against law-breakers, as the law then stood, was the authority for these directors of religious persecution.[111]

(ii.) A New Fellowship was Instituted

Besides breaking into the parishes of the appointed clergy, using their pulpits if they permitted, and conducting open-air preaching services, without ecclesiastical authority, Wesley constituted a new Church fellowship. These he called the Methodist Societies.[112] Those in the same city or neighbourhood were regarded as a united society, as in London, Bristol, and Newcastle-upon-Tyne. As they multiplied, their unity was maintained under Rules for their members. These are noticed above (p. 68). Provision was made by Wesley for Christian worship, teaching, discipline, and finance. While these arrangements were then intended by Wesley as supplementary to those of the Church of England, they were different from those provided by it. By many they came to be regarded as sufficient. Some Methodists continued to attend their parish churches. Many Methodists had never been connected therewith and never went to these

A CHURCH FOUNDER'S ACTS 211

services. For both these classes the teaching by Wesley in sermon and hymn, the fellowship with other Methodists, and the spread and building up of Methodism, became the chief delight of heart and mind and the object of their sacrificial gifts and labours. Wesley as an under-shepherd, with others appointed by him, gathered, fed, and led the People called Methodists, and built a new fold for part of the flock of the Chief Shepherd, Jesus Christ. At his Conference of 1749 he contemplated the result. All the Methodist societies throughout England might, he said, ' be considered as one body, firmly united by one spirit of love and heavenly-mindedness.' The London society might be ' accounted as the mother church ' and be consulted ' for the good of all the churches ' (Wesley's MS. *Minutes*, Wes. Hist. Soc. *Publications*, i. 63). Here Wesley uses for a local Methodist society or fellowship the New Testament name, Church.

(*iii.*) *Separate Church Buildings Erected*

Outward and visible signs of Wesley's constructive churchmanship appeared in 1739, that birth-year of Methodism. This was the erection or purchase of buildings for use by his followers. Whitefield had laid the foundation of a large room for the use of the colliers at Kingswood, near Bristol. This Wesley completed and used for them and other Methodists for church purposes. In the same year (1739) Wesley erected a larger building in Bristol. This is his famous ' Room,' some part of which may have been incorporated in a larger building on the same site built by Wesley in 1748. This is his ' new-built Room ' (*Journal*, iii. 376; viii. 159). It is the oldest of all

212 WESLEY, PHILOSOPHER AND FOUNDER

Methodist church buildings, which now number more than one hundred thousand in all parts of the world. Built originally for two Religious Societies which met in Bristol, Wesley's 'New Room' became the church building for his followers and the scene of remarkable developments in Church polity. The building was registered for worship under the Toleration Act. Wesley afterwards sanctioned the legal registration of many Methodist chapels.

Wesley also bought a disused building in London this year (1739), the Foundery, in Windmill Street (now Tabernacle Street), London. The Foundery was superseded by the noble church building in City Road, London, erected by Wesley in 1778. The Foundery and City Road Chapel were the home of the mother church Wesley wrote of. City Road Chapel is often styled the Mecca of Methodism. West Street Chapel, in Seven Dials, was leased by him in 1743.* In that year also his work in northern England was developed by the erection of the Orphan House, Newcastle-upon-Tyne.[133]

The dates of these early buildings, and Wesley's repeated action in this regard, are significant. Similar church buildings were later multiplied throughout the British Isles and the colonies. In several of those in Great Britain the Wesleys and other clergymen gave the Lord's supper to the Methodists. These buildings, except West Street Chapel, London, noticed above, had no consecration nor sanction by a bishop, and were flagrant violations of the authority he represented. Material structures, thus erected and governed and used

---

* This 'consecrated' building, formerly used by French Protestants, was the property of a charity.

A CHURCH FOUNDER'S ACTS 213

exclusively, indicate clearly the mind and purpose of those who erect them.

(iv.) *Church Workers Appointed*

The growing needs of Wesley's work as Church Founder led him to appoint church workers. Their duties correspond generally with those usually appointed in Churches. Some bore new names. The most notable of these were the Methodist preachers. Some of them were local preachers. These exercised their ministry only locally, and they continued their business or professional employment. Some were half-itinerants, and gave part of their time to evangelistic work. The itinerant preachers were generally employed by Wesley in the work of preaching, and in assisting him in his leadership of the Methodists. John Cennick of Kingswood was the first lay preacher (1739). Thomas Maxfield, who had been left in charge of the Methodist fellowship at the Foundery, London, 'turned preacher,' as Wesley said. His surprise and annoyance gave way before the advice of his mother, the capable, saintly Susanna Wesley, and before his own judgement upon Maxfield's gifts. He became one of Wesley's regular preachers (1740). Large numbers of such church workers were afterwards chosen by Wesley. He carefully trained them, and appointed them to labour in his circuits of Methodist Societies or Churches. The chief among them he styled Assistants, i.e. his assistants in superintending the circuits. Others he called Helpers.[114]

At his third Conference (Bristol, 1746) Wesley stated the tests to which he submitted these preachers. As will be shown, experiential knowledge of God was their chief qualification. A formal designation of these church workers to their solemn duties was evidently used, although Wesley at this stage declined to use 'more form and solemnity' in that act. These workers were not under any churchly authority except that of Wesley and the Methodist Conference, which appointed them. Their appointments to the highest duty in Christ's Church, 'to feed the flock of God,' aroused the ecclesiastical authorities. Bitter persecutions of the Methodists and the preachers followed, often instigated by the clergy.* Samuel Walker of Truro, a clergyman who became a friend of Wesley, stated the indisputable fact: 'Lay preachers, being contrary to the constitution of the Church of England, are, as far as that point goes, a separation from it.'

(v.) *A Supreme Court Constituted*

Beginning in London in 1744, Wesley annually summoned a Conference. He was President of more than forty of such gatherings. The purpose of the Conference was the definition of doctrine, the discovery of methods of church work, the appointment or dismissal of preachers, and the administration of united or connexional church finance. These gatherings were composed of himself and his brother Charles, with other clergymen and laymen. Most of these, but not all, were Methodist preachers.[111] The proceedings were conducted by question and answer. Wesley carefully prepared himself and his material for this annual convocation. In this original and most important

---

* Of this persecution, now deplored by most Anglican authorities, a summary is given in *A New History of Methodism*, vol. i.

church court of the Methodists his influence and utterances were supreme; but he regarded the Conference as paramount in the church constitution which he evolved. The *Minutes*—the record of the decisions reached and promulgated by the Conference—became of unique importance as a chronicle of Wesley's work as Church Founder and in the life and work of the increasing body of his helpers and adherents.[116] Dr. W. H. Fitchett thinks that the Conference was Wesley's most original contribution to church polity. Certainly as a supreme court, acknowledging no other authority and permitting no appeal from its decisions in any matter pertaining to the Methodists, the Conference unmistakably shows Wesley as a Church Founder.

In his Conference of 1747 Wesley defined explicitly his attitude and that of the Methodists towards the Church of England and churchly authority. This was after his perusal of Lord King's account of the Church constitution of the early Christians, to which we must soon refer. A lengthy quotation given in our Appendix is from the determinative declaration by Wesley at this Conference. He stated his view that a national Church was a mere political institution; that the Scriptures did not fix the episcopal order of Church government for all times and places; and that variety in this matter is permissible and had been practised, e.g. by the Reformed Churches.[117]

It should be observed that these acts of Wesley as Church Founder, as now recounted, occurred within a few years of the rise of Methodism. Some were tentative and experimental, and, like the establishment of the Conference, received final form at a much later stage, so far as Wesley was concerned. It was in the year 1746, seven years after the birth-year of Methodism, that Wesley perused the work on ecclesiastical history and polity which influenced him so profoundly. It confirmed his past acts, and convinced him in favour of further development on the same lines. The change made in some of his views can be gathered from his statement of them three weeks earlier in a letter to Westley Hall (*Journal*, iii. 229), and from the opinions now to be quoted. The influential work read by Wesley was Lord King's *Account of the Primitive Church*. Wesley says of it, ' In spite of the vehement prejudice of my education, I was ready to believe this was a fair and impartial draft ; but, if so, it would follow that bishops and presbyters are (essentially) of one order, and that originally every Christian congregation was a Church independent of all others.' Dr. A. W. Harrison rightly argues (*Wes. Hist. Soc. Proceedings*, xv. 9) that Wesley was compelled by this work ' to accept certain fundamental principles of Presbyterianism and even Independency as apostolic, and discovered that the absolute episcopal position was untenable.' [111] Wesley noted that bishops and presbyters were of the same order, or, more strictly, held the same office, in the primitive Church. In this work Lord King shows that the bishop was chosen by a majority of the Christians in a locality, and approved and ordained by the bishops of neighbouring localities. Among his co-presbyters he held a higher office than theirs. He was *primus inter pares*, first among equals. Wesley here notes another feature—that each Church was then independent of all others. It had the right of discipline over its members as a separate entity ; but it also claimed to be part of the universal Church. The unity of the latter was not shown by agreement in rites or ceremonies, or the minutiae of faith and practice, but by assent to the fundamental principles of the Christian faith. Students of Wesley know that there he took his stand. He claimed for Methodists, and for other Christians, inclusion in Catholic Christianity, and he claimed for all Christians liberty as to non-essentials. In his Conference of 1747 Wesley asked the specific question, ' Are not the Methodists guilty of making a schism in the Church ? ' His answer was, ' No more than rebellion or murder. They do not divide themselves at all from the living body of Christ. Let any prove it, if they can.'

(vi.) *Legal Acts to Secure Continuity*

Wesley early acquired buildings for Methodist Church purposes. Afterwards he vested these in trustees, e.g. his Room at Bristol and the Orphan House at Newcastle-upon-Tyne (1745).* His deeds provided that he—and Charles Wesley, if he was the survivor—should have the right to use the premises and to appoint persons to use them. After the death of the Wesleys, this right was to fall to trustees named in the deeds, who were to appoint preachers to use them ' to preach and expound God's holy word ' therein, as the Wesleys and their preachers had done.

A further important step was taken by Wesley in 1763. He and the Conference of that year issued a legal precedent or model of a deed containing the trusts upon which land was to be conveyed

* *Catalogue of Wesleyana*, ' Deed,' gives particulars and an illustration of Wesley's Deed of Declaration.

for buildings to be used for Methodist purposes.* Acting upon these trusts, the trustees were to permit the use of the buildings by the Wesleys and a clergyman, William Grimshaw, and the Methodist preachers appointed by the Conference. The doctrine, &c., permitted in these buildings by the trustees was rather vaguely defined. The teaching was to be ' no other doctrine than is contained in ' Wesley's *Notes on the New Testament* and four volumes of his published *Sermons*.

Further action, and the most effective possible, to secure the continuity and permanence of Methodism, was taken by Wesley in 1784. This act by Wesley confirmed his earlier ones, and made all coherent and operative. With competent legal assistance, Wesley prepared and enrolled in the High Court of Chancery a Deed of Declaration, Appointment, and Establishment of the Conference of the people called Methodists. As defined, composed, and empowered by this important deed, the Annual Conference was constituted, after the death of the Wesleys, the authority for receiving, appointing to and excluding Methodist preachers from the use of chapels, &c., held by trustees, as already described. The Conference was empowered to fill up vacancies in its membership caused by death, &c. This secured its continued existence in completeness, and the exercise of its functions. This Deed of Establishment was not revoked by Wesley. It cannot be denied that by it he intended to perpetuate the People called Methodists as a Church communion, separate from all others, self-governing and self-perpetuating.[19]

* *Minutes*, 1812 ed., p. 41. This Deed was that of the Manchester Chapel. The instructions of Wesley and the Conference as to the pulpit, &c., in the chapels are interesting : ' Let there be . . . no tub-pulpit, but a square projection with a long seat behind ' (*Works*, viii. 332).

(vii.) *A Church Constitution Provided for American Methodists*

Later in this same year, 1784, and acting consistently with his principles, Wesley performed acts which were startlingly assertive of his claims as Church Founder. He ordained an English Church clergyman, the Rev. Dr. Thomas Coke, to be superintendent of the Methodists in America, along with 'Mr. Francis Asbury,'* one of his preachers there. He ordained two other preachers to be elders or presbyters, and to give the Sacrament to the American Methodists. He also sent them forms of liturgical services extracted from the English Prayer-Book, to be used along with extempore prayers, according to their discretion. Wesley says that in these acts he was sustained by his acceptance of Lord King's treatise above referred to. Wesley saw clearly that he was violating English Church constitutional law. He wrote thus: 'If any one is minded to dispute concerning Diocesan Episcopacy, he may; but I have better work' (*Works*, xiii. 216). Here he exercised the function of a bishop, by ordaining Coke and others, although he was only a presbyter. He was convinced that by Scripture and primitive Church usage he had the right to do so. At the name of 'bishop' Wesley said that he shuddered. This was because of the unscriptural assumptions made by some who bore the name, and because of its historic associations. Men might call him opprobrious names, but, he said, 'they shall never call me bishop, by my consent' (*Letters*, 279). Nevertheless, Wesley believed, as he wrote to his brother Charles in 1785, that he was himself a scriptural

* So Wesley then styled him; *vide ante*, Book I., chap. iv.

ἐπίσκοπος (bishop) as much as any man in England, or in Europe. Wesley added, ' the uninterrupted succession I know to be a fable, which no man ever did or can prove, (*Ibid.*, 90). He therefore used the powers of such a bishop on this and other occasions shown. On the other hand, Wesley stated that he no longer desired an English bishop to ordain one of his preachers. ' If they ordain, they will expect to govern, and how grievously would this entangle us ! ' said Wesley. Every word of this famous letter, constituting a Church, a Free Church, should be studied. It is given in our Appendix.[100] As the American Methodists were free from the State, ' and from the English hierarchy,' as Wesley styled it, he declined to entangle them with either. Neither did he wish to control the Church for which he offered a constitution. Although he claimed to be, under God, the ' father of the whole family of Methodists,' including those in America, Wesley only offers his advice to them, in this letter, upon important matters in their Church.

(viii.) *Ministers Ordained for British Methodism*

The conviction and compulsion which Wesley felt had sustained him in providing for the needs of American Methodists prompted him to ordain several of his preachers for Methodist work in Scotland, and later for England also, and to supply them with a book of services for the Sacraments, and public prayers. This was the climax of Wesley's actions in denying episcopal authority and asserting his convictions as Church Founder. It was a graver act than the ordinations for America. Charles Wesley saw the high significance of those

acts, and wrote strongly of them. ' In his eighty-second year my brother . . . assumed the episcopal character, ordained elders, consecrated a bishop, and sent him over to ordain our lay preachers in America. . . . Lord (Justice) Mansfield told me last year that ordination was separation ' (Jackson, *Life of Charles Wesley*, ii. 391). These three ordinations operated in a distant country. To these Wesley added twenty-five other acts of ordination, of preachers in Scotland and England.*
A Book of Sunday Services, for optional use by English Methodists, was issued by Wesley in 1786, and again in 1788. This was a notable contribution to the equipment of the Methodists with a complete organization.† Finally, in 1787, Wesley deliberately used the provisions of the Act of Toleration, passed in 1689, which permitted religious services by Protestant Dissenters and Quakers. He decided that all Methodist chapels and travelling preachers should be licensed under that Act, the preachers being styled simply ' Preachers of the Gospel ' (*Journal*, vii. 339). This was done in many cases (*Journal*, viii. 76, note). Neither the clergy or members of the Church of England, nor the Methodist preachers and members, could miss the meaning of actions by Wesley such as these of ordination, the equipment of Methodism as a Church upon the lines, as Wesley believed, of New Testament Christianity, and the legal recognition of its church buildings.

* An ordination certificate, given by Wesley, is used as an illustration, on page 198 herein. For several originals and copies, see *Catalogue of Wesleyana* (1921), pp. 6, 15, 16.

† This Service Book is virtually Wesley's abridgement of the English Prayer-Book which he issued for the Methodists of the United States of America, except that, instead of the prayers there provided for ' the Rulers of these United States,' there are prayers for the monarch and the royal family.

Anglican and High Church critics of Wesley's actions as Church Founder make much of his sermon on 'The Ministerial Office,' the famous 'Korah' Sermon. In this he sharply rebukes some of his preachers who had given the Lord's Supper to the Methodists. Wesley's critics miss completely the point of his strictures. He condemned and rebuked such preachers because they had not been ordained, not even by him. It was not the fact that these preachers lacked ordination at the hands of an Anglican bishop which disturbed Wesley, and disturbed his critics then and since; it was the fact that he had not ordained them. 'Where did I appoint you to do this?' he asks. A considerable number of his ordinands, and those who had been ordained by them in America, were at that very time administering the Sacraments. None of these had been 'ordained,' or were entitled, according to English ecclesiastical law, to give the Sacraments.'[111]

These 'illegal actions,' of which Wesley is accused, must be explained. John and Charles were 'in orders' in the Church of England. Each had been ordained in due course 'deacon and priest.' Charles stood strictly for the Anglican view of the necessity of ordination by an Anglican bishop as the only means by which a man can become a minister. He ridiculed his brother's assumption of the power to ordain, as he had not been ordained as a bishop, who alone has that power according to the Episcopal system. Technically, and in harmony with the general Anglican teaching, Charles was strictly correct. John Wesley claimed to be an *episcopos*, a bishop. Those whom he ordained also accepted his assertion. The highest New Testament scholarship sustains his

A CHURCH FOUNDER'S ACTS 228

claim to be a ' bishop ' in that sense ; but not in the Anglican and High Church meaning of the term. According to that interpretation, he was simply a presbyter and had no right to ordain, since he had not been ordained as a bishop. Hence Charles Wesley's well-known jibe at his brother John, and at the Countess of Huntingdon, on this question :

> How easily are bishops made
> By man or woman's whim !
> Wesley his hands on Coke hath laid,
> But who laid hands on him ?

It follows that technically, and in the High Church meaning of words, the twenty-eight acts of ordination performed by Wesley were illegal, invalid, and meaningless. To those who accept the New Testament as their sufficient guide in faith and practice they were lawful, valid, and of all but the highest significance. The highest authority is ' the call ' of the Holy Spirit, approved by a duly constituted Church.

Judged by any other standard than this, Wesley's actions in this regard were irregular, not to say quaint. As early as 1760 he allowed his preachers, who had not been ordained by him or any one, to give the Sacraments at Norwich (Jackson's *Life of C. Wesley*, ii. 187). John Wesley ordained some preachers *for a locality*. They were ministers as long as they resided there. Some were ordained for Scotland and unfrocked when they crossed the Border. Such a Methodist preacher was an ordained minister *for a time* ; later, the same preacher, still entirely worthy, had neither the status nor duty of an ordained minister.* This was legitimate

* Hatch (*Organization of the Early Christian Churches*, 187) shows the same ' facility with which ordinations were made and unmade ' occurred in the early Churches.

ground of complaint by John Pawson, one of Wesley's best assistants and preachers. Pawson stated, 'I have nothing but love in my heart toward the old man. But, really, he will not bear the light at all.' So Pawson said about this.* Wesley was ever, he believed, a waiter upon Providence, opportunity, and suitability, and therefore felt himself justified in these varied acts and courses. His conduct, however, makes it absolutely impossible to claim for him obedience to ecclesiastical law or to assert episcopal or sacerdotal validity for any 'orders' which he conferred, or to trace an unbroken succession of those who received such orders and transmitted them.†

An Irresistible Conclusion

A review of these eight acts by Wesley, which have here been classified and summarized, show him definitely and unmistakably as a Church Founder. That he was such was early seen and stated by some. William Grimshaw was, like the Wesleys, a clergyman, and closely associated with them. He regarded Wesley's acts, and those permitted and encouraged by him among the Methodists, as indicative of their separateness from the Church of England. Grimshaw said in 1760 that the Methodists 'are as real a body of Dissenters from her as the Presbyterians, Baptists, Quakers, or any body of Independents' (Jackson,

* Tyerman, *Wesley*, iii. 498. Pawson was afterwards twice President of the Conference (1793, 1801).

† These two paragraphs were used in the *United Methodist*, October 16, 1919, and in *British Methodism As It Is, As It Was, As It Will Be*. A certificate of ordination, given by Wesley to one of his preachers, Gamble, and a certificate given by two of them, whom Wesley had ordained, to a Methodist preacher, Kilham, are given herein (p. 198).

Life of Charles Wesley, ii. 189). It is also noteworthy that Wesley deliberately included Methodism as a separate section of the Christian Church in the church history which he prepared and issued. In 1781, when he was seventy-eight, there appeared his work, in four volumes, entitled *A Concise Ecclesiastical History, from the Birth of Christ to the Beginning of the present Century.* This ' present century ' was the eighteenth. Wesley used Mosheim's church history, in a translation by Maclaine; but he impressed himself upon their work. He added a section, consisting of one hundred and thirteen pages, which he entitled ' A Short History of the People called Methodists.' It is a personal narrative by Wesley, and is distinct from other accounts by him. Wesley never re-called this remarkable work on Church history. Its appearance, with Methodist history as a part, is another fact of moment in Wesley's work as Church Founder.

We judge that these decisive acts by Wesley are still unknown to many present-day writers about him and his churchmanship. Certainly their meaning is not generally admitted. Canon Peter Green, of Manchester and Salford, esteemed for his candour and brotherly kindness, has mis-stated the attitude and intention of Wesley, at least that of the mature Wesley. Canon Green stated that ' Wesley meant his societies to be centres of social effort and evangelistic preaching and good works, from which the members would come up from time to time to their own parish church to make their communion.'* Wesley's acts do not bear this construction. Why should the Methodists go to their parish churches when Wesley and his Conference

* Quoted in *Methodist Times,* April 10, 1924.

P

had provided them with every aid to Christian thought, worship, and work, with sanctuaries, ministers, and optional forms of service? For a while, even after Wesley's death, some Methodists did not hold their services in ' church hours '; and some, who had been accustomed to attend those sanctuaries for the Lord's Supper, continued to do so. Many never went. By the middle of the next century very few did so; and generally, Methodist services were held at suitable times, without reference to the Church of England. It came to be recognized that Wesley's arrangements, adapted as necessary, sufficed for his followers. It is good to note that responsible historians of the Church of England recognize that Wesley's acts must be interpreted according to their clear tendency. This was separation from and independence of any other church organization. They hold that ' from the very first, the Wesleyan movement, so far as it concerned organization, never was, and never could have been, a Church movement.' They ask, ' What was the tendency of the movement? Where did the followers of Wesley find their religion? Where was their true motive power?' Their reply is conclusive: ' Surely not in the Church system, but in their own separate organization' (Overton and Relton, *Hist. of English Church*, vii. 74). Indirectly, such writers pay tribute to Wesley as a Church Founder.

III
WESLEY'S REGULATIVE PRINCIPLES AS CHURCH FOUNDER

THE acts of Wesley as Church Founder, the human Founder of Methodism, occurred at intervals during more than fifty years, the period from 1738 to 1791. They varied in their importance and significance, while all were governed by his concepts as a Christian philosopher. We have now to trace the underlying principles which unify these several acts of Wesley. The principles we trace are four: The supreme importance of Spiritual Intuition and Moral Consciousness; Divine Guidance received through the Holy Scriptures; the Verdict of the Common Sense of Christians; and Practical Value as discovered by Use. Guided by these principles, Wesley laid the foundations of Methodism. It may be added that the subsequent development of the organization was upon the same Principles.*

(i.) The Primacy of Spiritual Intuition and Moral Consciousness

Students recognize that no problem emerges in a man's belief or conduct which has not already

* Cf. Wesley's remarkable booklet of 1745 (*Works*, viii., 351), the golden *Advice to the People called Methodists*. Much read by those who wish to know Wesley and be genuine Methodists, it deserves Dr. J. S. Simon's high praise (*John Wesley and the Religious Societies*, 294).

appeared in his thought. The primacy of spiritual concerns was gained in Wesley's mind as a result of thirteen years of thought which culminated in his evangelical conversion. After that crisis in 1738 the spiritual was dominant in Wesley's whole personality and conduct. He and his brother Charles both owed their spiritual quickening or evangelical conversion to the agency of persons—Böhler, Holland, Bray and Mrs. Turner, whose chief qualification was their spirituality. Wesley became forthwith the sworn foe of materialism in all its forms. Mechanism, determinism, and fatalism he hated with a perfect hatred. Whether as a philosophical doctrine, Necessity, or as a theological dogma, Calvinism was opposed by Wesley continuously, and with all his resources. He held that that view of God and man was not true, since it does not arise from the facts of experience; and it ought not to be true since it does not agree with the moral ideal embodied in Jesus Christ. God 'does not necessitate one to be good and another to be evil,' he declares in his *Thoughts Upon God's Sovereignty*. Wesley was as sure as a thinker can be, that form and action are not predetermined, but are the result of the movements of a living free Spirit in God and man. ' God is Spirit,' and ' Wherever the Spirit of the Lord is, there is open freedom,' says the New Testament. Monsieur Paul Sabatier has summed up the continued contrast and opposition between materialistic views of God and His work and worship, and the primacy of the spiritual in Him and them, in the illuminating title of his masterpiece, *The Religions of Authority and the Religion of the Spirit*. It is the latter for which Wesley stood. With Wesley the spiritual was primary.

REGULATIVE PRINCIPLES

It was axiomatic in all Wesley's thought and action that God moved upon him and within him by His Spirit. What he was then aware of was of supreme importance and authority for him and through him, if permitted by the other principles stated above. Wesley was a mystic. For him the line of life, and light, and power was vertical, not horizontal. These issued from God as the ever-living, acting Source. The spirit of Wesley felt and saw God as Spirit, in the sense in which human ' spirit with spirit can meet,' and what he felt and saw had for him ultimate final authority, when tested and fully confirmed in ways to be stated. He was a judge of the meaning and value of these intuitions and spiritual feelings. Consequently, he declined to be fettered by human authority as to time, place, or method of interpretation or work. He says, ' I am to obey God rather than man.'[1] This exercise of the individual judgement is, as Dean Inge declares, the essence of Protestantism (*Personal Idealism*, 105).

Wesley held firmly that others must act upon this principle of the primacy of the spiritual. In his Conference of 1745 Wesley asked, ' Is the shepherd free to leave his sheep ? Or the sheep to leave their shepherd ? ' Wesley answered for himself and for others thus : ' Yes, if one or the others are convinced it is for the glory of God and the superior good of their souls.' (*Minutes*, 1745, Wes. Hist. Soc. *Publications*, i. 25).[2] He regarded the ecclesiastical constitution of the Church of England as being no more the fundamental principles of a Christian Church ' than the tiles are the most fundamental principles of a house ' (*Works*, xiii. 204). When he was eighty-five years old, Wesley claimed that he had not premeditatedly nor willingly varied from the Church of England in anything, 'till we were convinced we could no longer omit them at the peril of our souls' (*Journal*, vii. 422): but he did 'vary,' in harmony with this principle of the primacy of the spiritual. Hence he condemned the persecution of any one for his opinions as to doctrine, or as to modes of church work. He held that Religion is not mere opinion, not even right opinion. He reckoned mere orthodoxy as among trifles. 'We know, indeed,' he added, 'that wrong opinions lead to wrong tempers, or wrong practices; and that, consequently, it is our bounden duty to pray that we may have a right judgement in all things. But still a man may judge as accurately as the devil and yet be as wicked as he' (*Works*, vii. 315). He said also, 'As to all opinions which do not strike at the root of Christianity, we think and let think'* (*Works*, viii. 340).

It is gratefully recognized that the labours of Charles Wesley as evangelist and hymnist were second only to those of John Wesley in usefulness and importance in early Methodism. Nevertheless, guided by his master principle, Wesley advanced at critical stages in the development of Methodism without the help of his brother Charles, and sometimes in sharp divergence from him. Charles was more conservative in temper and more obedient to human authority than John. At times Charles Wesley declined to act upon the principle that spiritual interests are primary and spiritual sensitiveness is the chief qualification for Christian workers. On one occasion he threatened to leave the Conference of Methodist clergymen and others, if unordained preachers or others were permitted to

* This memorable phrase occurs repeatedly in his *Journal* also.

give their judgement. Wesley presided, and he thereupon said to a friend near to him, 'Give my brother Charles his hat.' As John Bennet's *Minutes* and other documents show, Wesley composed his Conferences without regard to clerical qualifications. Spirituality and helpfulness were the tests. When Charles Wesley, and others of a clerical mind, objected to some of the work done by Methodists in obedience to their convictions, Wesley declared that 'Soul-damning clergymen lay me under more difficulties than soul-saving laymen' (*Arminian Magazine*, 1779, p. 375).[134] In selecting one of his preachers to be his assistant or superintendent of the Methodists in a circuit or group of societies or local churches, Wesley required that he should be eminent for spiritual-mindedness and moral worth; qualified for his charge not so much by superior gifts as by walking closely with God (*Minutes*, 1749, Wes. Hist. Soc. *Publications*, i.). His preachers were not incapable, nor ignorant; but they must be true Christians, whatever they might lack.

This principle regulated Wesley's actions as to the use of the Sacraments by Methodists. He was convinced of the absolute necessity for preaching the Christian gospel, alike by ordinary and special agents, in every place and at every time. He did not attach the same degree of importance to sacramental services. He believed that to provide occasion and opportunity for the utterance of the Spirit of God to the human spirit was the most urgent duty, whether a symbolic service was used or not. The presence of an ordained minister, or the use of certain forms or words, was not necessary, he held, to the validity of a means of grace or the effectiveness of the work of God; while in his *Rules* for the Methodists, summarized before (p. 68), he conditioned continuance in the Methodist fellowship upon the use of the means of grace, including the Sacrament of the Lord's Supper. As to the last-named service of unique helpfulness, Wesley's example is impressive. All through his life he practised frequent communion. By his sermons (e.g. No. xii., ' The Means of Grace '), by many hymns, and by providing for the Methodists in America, and later in England, amended and strictly Protestant forms of service, Wesley recognized that the Sacraments may be the means of unique blessing to the recipients. He advised his American ministers to give the Lord's Supper to the Methodists every Lord's Day. He was sure that the Lord's Supper may be a ' converting ordinance,' and appealed to the experience of many Methodists that ' the very beginning of your conversion to God (perhaps in some, the first deep conviction) was wrought at the Lord's Supper ' (*Journal*, ii. 361). He was therefore wishful that Methodists should partake of the Lord's Supper regularly and frequently. Many of the clergy would not give that ordinance to Methodists, or were unworthy to give it. Nor were their numbers sufficient, because of the rapid growth and wide diffusion of the Methodists. Accordingly, Wesley met the situation by ordaining several of his preachers that they might give the Lord's Supper to the Methodists.[125]

These facts and others show that Wesley was not a Sacramentarian, nor had his teaching that character. He did not condition immediate contact with God in Christ by the Holy Spirit upon any means of grace, however helpful and important.[126] On the other hand, Wesley denounced those who practised 'stillness' or independence of the means of grace, and also the Quakerism of his age. As to these matters, the question is one of place and proportion. For Wesley himself, as taught by his experience examined above (cf. page 90), and the experience of others, the spiritual was first and chief. With St. Paul, he believed and taught that, helped by the Holy Spirit, the human spirit can have direct contact with God; that faith must come from what is heard, and what is heard comes from the word and mind of Christ, and this is interpreted and assured to the spirit of man by obedience to God (John vii. 17; 1 John i. 3). Wesley therefore continually heard St. Paul's question concerning the salvation of men, ' How are men to hear without a preacher ? ' Wesley preached far more frequently than he held sacramental services, although he believed ' that no fitness is required at the time of communicating but a sense of our utter sinfulness and helplessness ' (*Journal*, ii. 362). He sent out many preachers, itinerant and local, to call men to God; he ordained some to give the Sacraments. In this abundant use of the spiritual, immaterial appeal, Wesley followed, not the priests and the temple service of the Old Testament, but Ezra, Isaiah, and the prophets, the apostles of the New Testament, and our Lord and Saviour Jesus Christ.

The same principle guided Wesley in his constitution of the highest court of the Church he founded. When Wesley, by his Deed of Declaration in 1784, constituted a Conference to maintain the Methodists as a separate, self-governing Church, he composed the Conference of ordained ministers and of preachers who lacked that recognition. More than eighty of these had not been ordained, even by him. They were not empowered to give the Sacraments, and generally did not give them. Some of them were young preachers of only one, two, or three years' service in his Connexion. Sixteen had 'travelled' fewer than four years. To this mixed Conference, very mixed if judged by mere ecclesiastical standards, Wesley committed Methodism. The doctrine of the Church he thus founded (except as generally defined in his *Notes on the New Testament* and forty-four *Standard Sermons*), its discipline, the stations or appointments of the preachers, and the admission to and expulsion of them from the ministerial office, were all entrusted to this Conference and its successors. The Methodist Conference as constituted by Wesley, with all its powers, was composed of lay preachers as to four-fifths of the legal members of it; but they were all, he believed, godly men, whether ordained or not. This fact is very suggestive.* So is the fact that Wesley held that the Christian pastor is a guide, not a ruler, and should be chosen by those who follow him. He says, 'As every one must give an account of himself to God, every man must judge for himself, especially in a point of so deep importance as this is—the choice of a guide for his soul.' Obedience to a minister is due, he held, in a limited degree only: 'Not in things enjoined of God; not in things forbidden by Him; but in things indifferent: in all that are not determined, one way or another, by the oracles of God' (Sermon xcvii.).

(*ii.*) *Divine Guidance through Holy Scripture*

The closing words of the last sentence, 'the oracles of God,' lead us to another of the regulative

* Paragraph quoted from *British Methodism As It Is*, p. 107.

REGULATIVE PRINCIPLES

principles of Wesley's work as Church Founder. He held that spiritual things taught by God to the human spirit must accord with those taught in the Scriptures, as these culminate in the living Word of God, Jesus Christ, the Pioneer and Perfecter of Faith. Wesley built upon 'the apostles and prophets as foundation, with Christ Jesus as the corner stone, in whom the whole structure is welded together and rises into a sacred temple.' Wesley was a Mystic like St. John and St. Paul, with immediate knowledge of the Mind of Christ; but he tested and valued this subjective knowledge by its agreement with the objective standard, the revealed Word of God in the Holy Scriptures. His appeal to the Scriptures is insistent, constant, and final. He regarded 'searching the Scriptures' as one of the divine ordinances. He sedulously used it and enjoined it upon every Methodist. The first Methodists at Oxford were derided as Bible moths; but the name testified to their intense love and constant use of the Scriptures. Every experience of God granted to Wesley, or to any in his fellowship, must be tested by comparison with such recorded in the Bible, which he regarded as a progressive revelation, interpreted for the needs of every age by the Holy Spirit, through the people of God. Wesley had no higher ideal than to raise real 'Bible Christians'* (*Letters of John Wesley*, 156). Besides his *Notes on the New Testament* (referred to on page 73), Wesley prepared for the Methodists his *Explanatory Notes upon the Old Testament*. This large work, which filled more than two thousand six hundred quarto printed pages, was compiled chiefly from the works of Matthew Henry

---

* Early in the nineteenth century some Methodists used this beautiful name (1815-1907), until they became part of the United Methodist Church.

and Poole. It was issued in sixpenny parts, week by week—another anticipation of modern enterprise by Wesley as publisher and educationist. The heavy labour and cost of this effort to popularize Bible reading and knowledge indicate Wesley's love and reverence of it as an authority.[1]

Wesley did not worship the mere text of Scripture, nor regard the English Bible as a book idol. He was not in this matter, or any, a literalist. The reader is referred to what is stated on page 74, regarding Wesley's attitude towards the Bible as literature. Notwithstanding these distinctive views, indeed partly because of them, he claimed that he had Scripture warrant for his actions in building Methodism. The means which Wesley stated for the quickening, education and sanctification of man's moral nature; the prominence he gave to preaching, hymns, and singing; the simplicity, variety, and adaptability of Methodist religious services; his use of Christian fellowship and human experience of all kinds, and the narration of it; his use of all types of workers, men and women, and of their gifts of all kinds, in the offices of the Church; and his use of the group mind in Church courts—all these were built by Wesley upon the ways of the first Christians, as recorded in the New Testament, or were, he believed, developments therefrom, or were not contrary thereto. From the beginning of his work as Church Founder, Scripture was his guide and authority. 'God in Scripture commands me,' he wrote to Hervey in 1739, in the famous letter wherein he declared that he looked upon all the world as his parish; 'I allow no other rule, whether of faith or practice, than the Holy Scriptures' (*Journal*, ii. 217). Many years later, when Wesley acted in violation of the laws of the Church of

England and ordained some of his preachers to give the Sacraments, it was because he believed that he was a bishop according to New Testament teaching.

A man of many books, alike as an incessant reader and writer of them, Wesley declared himself to be *homo unius libri*, a man of one book, and that book the Bible. In the preface to the first volume of his *Standard Sermons*, he gives his *apologia* for his work as Church Founder, for that of a seeker after God and wisdom, and an Evangelist, and there he wrote an imperishable eulogium of the Bible, inspired by that imperishable subject (*Works*, v.). Church history, tradition, and the utterances of Church Councils, were only authoritative with Wesley if they were accordant with and illustrated the plain teachings of the Bible. He wrote to Dr. Dodd in 1756 thus, ' My father gave me, thirty years ago, to reverence the ancient Church and our own. But I try every church and every doctrine by the Bible.'

(*iii.*) *The Verdict of the Common Sense of Christians*

A third regulative principle which emerges from a consideration of Wesley as Church Founder is the use he made of the appeal to the verdict of the Christian conscience. The aged Wesley told Freeborn Garrettson, a quondam slave-owner of North America, who was ordained as a Methodist preacher, that it is a very desirable thing that the children of God should communicate their experience to each other, and it is generally most profitable when they can do it face to face (*Letters of John Wesley*, 268). He regarded it as necessary as well as desirable. His opinions, and those of others who acted with him or whom he guided, he tested and appraised by the moral sense of a Christian community. Finally, this appeal was to the Catholic or universal mind of the children of God, the Christian conscience. He used a limited test of consensus, *consensus communis fidelium*, the consent of the community of the faithful.* The reader is referred to Wesley's successful restoration of Christian Fellowship in the Church by the Class-meeting, the Love Feast and the Conference, as before described (page 145). He invited the Methodists to recount their experiences and notions in the class or fellowship meeting. Their individual convictions and testimonies were tested by coherence with the general body of truth accepted by the faithful, since the universal is true. It was Wesley's belief that every renewed human spirit may know and teach some truth, while the trained mind and special natural powers are necessary for the exposition and conveyance of the truth. The commonalty of the faithful can appreciate the evidence and supply the verdict, as a jury; while the expert, like the judge, must sum up the case and pronounce the consequence of their findings. Accordingly, Wesley admitted converted clergymen, unordained preachers, and church officers to his annual Conferences on Methodist doctrine and discipline.

In such gatherings Wesley, humbly and sincerely regarding himself as an expert in these august matters, uttered the decisions. These were always open to appeal, as to the truth to be accepted, and preached, and practised by the community. Wesley, as we have shown, was learning, and was ready

* For the use of this in theistic philosophy, see Professor A. Caldecott's work, *The Philosophy of Religion in England and America*.

to be taught by the humblest of the faithful. He was willing to learn from any one concerning spiritual things. He believed that these must be read with the spiritual eye, although he constantly paid tribute to the mind of man as the organ of intellectual apprehension. Accordingly, sane saints and strange quaint people, with whimsies and fancies, find a place in his incomparable *Journal*. He listened to them all, lest he might miss a word or tone of the authentic voice of God. He tested old and new alike by an appeal to the Bible and the common sense of the Christian community. The court of final decision for Methodists, which Wesley constituted and they accepted, was the annual Conference. It was his most notable contribution to churchly apparatus. As suggested, its method may be compared with the British legal procedure to discover facts and administer justice. In a sense, it was true of Methodism, as Brougham quoted from an anonymous jurist, ' that all we see about us, kings, lords, and commons, the whole machinery of the State, all the apparatus of the system, and its varied workings, end in simply bringing twelve good men into a box '—the jury box of the Conference, with a learned, trained, elected President as the ' judge.' [144]

Had Wesley denied the right of the humblest Methodist to judge of things spiritual, and to testify concerning them, he would have violated his principles as a Mystic with whom the spiritual sense is primary, as a New Testament scholar, and as a Protestant Churchman. ' Remain in Christ,' wrote St. John to the first Christians (1 John ii. 27), ' for His unction teaches you about everything and is true and is no lie ; remain in Him as it has taught you to do.' But Wesley did not deny this inherent right of judgement possessed by every Christian, as spiritually illuminated. He exercised it himself and invited others to do so. In this connexion, as in several, he has been gravely misunderstood and misrepresented. He did not pose as an oracle, although he did not suffer the foolish readily. He remembered the injunction of our Lord, that pearls must not be thrown before swine. Wesley brought together competent Christian jurymen— so one likes to think of them—in his Conferences, large and small. On occasion, he added the expert or technical counsellor who might be required. For such a court, so composed, he prayed and urged others to pray, that it might have complete insight and understanding of the open secret of God's will . . . and the Spirit of wisdom and revelation for the knowledge of Himself, illuminating the eyes of the heart (Eph. i.).

> Here is knowledge rare and hidden
>   From the wise,
>   Who despise
> All our inward *Eden*;
> Thou to us the truth hast given,
>   We in Thee,
>   Happy we!
> Know the way to heaven.
> —*Poetical Works*, vii. 148, ' The Collier's Hymn.'

The *Minutes* of Wesley's early Conferences, notably those of 1745 and 1746, show all the features indicated above.

That Wesley did really confer with others, and appealed to the common sense of faithful fellow Christians, was seen in his Conference of 1745 (*Minutes*, Bennet's copy):

Q. Should we still consider ourselves as little children, who have everything to learn?
A. Yes, so far as to have our minds always open to any farther light which God may give us.

REGULATIVE PRINCIPLES 241

Q. What general method may we observe in our following Conferences ?
A. To read and weigh at every Conference each article of those preceding. To speak freely and hear calmly touching each, that we may either retract, amend, or enlarge it.
Q. Should not the time of this Conference be a time of particular watching and self-denial ?
A. It should.
Q. Should we not desire all who can of the Society to join with us to-morrow in fasting and prayer ?
A. We will desire them so to do.
Q. Ought not every question which shall be proposed to be examined from the foundation ?
A. Without question it ought. If there was any defect therein at the last Conference, let us amend it now.
Q. How can we effectually provide that everyone may speak freely whatever is in his heart ?
A. By taking care to check no one, either by word or look, even though he should say what was quite wrong.
Q. How shall we provide that every point may be fully and thoroughly settled ?
A. Let us beware of making haste or showing any impatience, whether of delay or of contradiction.

Joseph Sutcliffe shows how fully Wesley obeyed these counsels at his last Conference, 1790 (*Wes. Hist. Soc. Proceedings*, xv. 57).

Sometimes between the sessions of a Conference each member was asked to consult the Scriptures on the matter under discussion and bring his findings on the following day. Was not Wesley restoring the methods of the primitive Christian Church, as recorded in Acts by the first church historian, St. Luke ?

This appeal to the judgement of the Christian community Wesley used in local church matters. The whole membership of the little society or church, not its ' leaders ' alone, were the jury. The local church was the unit of the fellowship, and served as the disciplinary court for its members. These were expelled by Wesley with its consent and approbation (*Journal*, ii. 430). When the grave issue was raised of the separation of the London Methodists from the Moravians, Wesley summoned all the members of the inner fellowship—the Bands —to consider and decide the course. He adds that God did not cast out their prayer nor leave Himself without witness among them. A unanimous decision was reached that the time had not come for separation. It came afterwards (*Journal*, ii. 369).

Wesley gave the right to the trustees of his meeting-houses or Church buildings to inhibit a preacher from using them if he became erroneous in doctrine, as judged by the standards of the teaching fixed by Wesley's Conference. These trustees were almost always laymen. They were not ordained, even by Wesley. Here again was a recognition of the Christian believer's right of judgement. Near the end of his wonderful career, in 1788, as at its beginning, Wesley clearly recognized the right of the local church. In that year he re-published a service book, *The Sunday Service of the Methodists, with other Occasional Services*. This might be used (so Wesley and the Conference decided) in Methodist sanctuaries, at the discretion of the chief preacher at certain times, 'if the generality of the Society acquiesce with it.'¹⁹ It was so used in English Methodist sanctuaries.

(iv.) *Value as discovered by Use*

Finally, Wesley as Church Founder used items of church polity and method as they were found useful. Antiquity, human authority, and ease in working must, with him, give way to practical utility. In this way he was a pragmatist, although neither in doctrine nor polity would he have used the dictum of Alexander Pope:

> For modes of faith let graceless zealots fight,
> His can't be wrong whose life is in the right.

Wesley stood for accuracy in thought and expression, but one of his tests of any theory or method was the ethical result or the service rendered. That a proposal worked well and produced effects of the highest moral worth was a strong recommendation to Wesley. This was the justification of his teaching. He asked the Bishop of London (Dr. Gibson) to consider the results of it in reformed lives, a 'cloud of witnesses who at this hour experience the gospel which I preach to be the power of God unto salvation' (*Works*, viii. 495).

Wesley applied the like test to church workers. However eminent or humble, all must submit to this. They might possess 'gifts' and 'graces,' but if their work had not 'fruit,' Wesley did not readily receive them as genuine, nor use them as fellow labourers. In 1745 he wrote to an Irish clergyman, 'I think he is a true evangelical minister, Διάκονος, "servant" of Christ and His Church, who οὕτως διακονεῖ, "so ministers" as to save souls from death, to reclaim sinners from their sins' (*Letters*, 111). This is the burden of his trenchant sermon, 'A Caution against Bigotry.' It is based on Christ's teaching in Mark ix. 38, 39. There Wesley argues that outward connexion with a church, or with a party in it, or adherence to an opinion, or the use of certain practices, or even the use of correct doctrine, is not the final proof of a Christian worker. 'Does he cast out devils?' Wesley's text declared that this was the fact concerning one who did not associate with the recognized disciples of our Lord, and this secured him permission by our Lord to continue his work; for, Christ added, 'there is no man which shall do a miracle in My name that can lightly speak evil of Me.' Of such a man in that age and place Wesley says, ' forbid him not ; no, not at the peril of your soul. . . . No man can do these works unless God is with him ; unless God has sent him for this very thing. . . . If a man has brought sinners to repentance and yet the Bishop will not ordain him, then the Bishop does forbid him to cast out devils. But I dare not forbid him ; I have published my reasons to all the world.'[140]

Wesley's test as to the teaching and the teachers was applied by him to methods and organization. The spirit and intention, always primary with Wesley, must be allowed to create its own organ and way of work, and this must be amended, developed, or discarded as it proved useful or of little or no service. Wesley did not use an arrangement permanently unless it had worked well. At one period his itinerant preachers were moved about every two months ; later, yearly, and limited to a three years' stay. At first the preachers were of four classes : clergymen, itinerants, half-itinerants (such as were employed partly as preacher and partly in trade), and local preachers. Two of these classes, clergymen and half-itinerants, disappeared from the Methodist system, since use did not approve them.

A similar course was taken in regard to internal local church arrangements : e.g. as to the grading of members and the grouping of them. At first the name of each Methodist had a mark attached on the class-paper to indicate the stage of his religious life. He was defined as a penitent, as a justified or sanctified believer. This grading system disappeared in Wesley's lifetime. For a considerable time the Methodist members met weekly, with a leader, in Bands as well as Classes. The Band was an inner fellowship. This also disappeared.

REGULATIVE PRINCIPLES 245

Similarly, new offices were created to meet needs. They were continued if they proved useful, not otherwise. Such were the office of Local Preacher, of Stewards of various kinds, and of Trustee. Wesley's view of a Christian community was that the living Spirit of God dwelt in each member, and among them, and guided them into all truth both for belief and activity. Wesley's idea and that of the Methodists was that lately expressed by Professor C. Ryder Smith: 'that Church government is a tool, and that a tool may be refashioned from time to time to suit the work that it has to do.' [141]

This is Wesley's test of utility. Hence the fact that many in all church communions who wished to build New Testament Christianity as catholic, as Protestant but positive and comprehensive, all claimed Wesley as a leader. None had to cry, 'Back to Wesley!' nor 'Forward and leave Wesley!' Their call was ever 'Forward with Wesley!' while they used his prayer, 'I am willing to do, let me know Thy will.' The essential, authentic, mature Wesley has the note of timelessness. Like Shakespeare in his sphere, Wesley was not for an age, but for all time.

The Test of Survival

In closing this study of Wesley it is claimed that time has paid tribute to him as Christian Philosopher and Church Founder. A few years hence will see the second centenary of his evangelical conversion in 1738, and of the founding of the mother Methodist Church in 1739. Dr. W. H. Fitchett of Australia reminds us in his *Wesley and His Century* that the spiritual impulse imparted through Wesley has survived all the schisms in his work, and has characterized each separate fragment. ' Sea transit has not killed it ; new social and geographical environments have not arrested it. Methodism has crossed all the seas of the planet, and taken root on every soil. It has varied its name, its forms, its methods ; but, under all its forms, it has kept steadfastly loyal to its original ideal. And everywhere it is marked by that same strange continuity of spiritual impulse.' More than this is true. The Christian philosophy of Wesley, and his principles as Church Founder, have permeated all fields of thought and affected Christendom. The interpretation of the universe in terms of Christian experience, which he was permitted to restate, grows in acceptance everywhere.[141] His teaching concerning God as Holy Love, and concerning Jesus Christ and the Holy Spirit, has prevailed and spread. So has that concerning every man's need of God and the possibility of response to God by every man. Determinism seldom appears in philosophy, nor Calvinism in theology. Evangelical Arminianism is commonly taught. Wesley's doctrine of Christian perfection, the complete but growing love of God and man, is now welcomed as the hope set before us. The features of Wesley's church polity—connexionalism, interpretation by the living church as the organ of the Holy Spirit, legislation and government by conferences of representatives—are likewise to be found in all the Protestant Churches.

All this is not to the praise of Wesley, but of God, who wrought by Wesley. Of all that is worthy which has issued from his mind and service, Wesley must always be thought of as expressing adoring wonder. He was amazed at the divine use of himself as a human instrument. He used frequently the mystical comment of his brother Charles on the same feeling as expressed by the patriarch Jacob :

> O the fathomless love,
> That has deigned to approve
> And prosper the work of my hands!
> With my pastoral crook
> I went over the brook,
> And, behold, I am spread into bands!

APPENDIX
ADDITIONAL NOTES, AND LITERARY AUTHORITIES USED IN THIS WORK

I. ILLUSTRATIONS

i. (*Frontispiece*) JOHN WESLEY IN HIS MATURITY. This unique portrait of Wesley, head and face only, is from the original painting, a three-quarter figure, in Kingswood Wesleyan Methodist School dining-hall, Bath, per a Woodburyprint photograph in the author's collection. The artist was John Russell, R.A. He was the first Methodist who obtained that distinction. Unlike many who portrayed Wesley, Russell was often at Wesley's services, knew him intimately, and loved him. The portrait, painted in 1773, is of Wesley when he was seventy, and may be regarded as the most natural and attractive of more than four hundred different representations of his expression.

ii. (p. 84) WESLEY AS TEACHER-EVANGELIST. This portrait of Wesley by Nathaniel Hone, R.A., represents Wesley as he preached in the open air. His age was sixty-seven. The Bible in his right hand is the edition by Field. The engraving from which our illustration is reproduced is a singularly beautiful one by John Greenwood, in 1770, in the possession of the Methodist Publishing House, London. It is No. 9, and has the inscription, 'Done from the original picture, in possession of Thomas Woolridge, Esq., of East Florida,' U.S.A. This picture must be distinguished from another by Hone, engraved by Bland. In that the figure of Wesley is on the right-hand side. Wesley is there said to be aged sixty-three. The original painting of that is in the National Portrait Gallery, London. Our illustration is from Greenwood's best engraving of another painting by Hone, which went to the United States. Besides this engraving of that (No. 9), Greenwood made another (No. 65), also in the 'Portraits' collection at the Methodist Publishing House. Details in the pictures and inscriptions distinguish them. Of No. 65, Dr. J. Alfred Sharp has a unique reproduction on glass. Wesley's title of his Scotch ministerial office, 'Chaplain to the Countess Dowager of Buchan,' appears on the engraving now reproduced.

iii. and iv. (p. 198) TWO METHODIST CERTIFICATES OF ORDINATION OF A PREACHER TO THE OFFICE OF MINISTER. One is by Wesley, of Robert Gamble, in 1788; the other is by two ministers ordained by Wesley (Joseph Cownley and Charles Atmore), who ordained Alexander Kilham,

NOTES AND AUTHORITIES 249

in 1792, the year after Wesley's death. Kilham was a founder of the Methodist New Connexion (1797-1907), now part of the United Methodist Church.

v. Facing page 264 is a SKETCH PLAN OF STREETS, indicating sites of buildings associated with the evangelical conversion of John and Charles Wesley.

II. ADDITIONAL NOTES AND LITERARY AUTHORITIES

INTRODUCTION

[1] (p. 15) Cf. Professor W. R. Sorley's Gifford Lecture, *Moral Values and the Idea of God* (2nd ed., 1921), and Professor J. S. Mackenzie's volume, *Ultimate Values in the Light of Contemporary Thought* (1924).

[2] (p. 16) In *Seven Ages*, by A Gentleman with a Duster (1923): 'Wesley roused the soul of England from its slumber of death. The three great words of his discourse were God, Christ, Sin. He had the grace of a scholar, the charm which goes with a slightly quizzical humour, and that immense attraction which emanates only from a perfectly sincere spirit. On all sides of Wesley were religious buffoonery, mockery, coldness, apathy, hypocrisy, and self-deception of a quite staggering order. But he retained his serenity, and met the violent abuse of his brother clergymen with a smile. That Wesley, with his intense conviction of the truth of religion, should have preserved this sense of humour in an age so full of barren formalism and downright infidelity in the Church itself, is memorable evidence to the beauty of his character and the fineness of his mind.'

[3] (p. 19) *English Thought in the Eighteenth Century*, by Leslie Stephen, is a valuable study of the eighteenth century; but its judgements must not be accepted without reserve. Gladstone challenged several concerning Butler (*Subsidiary Studies*); and Dr. W. H. Fitchett (*Wesley and his Century*), and Dr. E. H. Sugden (*Wesley's Standard Sermons*), those on Wesley. The social and moral conditions are shown in the *Cambridge Modern History*, vi., and *Social England* (Traill and Mann), v.

[4] (p. 22) *Works*, in 4 vols., ed. by A. C. Fraser (1901). See also Professor R. F. A. Hoernlé's exposition of Berkeley's teaching and of the general subject, in *Idealism as a Philosophical Doctrine* (1924).

[5] (p. 22) 'This is the way in which things appear to me. In the intelligible place the Idea of the Good is the last object of vision and is scarcely to be seen; but, if it be seen, we must collect by reasoning that it is the cause to all of everything right and beautiful, generating in the visible place, light, and its lord, the sun; and in the intelligible place, it is itself the Lord, producing the truth and intellect; and this must be beheld by him who is to act wisely either in his own or public affairs' (Plato, *Republic*, vii., ' Truth and Its Shadows,' Socrates *loq.*).

[6] (p. 22) The idealism taught by Berkeley begins with the mind of

man, rather than with universal ideas. He showed the spiritual nature of Reality, i.e. God, the universal Mind, by insisting upon the spiritual nature and certainty of finite minds, and the analogy between individual finite minds and infinite Mind. In Berkeley's philosophy the objects of human knowledge are ideas. Ideas are imprinted on the senses; or perceived in the attention of the mind to the passions or its own operations; or are formed by memory or imagination. Beside ideas or objects of knowledge, says Berkeley, there is ' Something which knows or perceives them and exercises the functions of willing, imagining, and remembering about them. This perceiving, active being is the mind, spirit, soul, or self.' That thoughts, passions, or ideas formed by the imagination, could not exist apart from a mind is allowed by all; but Berkeley also asserted 'that the various sensations, or ideas imprinted on the sense, and whatever objects they compose, cannot exist otherwise than in a mind perceiving them.' *Esse est percipi* (To be is to be perceived). Existence is in being perceived (*Works*, i. 259). The reality called pain is not in that which is the instrument or occasion of the pain, but is in the mind which perceives the pain. All experience is mental. The percipient mind may be my own, or that of another created spirit, or the eternal Spirit.

⁷ (p. 23) Cf. Jesus Christ's remarkable statement (John v. 17), 'My Father has continued working to this hour, so I work too'—Moffatt's translation. This is generally used by me in this work.

⁸ (p. 23) This significant phrase from Virgil (*Aeneid*, vi. 727), first quoted by Berkeley in 1713 (*Works*, iv. 180), was chosen (*circa* 1871) as the appropriate motto of the physical science college, now Armstrong College, Newcastle-upon-Tyne (Durham University). Poetry, philosophy, and science were thereby linked, and very significantly. Philosophy and poetry are more nearly related than is sometimes allowed. Wesley, like the eighteenth-century thinkers who preceded him, is shown later as having a poetic counterpart.

Among modern English poets Wordsworth seems to the present writer to be the poetic counterpart of Berkeley. The spiritual interpretation of Nature is common to both of them. Sometimes the poet seems almost to reproduce the language of the philosopher. Cf. the well-known passage from Wordsworth's poem, ' Lines composed above Tintern Abbey ' :

> I have felt
> A presence that disturbs me with the joy
> Of elevated thoughts ; a sense sublime
> Of something far more deeply interfused,
> Whose dwelling is the light of setting suns,
> And the round ocean and the living air,
> And the blue sky, and in the mind of man ;
> A motion and a spirit that impels
> All thinking things, all objects of all thought,
> And rolls through all things.

Once in the same poem Wordsworth nearly expresses Berkeley's formula, *esse est percipi*, existence is by being perceived, as thus :

> the mighty world
> Of eye, and ear,—both what they half create,
> And what perceive.

⁹ (p. 25) The importance of the ontological argument is recognized by present-day thinkers as a valuable aid to religious belief. Professor Sorley (*Moral Values and the Idea of God*, 307) holds that the power of that argument is in the demand of the mind that the best and most perfect Being which we can conceive shall not be severed from reality. Sir Oliver Lodge lately said, ' I will never believe that it is given to men to conceive a nobler idea than the reality of things.' This conviction has a moral quality. It is not purely metaphysical. Conscience and feeling enter into it. The ontological argument, pure and simple, is inconclusive. Professor R. F. Alfred Hoernlé, in a paper read at the Aristotelian Society, November 1922 (*Proceedings*, N.S. iii.), showed that Anselm's argument cannot be understood, nor is it effective, except on the basis of *fides*, faith, i.e. belief in God, accompanied by experience of God on the part of the person who uses the argument. The original purpose of Anselm's statement of the argument was, *Fides quaerens intellectum*—faith seeking understanding, or, faith seeking to understand itself. Anselm knew God by faith (*fides*), and used the argument to support faith by thought (*intellectum*). The faith which thus gives assurance to the mind must, in the end, be known by first-hand experience. There is no other way than by being a religious person. The Being whom Anselm defined as that than which no greater can be thought, *quo majus cogitari nequit*, is the same Being whom he worshipped.

¹⁰ (p. 26) Cowper the poet, and ' the flower of the Evangelical Revival,' may have had such a philosopher-divine as Clarke in mind when he wrote the following lines in *The Task*. He names Clarke's friend, Sir Isaac Newton, therein.

> Philosophy, baptized
> In the pure fountain of eternal love,
> Has eyes indeed ; and viewing all she sees
> As meant to indicate a God to man,
> Gives *Him* His praise, and forfeits not her own.
> Learning has borne such fruit in other days
> On all her branches ; piety has found
> Friends in the friends of science, and true prayer
> Has flowed from lips wet with Castilian dews.
> Such was thy wisdom, Newton, child-like sage ;
> Sagacious reader of the works of God,
> And in His word sagacious.

¹¹ (p. 26) *The Works of Bishop Butler*, a new edition with Introduction and Notes, by J. H. Bernard, D.D., 2 vols. (1900). Gladstone edited an edition in 1896. His *Studies Subsidiary to the Works of Bishop Butler*

is published separately. A. Whyte's small volume is useful, *Bishop Butler, An Appreciation, with the Best Passages of his Writings* (1903).

[12] (p. 27) *Natural Theology, or the Evidences of the Existence and Attributes of the Deity,* by William Paley, D.D., with Introduction by Lord Brougham, F.R.S., and Notes by Sir C. Bell, F.R.S. (1845). An edition, edited by F. Le Gros Clarke, F.R.S. (1885), adds the results of recent scientific research. Much of Paley's reasoning is supported, and his investigations are greatly enriched, by the work of Profess)r J. Arthur Thomson, M.A., LL.D., in *A System of Animate Nature* (Gifford Lectures, 1915-16); cf. also a very valuable chapter on the contribution made by Science to Religion in Professor Thomson's later work, *Science and Religion* (1924). The force of this argument, which Wesley valued and used (cf. his *Survey*), is more appreciated in our age by scientific thinkers than in the last generation. Bacon stated it in his essay on Atheism. 'It is true that a little philosophy inclineth men's minds to atheism, but depth in philosophy bringeth men's minds about to religion; for while the mind of man looketh upon second causes scattered, it may sometimes rest in them and go no further; but when it beholdeth the chain of them confederate, and linked together, it must needs fly to Providence and Deity.'

[13] (p. 27) Theistic argument as drawn from the cosmic and moral order has been greatly deepened and strengthened in our own age by divines and philosophers who recognize the significance of Jesus Christ. He entered into the cosmic order, which culminates in the moral order. He is the sum of both, although unique. He is declared in the records concerning Himself to be the Man, Jesus Christ, or Jesus Christ, Man. He is at once the standard and the judge of human life and conduct, since He is the embodiment of essential right in its individual and social relations. As Dr. W. T. Davison says, ' Jesus Christ must be regarded as the incarnate conscience of humanity.' He said, ' Believe in God and also in Me.' We must also believe in God because we believe in Jesus Christ. ' He who has seen Me has seen the Father ' (John xiv.) Cf. the relevant sections in Dr. W. T. Davison's work, *Christian Conscience*; J. Caird's Gifford Lectures on *Idealism and Christianity*; Professor C. C. J. Webb, *God and Personality* and *Divine Personality and Human Life*; and in Professor W. E. Hocking's *The Meaning of God in Human Experience*. Dr. D. W. Forrest, in his *Christ of History and of Experience*, and Dr. Hastings Rashdall, in his *Theory of Good and Evil*, show the unique value of Jesus Christ for thought, morals, and religion. In doing the same, Dr. Scott Lidgett, in his invaluable work, *The Christian Religion—its Meaning and Proof*, shows the defects of Paley's argument, and the permanent value of the Argument from Design (Bk. II. iv.). Dr. Lidgett uses, and criticizes, the learned work of Dr. J. T. Merz, of Armstrong College, Newcastle-upon-Tyne, *The History of European Thought in the Nineteenth Century*. It

NOTES AND AUTHORITIES 253

should be added that our Lord asserted also His distinctness from man and his nature (cf. Matt. xi. 27 ; John xvii.).

¹⁴ (p. 28) Kant was the successor of Butler in giving prominence and eminence to the human conscience and its metaphysical implications. While denying that man can have knowledge of the soul, the world, and God, Kant admitted a metaphysic of morals. On conscience, the moral law in man, Kant rested his assumption of the existence of a supersensible Reality, and found therein indications as to the divine nature, which faith may accept. Hence Kant's doctrine of conscience leads students towards Infinity (*Critique of Practical Reason*, Abbott's trans., 4th ed.).

¹⁵ (p. 28) Cf. Augustine, *Confessions*, i. 1 ; ' Thou dost arouse us to delight in praising Thee ; for Thou hast made us for Thyself, and our heart is restless, until it finds rest in Thee.' Cf. also Maclaren, *Exposition of Holy Scripture* (Isa. lv. 8, 9) : ' If our thoughts were not in a measure like God's thoughts, we should know nothing about Him. If our thoughts were not like God's thoughts, we should have no standard for life or thinking. Righteousness and truth and beauty and goodness are the same things in heaven and earth, and alike in God and man. We are made in His image, poor creatures though we be. The criminality of our unlikeness to Him rests upon our original likeness.' Wesley's views are summarized by Dr. E. H. Sugden (*Wesley's Standard Sermons*, ii. 207).

¹⁶ (p. 28) Butler knew the problem presented by pain and evil in the cosmos. Pain is regarded by Butler and Paley as part of a system which is designedly and generally beneficent. The sum of pain is small compared with that of happiness, and it appears to be an accompaniment, perhaps it is in part a condition, of development, both of the individual and the race. Physical death is an item in the scheme. Birth has death for its correlate. . . . Successive generations die to give place to others (Butler, *Works*, ii. 28). Under natural conditions, pain is never inflicted for its own sake. It is a result of error, and serves as a warning against possible dangers, as a stimulus to the exercise, and thereby to the growth, of faculties, and also as punishment for the neglect or misuse of them. It is found that pain develops benevolence and promotes compassion and sympathy. Love appears to need pain for its highest manifestation in self-sacrifice. So far as we can see, these virtues could not be developed otherwise than by pain and suffering ; cf. ' The Moulding of Souls,' in Bosanquet's *Value and Destiny of the Individual*. There is a relation, sometimes a direct causal relation, between the sin of man against conscience and God and the pain and suffering which follows sin. This, too, Butler and Paley regarded as designed, as part of man's discipline on earth. Wilful ignorance of the laws of nature, which are God's laws, is culpable, and brings suffering. Man everywhere recognizes the disciplinary elements in his pain and suffering. Moreover, as Butler thought,

man is designed for society. Mankind is a social organism, a body with members. All are benefited by the virtue, and suffer by the vice, of each. The innocent suffer with, sometimes for, the guilty; the guilty are served and saved by the mediatorial sufferings of the innocent. Mediatorship is traced by Butler as an office discharged by man for man. The mediatorship of our Lord and Saviour Jesus Christ, who voluntarily accepted suffering and punishment on behalf of, and instead of others, is the supreme instance of this feature of the cosmic and moral order (Butler, *Works,* 'Analogy,' v.).

[17] (p. 29) Browning may be regarded as Butler's poetic counterpart (cf. Jones, *Browning as a Philosophical and Religious Teacher*). In *Paracelsus* Browning's summary of the cosmos is:

> All tended to mankind
> And, man produced, all has its end thus far;
> But in completed man begins anew
> A tendency to God.
> In man's self arise
> August anticipations, symbols, types,
> Of a dim splendour ever on before
> In that eternal circle life pursues.

Butler and Browning both regarded Nature as a designed course and constitution, having moral significance. They thought of it as an analogy and, in part, a revelation of divine truth. Browning says, in *Christmas Eve*:

> Take all in a word: the truth in God's breast,
> Lies trace for trace upon ours impressed;
> Though He is so bright and we so dim,
> We are made in His image to witness Him.

That nature and experience are used by God as a school, as a probationary process, test, and opportunity of growth of the human spirit and the human race, is a large part of the teaching of both these thinkers. God has 'fixed man 'mid a dance of plastic circumstance, to give his soul its bent; to try him and turn him forth sufficiently impressed' and prepared for a future existence. They saw also that God is not apart from the ordeal which man endured, nor from the soul which is being thereby tested and perfected. A 'non-interfering Deity' is insufficient for the facts of life and faith, according to Butler and Browning. So the latter makes Paracelsus declare:

> God! Thou art love! I build my faith on that,
> Even as I watch beside Thy tortured child,
> Unconscious whose hot tears fall fast by him,
> So doth Thy right hand guide us through the world
> Wherein we stumble.

[18] (p. 31) This experience of Butler in his dying hours is given on the authority of Venn, and repeated in Dean Kitchin's volume, *Seven Sages of Durham*. Alexander Whyte, in his *Bishop Butler* (p. 87), says, 'The

NOTES AND AUTHORITIES 255

narration carries its truth on the face of it, and a narrative we would not have wanted for anything.' The Bishop of Durham (Dr. H. Hensley Henson), writing of Butler in a letter to the present author, notes ' the indefinable spirit of awful reverence which exales from his pages, and makes me, when reading Butler, become solemnized as by a greater than any human Presence.'

[19] (p. 32) Beau Nash, the strange leader and exacting ruler of fashion and folly, was styled ' King of Bath.' On his gains by gambling he held high revel in that city, and drove about in royal style. Here he rudely pushes through the crowd of listeners to stop Wesley preaching. The famous encounter was evidently in the open air, probably in Richard Marchant's field. Neither the Pump Room, where Nash's portrait and ' Rules ' now hang, nor the Assembly Room, would contain the ' thousand new hearers ' of that day. When he asked why the people came to hear Wesley, he got his answer from an unnamed sufferer from man's ancient hunger. Wesley, in his letter, says : ' A bystander said, " Sir, let an old woman answer him." Then turning to Mr. Nash she said, " Sir, if you ask what we come here for ; we come for the food of our souls. You care for your body. We care for our souls." He replied not one word, but turned and walked away ' (see *Letters of John Wesley*, p. 99).

Book I.—WESLEY AS A CHRISTIAN PHILOSOPHER

Chapter I.—New Light on Wesley and His Quest for God

[20] (p. 37) The brief statement of J. H. Rigg in his *Living Wesley* is an exception as to the general omission of this aspect of Wesley. It appeared first in 1875. John Snaith, a Primitive Methodist minister, said in his *Philosophy of the Spirit* (1914), that ' Wesley was without an equal as a philosopher and evangelist ' in the eighteenth century (p. 211).

[21] (p. 37) The Standard Edition in 8 vols., edited by Curnock and experts (1908–16), is the only complete form, and is here used throughout. This edition is based upon, and includes very much from, Wesley's diaries.

[22] (p. 38) This set of Resolutions, often quoted since their discovery (*circa* 1912), has hitherto been translated incompletely. Wesley was eighty years of age when he recorded them. They recall such vows made about sixty years before (*Journal*, i. 47). These Resolutions appear on the front page of a volume of Wesley's Diary, which records his doings each day, often each hour, from December 1, 1782, to January 31, 1790. The words translated below are partly in abbreviated long hand, in shorthand, Latin, and Greek. We put our translations in brackets.

I resolve, *Deo juvante* (with God's help)
   1. To do no will (of man), but look at His, or none, (as) sole judge or justification.

2. To dedicate an hour, morning or evening,
   No Excuse, Reason, or Pretence.
3. To converse κατὰ θεόν (according to God); no anger;
   No εὐτραπηλία (frivolous talk or buffoonery).
4. To pray every hour, seriously, deliberately, fervently.

¹³ (p. 38) One of his favourite hymns, written by his brother Charles, which begins with ' Open, Lord, mine inward ear,' has this verse :

> From this world of sin and noise,
>   And hurry, I withdraw :
> For the small and inward voice,
>   I wait with humble awe ;
> Silent am I now and still,
>   Dare not in Thy presence move ;
> To my waiting soul reveal
>   The secret of Thy love.

¹⁴ (p. 40) Cf. the letter to his mother, dated March 19, 1726–7, given fully in *Letters of John Wesley*, pp. 44–7, and other letters there ; also the manuscript, referred to on p. 55 now in the British Museum, entitled ' An Account,' &c.

¹⁵ (p. 40) A system invented by Dr. John Byrom, F.R.S., of Cambridge and Manchester, a minor poet, and a friend of the Wesleys. Wesley appears to have used it from 1736 to 1791. Cf. *Byrom and the Wesleys*, by Rev. Dr. Hoole (1864), and ' The Wesleys and the Winged Art ' by William J. Carlton (*Wesleyan Methodist Magazine*, 1915).

¹⁶ (p. 40) Wesley's cipher may be compared with Lord Bacon's and with that used by Pepys in his famous diary. In all, about twenty-seven years of Wesley's life (portions only of some years) are covered by his private cipher and shorthand diaries which have been recovered. These contain the first entries of his thoughts, feelings, and activities. The tiny notes were afterwards elaborated in ' narratives ' and ' accounts ' in his *Journal* and letters. These fuller authorities cover about sixty-six years (1725–91). The diaries show the most important, the formative and mature, periods of his life. Most of these small invaluable volumes are in the Colman Collection, Norwich. To handle them is to feel oneself very near to Wesley. Other diary volumes are in the London Collection of the Wesleyan Methodist Church at 25 City Road. Other portions are in Methodist colleges in England and the United States.

¹⁷ (p. 43) Hugh Price Hughes showed much insight in his interpretation of Wesley's mind and churchmanship. He stated that Wesley was the first great religious leader who heartily accepted the Baconian principle of verification in the region of theology. As to Wesley's churchmanship, Hughes said, ' To say that John Wesley never left the Church of England when he ordained bishops for America, presbyters for Scotland, and

NOTES AND AUTHORITIES 257

presbyters for England, is to talk meaningless nonsense. I know that he was very reluctant to do so ; but his extreme reluctance only proved that he was the unwilling instrument of the divine purpose ' (*Life*, by his daughter, p. 488).

CHAPTER II.—LIFE AND WORK AS PHILOSOPHER OUTLINED

[18] (p. 44) His baptismal name was John Benjamin, but he never used the second name. For the Wesley and Wellesley pedigree, see the MS. in Bodleian Lib., Oxford (MS. Eng. Lang. d. 20) ; see also the *Wes. Hist. Soc. Proceedings*, xii. 25. A list of names and dates of birth and death of eighteen of the nineteen children of Samuel and Susanna Wesley is given by J. G. Stevenson, M.A., in *Wesley Memorial Volume* (ed. by O. A. Clark ; Phillips & Hunt, New York, 1881). Charles Wesley was their youngest child but one.

[19] (p. 45) An impression of Wesley's preaching and methods is offered in the chapter, ' Secrets of Whitefield and the Wesleys,' in the volume *Evangelism : a Re-Interpretation*, ed. by Rev. E. Aldom French.

[20] (p. 45) See *Wesley's Chapel and Wesley's House* (London), by Rev. J. Telford, B.A.; *John Wesley and Kingswood* (Bristol), by the present author ; and *The Orphan House of Wesley* (Newcastle-upon-Tyne), by W. W. Stamp.

[21] (p. 46) The Methodists in all countries, all of whom regard Wesley as Church founder, now number eleven millions of enrolled members (*vide* Ecumenical Methodist Conference *Report*, 1921, p. 431) ; cf. *A New History of Methodism*, ii. 531. The number of adherents is estimated at 35 millions.

[22] (p. 46) See ' A Pen Portrait,' in *Letters of John Wesley*, p. 5. ' Little John ' was a favourite name for him in the Calvinistic and Arminian controversy. His height was 5 ft. 5¼ in. See also, ' The New John Wesley,' in *Holborn Review*, 1917, pp. 349–57.

[23] (p. 47) W. T. Stead repeated the usual mis-statements about Wesley's ' marvellous body, muscles of whipcord, lungs of leather, and heart of a lion !' (*Review of Reviews*, March 1891). Particulars of sixty-nine attacks of sickness suffered by Wesley, referred to in the text, are given in the late Rev. R. Butterworth's article in *Wes. Hist. Soc. Proceedings*, xiv. 62.

[24] (p. 47) ' Gaiety ' is a word used about Wesley's manner sometimes. Alexander Whyte asks Wesleyans not to resent it (*Walk . . . of Jesus Christ our Lord*, 244). Alexander Knox of Delganny, Ireland, knew Wesley intimately during the last twenty-three years of Wesley's life. Southey secured his impressions of Wesley. These, written about 1826, harmonized with the statements of Knox used in biographies of Wesley immediately after his death. They received abundant corroboration. Knox says of

R

Wesley, ' His countenance, as well as conversation, expressed an habitual gaiety of heart, which nothing but conscious virtue and innocence could have bestowed. He was in truth the most perfect specimen of moral happiness which I ever saw ; and my acquaintance with him has done more to teach me what a heaven upon earth is implied in the maturity of Christian piety, than all I have elsewhere seen, or heard, or read, except in the sacred volume. . . . It was too obvious that his bodily frame was sinking ; but his spirit was as alert as ever. . . . He was the life of the company he happened to be in. . . . Such unclouded sunshine of the breast, in the deepest winter of age, and on the felt verge of eternity, bespoke a mind whose recollections were as unsullied as its present sensations were serene. . . . For the last fifty years . . . is he not uniformly the same man—devoted to what he deemed his duty : alike regardless of privation or endurance, and yet beaming with happy cheerfulness, and glowing with unbounded philanthropy ? ' (Southey's *Life of Wesley*, ed. by Maurice H. Fitzgerald, vol. ii. 344–9.) Mr. Augustine Birrell disagrees with the statement that the character of Wesley lacks charm (*The Collected Essays and Addresses of Augustine Birrell*, 1922, i. 310).

¹⁵ (p. 50) Baring-Gould's statements and style may be estimated by his references to the Church of England, of which he was a minister. Of eighteenth-century bishops he says (p. 26), ' they stood still, stared and asked, " Why cannot this stupid people rest content with the rations of swipes and slops that we supply ? " ' Baring-Gould says that Wesley's ' vanity showed itself in wearing his hair long, in curls flowing over his shoulders and down his back ' (*Evangelical Revival*, p. 80). The fact is that Wesley wore his hair long to avoid the lavish expense of the period on hairdressing. He gave the sum he saved to the poor. A fever, when he was seventy-two, robbed him of his hair. Thereafter he wore the wig seen in his later portraits. Cf. articles on the eighteenth-century custom in *Wes. Hist. Soc. Proceedings*, vi. 21, 28, 48, and also Rev. Thos. E. Brigden and Rev. M. Riggall on ' Wesley and the Conference on Wigs, Hair Powder, Curls, and Barbers,' and their charges (*ibid.*, xiii. 138).

Baring-Gould repeats (p. 80) the charge of ambition against Wesley. This was alleged, but never proved, by Coleridge and Southey. Indeed, the latter withdrew it, wrote to Nichols in 1835 that he was mistaken, would correct this in his *Life of Wesley* in a new edition and promised Adam Clarke to do so (cf. Rev. J. Telford's *Life of Wesley*, 361). Again : Wesley's genuine self-denial and abounding generosity, referred to in our text (p. 47), are cruelly misrepresented by Baring-Gould (p. 89). He did this on the false testimony of the notorious James Lackington. This man owed to Wesley his start towards financial prosperity. Through him, he gained entrance to Methodist circles. He misused this knowledge in scandalous and vile ways. Later, Lackington bitterly repented of all this, and stated repeatedly his retractations in his published volume

Confessions. Baring-Gould quotes from this later volume on p. 106; but we trace no reference to Lackington's many retractations. Further, Baring-Gould quotes one of two utterly unworthy letters, forged in the name of Wesley (p. 86). They are quoted in Lackington's *Memoirs.* All that Baring-Gould says in using one of these forged letters is this: 'If genuine, its admissions are valuable.' Now Lackington, in his *Confessions* (p. 151), stated that both these letters were forgeries: 'I am convinced that those two letters which are ascribed to him (Wesley) were fabricated to answer some base purpose.' But Baring-Gould makes no mention of this confession, although he used the *Confessions* for other purposes. Historical students know the worthlessness of such vitiated criticisms as these by Baring-Gould of Wesley. They ought not to have been published by him. Happily, they have no authority except that of their writer.

[16] (p. 52) Landscape scenery, noble houses and buildings are often described by Wesley; e.g. *Journal,* v. 139, 263, 337, 340, 375, 431. Even a bird, which sings while he preaches, is caged in his record (v. 276).

[17] (p. 53) Mr. Rudyard Kipling (*Just-So Stories,* 'The Elephant's Child') pays tribute to this method:
I keep six honest serving-men
  (They taught me all I know);
Their names are What and Why and When
  And How and Where and Who.

[18] (p. 55) One of several translations made by him from Tersteegen and German hymn-writers, given in *Poetical Works of John and Charles Wesley* (13 vols.).

[19] (p. 55) Additional MS. 7119—136 a—1, 'An account of an Amour by John Wesley.' This 'Account' belonged to Noah Vazeille of Stratford, Essex, son of Mrs. Vazeille of London, who was married to Wesley in 1751. A summary of the 'Account' is in the *Journal,* iii. 418-22. Professor Augustin Leger made the 'Account' the basis of his thesis for the Doctorate of Literature in the University of Paris, *circa* 1909. An English translation of this, as *Wesley's Last Love,* appeared in 1910.

[40] (p. 60) In his paper, 'Problems of Classification in Religion,' read at the Aristotelian Society, London, January 1923 (*Proceedings,* xxiii. 71). afterwards expanded into his volume, *Imperialistic Religion and the Religion of Democracy.*

[41] (p. 60) Wesley's tirades against Behmen and Mysticism were against aberrations; cf. his admiration for John Smith, the Cambridge Platonist, and, in his later years, for William Law; also his own hymns and mystical teaching.

[42] (p. 61) *Poetical Works,* i. 328. The whole poem of 48 lines, entitled 'Against Hope, believing in Hope,' was published in 1742. It is a characteristic Wesley production. Parts of it are now used by many religious

communities, Anglican, Methodist, and Unitarian. See Canon Julian's *Dictionary of Hymnology* and Rev. J. Telford's *Methodist Hymn-Book Illustrated*.

⁴³ (p. 61) Methodists, a name worn by a group of physicians in the Middle Ages (Murray's *English Dictionary on Historical Principles* and Wesley's tract, *Short History of Methodism, Works*, viii..847), was given to Wesley and his followers in Oxford University by a wit of Christ Church College. Wesley says (*Works*, vii. 203) they were reproached for being Bible Christians, and termed Bible bigots and Bible moths, ' feeding upon the Bible as moths do upon cloth.' The title 'the people called Methodists' is first used by Wesley, I think, in 1742, when he published his pamphlet, *Character of a Methodist (Works*, viii. 339). He never used the name Wesleyans. He says, ' By Methodists I mean; a people who profess to pursue (in whatsoever measure they had attained) holiness of heart and life, inward and outward conformity in all things to the revealed will of God, who place religion in an uniform resemblance of the great object of it ; in a steady imitation of Him they worship, in all His imitable perfections ; more particularly, in justice, mercy, and truth, or universal love filling the heart and governing the life ' (*op. cit.*, 352).

CHAPTER III.—LITERARY DOCUMENTS OF WESLEY'S CHRISTIAN EXPERIENCE

⁴⁴ (p. 63) His letters on literary style are an interesting group. See *Letters of John Wesley*.

⁴⁵ (p. 63) Many hundreds of literary quotations which occur in his *Journal* have been traced to their sources in eight papers by C. L. Ford, B.A., in *Wes. Hist. Soc. Proceedings*, i. and vii. Eight other papers by F. M. Jackson, in *Proceedings*, iv., give an annotated catalogue of books mentioned by Wesley in his *Journal*.

⁴⁶ (p. 64) Green's *Bibliography* of the Wesley literature shows that John Wesley produced 233 original works and extracted or edited one hundred others. It contains summaries of 417 works in its 257 pages. The twenty original works by Charles Wesley all owed much to revision by his brother John. Cf. Green's vol. (1905), *John Wesley, Evangelist*. Wesley's works in Canon Overton's list occupy seven pages. Cf. Richard Baxter, who is credited with 176 works (see *Richard Baxter*, by the present writer).

⁴⁷ (p. 65) The Standard Edition of the *Journal* makes these available. An invaluable index of its contents, prepared by Mr. A. Wallington, has 246 columns of entries.

⁴⁸ (p. 66) *An Earnest Appeal*, 1744 (48 pp.). *A Farther Appeal*, 1744–5, parts i., ii., iii. (107, 78, and 60 pp.). Wesley's treatise on *Original Sin* is larger than the *Appeals* ; but it is not as effective or brilliant.

NOTES AND AUTHORITIES

⁴⁹ (p. 66) Cf. his appeal, 'I want thee for my Lord' (*Works*, v., Serm. 5), and his apostrophe, 'O want of bread!' (*Works*, vi., Serm. 47).

⁵⁰ (p. 66) See Prior's poem, 'Charity' (Wesley wrote 'breast' instead of 'heart' in the 4th line). The other exquisite poetic quotation at the beginning of the *Earnest Appeal*, 'Eternal sunshine of the spotless mind,' is from Pope's poem, 'Eloisa to Abelard,' 209-14.

⁵¹ (p. 68) The letters of 'Mr. John Smith' to Wesley are given in Moore's *Life of Wesley*, ii. 475.

⁵² (p. 69) This booklet, of which millions of copies have been used, was first printed at Newcastle-upon-Tyne (John Gooding, on the Side, 1743, pp. 12). The first issue bore Wesley's name alone; subsequent issues, that of Charles Wesley also.

⁵³ (p. 71) Charles Wesley's wonderful mystical fantasy, 'Wrestling Jacob'—a hymn beginning, 'Come, O Thou Traveller unknown'— is in most anthologies. 'Hark, the herald angels sing,' 'Christ the Lord is risen to-day,' and 'Jesu, Lover of my soul,' are used everywhere. The last was sung at a dedication service of the grave of the Unknown Warrior in Westminster Abbey, 1922. 'Love Divine, all loves excelling,' another of his hymns, was sung at the British Empire Exhibition, Wembley, London, at the united service commemoration, Empire Day, May 24, 1924. That day is also Wesley's Day.

⁵⁴ (p. 71) Students should know the complete edition—*Poetical Works of John and Charles Wesley*, ed. by G. Osborn, 1868, 13 vols. Cf. Canon Julian's *Dictionary of Hymns*, p. 1259; also *The Methodist Hymn-Book Illustrated*, by Rev. J. Telford, B.A., and *Methodist Hymns in their Literary Relations*, by Rev. Henry Bett, M.A., also *The Hymns and Hymn-writers of the Church*, an annotated edition of the Methodist Hymnal of the Methodist Episcopal Church, U.S.A., by Charles S. Nutter, D.D., and Wilbur F. Tillett, D.D., LL.D.

⁵⁵ (p. 72) e.g. the famous canto beginning:
> O for a thousand tongues to sing
> My great Redeemer's praise.

It is from Charles Wesley's poem of seventy-two lines. It was written on the first anniversary of his spiritual change or conversion, and records that and another experience (*Poetical Works*, i. 299).

⁵⁶ (p. 73) Wesley's teaching in these standard *Sermons* has been collated, compared, and corrected in the light of his other utterances, and of later biblical science, by the Master of Queen's College, University of Melbourne (the Rev. Edward H. Sugden, M.A., B.Sc., D.Litt.). Cf. *Wesley's Standards in the Light of To-day*, by Rev. H. Maldwyn Hughes, M.A., D.D. (Principal, Wesley House, Cambridge).

⁷⁷ (p. 73) The first seven chapters of Matthew show that Wesley made 113 alterations in the text which agree in whole or part with those of the R.V. (Rev. Thos. E. Brigden, *A New History of Methodism*, i. 222). Tribute was paid to Wesley as a translator of the New Testament by Professor James Moffatt, M.A., D.Litt., D.D., at a conference of Free Church ministers on the Bible, at Hampstead, London, in 1925, at which the ex-president of the Metropolitan Free Church Federation (Rev. Samuel Horton) presided. Dr. Moffatt referred specially to Wesley's rendering of Matthew v. 8.

⁷⁸ (p. 77) Wesley quoted the Bible account of the creation of man, but allowed in his statement for the process of development as to his body. He said, ' The scriptural account is this : God made the body of man out of the earth, and breathed into him the *Breath of life* ; not only an animal life, but a spiritual principle, created to live for ever. Even his body was then perfect in its kind ; neither liable to death nor pain. But what the difference was, between the original and the present body, we cannot determine. . . . Certainly, with regard to the structure of the Body, the difference is not extremely great between man and other animals. . . . There is a wonderful *agreement* between the bodies of men and beasts, not only with regard to the structure, but also the use of the several parts. How they differ, will be mentioned hereafter ' (*Survey*, i. 179, 191, 193). At one point Wesley seems to teach the creation of man at the first by a divine fiat—' in that moment.' Even there he speaks of man ' rising by degrees ' and as ' finished part by part.' He uses Bonnet's *Contemplation of Nature*, quoted above, from p. 60 to p. 331 in vol. iv. Cf. Darwin, *Origin of Species* (1859), *Descent of Man* (1871). Darwin's theories have been seriously modified by later investigators ; but his restatement of the evolutionary principle persists ; cf. Wallace, *Letters and Reminiscences*, ed. Sir James Marchant, vol. ii. 6, 31, 181, 249.

That Wesley gave countenance to this anticipation of the theory of Evolution, as a process in creation, was noticed by the present writer, *Letters of John Wesley* (1916), 448. This attracted attention. A discussion, ' pro and con,' was conducted in the columns of an American Methodist journal (*Nashville Christian Advocate*, August 1922). Rev. Dr. R. E. Blackwall, of Wargentown, Va., defended the view of Wesley's thought here given. The Director of Research in the American University, Washington, D.C., the Rev. Frank W. Collier, Ph.D., did likewise, in 1924, in a valuable booklet, *Back to Wesley*. The Rev. Professor Charles Wesley Hargitt, Ph.D., of Syracuse University, U.S.A., took the same view of Wesley's *Philosophy*, in an article in *Zion's Herald* (Boston, U.S.A.), 1925, p. 106, entitled, ' John Wesley—Evolutionist.' Professor J. Y. Simpson, D.Sc., F.R.S.E., in his *Spiritual Interpretation of Nature*, cites Wesley and this anticipation of evolution, or gradual, orderly, and progressive change as the creative process used by God. This theory was earlier expounded in the Wesleyan Methodist Fernley Lecture of 1887,

NOTES AND AUTHORITIES 263

by Rev. W. H. Dallinger, LL.D., F.R.S., *The Creator and what we may know of the Method of Creation*. When the present work was completed, the writer received with pleasure a booklet, *The Philosophy of John Wesley*, by F. Louis Barber, M.A., Ph.D., Victoria University, Toronto.

⁴⁹ (p. 79) This work is *The Procedure, Extent, and Limits of the Human Understanding* (1728). Browne has a place in Professor W. R. Sorley's *History of English Philosophy*, and in that of Leslie Stephen, who slashed him (*English Thought in the Eighteenth Century*, i. 113).

CHAPTER IV.—CHRISTIAN EXPERIENCE AS SEEN IN WESLEY AND OTHERS

⁵⁰ (p. 85) Cf. Charles Wesley's experience prior to his evangelical conversion, as given in a poem of 132 lines entitled, ' The just shall live by faith ' (*Poetical Works*, i. 332). He said :
> For ten long, legal years I lay
> A helpless, though reluctant, prey
> To pride, and lust, and earth, and hell ;
> Oft to repentance vain renewed,
> Self-confident for hours I stood,
> And fell and grieved, and rose, and fell.

⁵¹ (p. 85) In 1789 he published a sixth edition of this remarkable book, only two years before his death. Cf. the summary by the Rev. Professor J. Arundel Chapman, M.A., B.D., in his booklet, *John Wesley's Quest*.

⁵² (p. 86) Thomas à Kempis, of *The Imitation of Christ*, was one of these. At this stage he approved some ' main points.' Later he found that this wonderful book of devotion recorded direct experience of God in Christ. Wesley published and gave away many thousands of copies of this work. He named it *The Christian's Pattern*.

⁵³ (p. 86) A facsimile of this page, in the cipher original, with a translation of the part quoted, is given in Wesley's *Journal*, i. 56.

⁵⁴ (p. 88) Moravia was part of the Austrian crown lands. Wesley generally calls its people Germans.

⁵⁵ (p. 89) For this correspondence see Wesley's *Journal*, viii. 319. It is interesting to compare accounts of this unfortunate episode. The Methodist biographer, Tyerman, blames Wesley ; the Anglican, Canon Overton, deeply deplores the estrangement between two of the holiest and ablest men of the day.

⁵⁶ (p. 89) The late Principal Alexander Whyte of Edinburgh is the most recent expositor of Law and Behmen. His volume (1893), *Character and Characteristics of William Law, Non-Juror and Mystic*, selected and arranged with an Introduction, is a mine of wealth, theological and practical.

264 WESLEY, PHILOSOPHER AND FOUNDER

⁶⁷ (p. 92) The exact locality of this historic scene has been much discussed. It is of interest to visitors from all parts of the world. Only less interesting is the site connected with Charles Wesley's conversion, in the same month and year. Both sites are within a few hundred yards of each other, and of St. Botolph's Church, Aldersgate Street, London, E.C.1. Behind the short statement in the text (p. 92) is much research work on the literary and topographical authorities. Cf. the article by H. J. Foster (*Wesley Studies*, 1903, p. 81) and *Wes. Hist. Soc. Proceedings*, 1906, p. 332; also Rev. J. Telford's Lives of John and Charles Wesley, and the maps and plans cited below. A sketch plan of the district is given on the opposite page, with certain sites marked.

This question is involved with the doings of James Hutton, a London bookseller and Moravian leader. The *Memoirs of James Hutton*, by D. Benham, 1856, shows that on completing his apprenticeship, in 1735 or early in 1736, Hutton set up as a bookseller at 'the Bible and Sun,' a little westward of Temple Bar. He ' also engaged a room in Nettleton Court, Aldersgate Street, where he met a small society of people every week for mutual edification ' (p. 12). He formed another society which met in his house. All this was while John and Charles Wesley were serving as missionaries in the New England colonies. Other societies beside this existed in Aldersgate Street district.

John Wesley returned from Georgia to England, where he landed on February 1, 1738. He met the elder Huttons, who were Anglicans, and the above-named James Hutton, their son, in London. He was constantly the companion and the guest, says Curnock, of James Hutton (see *Life*, 33-9).

These developments did not involve the cessation of the society, formed by Hutton, which met in Nettleton Court (*ibid.*, 12). It was meeting regularly in 1737. This is shown by West in his autobiography (published in the Moravian *Messenger*, 1875, quoted by Curnock, Wesley's *Journal*, i. 475). West says, ' About this time (1737) I heard of a religious society which met weekly in Nettleton Court, Aldersgate Street, and it was not long before I joined them. The brethren James Hutton and John Edmunds were of the number.' Curnock says (Wesley's *Journal*, i. 475) ' the probability is that he (Wesley) would accompany his host (James Hutton) to the society he had founded, which, it is clear, met in Nettleton Court. On the whole the balance of evidence is in favour of the Nettleton Court site,' as the place where Wesley's evangelical conversion occurred on May 24, 1738; but no evidence has been traced as to Hall House as the building in which the event occurred.

Nettleton Court, a long, narrow passage, entered from the east side of Aldersgate Street, is shown on Rocque's Map of London in 1746, only eight years after these events; also on Norwood's, 1799, but without name. It is not shown in Lockie's topography, 1816. A map of 1848 does not show *that* Nettleton Court, but a short one. This is still there, off

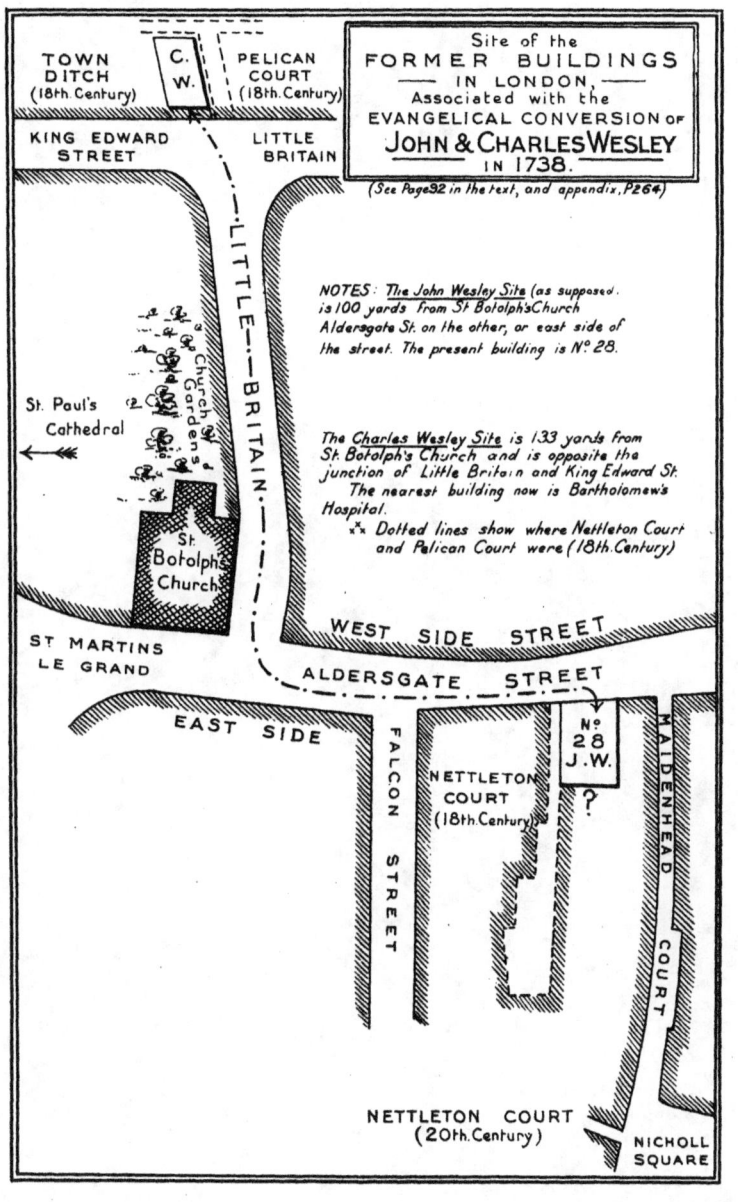

Nicholl Square, via Maidenhead Court, which is next to No. 30 Aldersgate Street. The present and the ancient Nettleton Court may have been connected at the back. Mr. P. J. Lupton (*circa* 1900) thought he had traced the site of an old building, Hall House, in Nettleton Court, in which he believed Wesley's conversion occurred. Lupton was a trustee of Wesley's Chapel, in City Road, and a business man in Aldersgate Street Ward. He pointed to the south-east angle of the site of a building, No. 28, in the street, as the site. From 1894 onwards a building used as a restaurant stood there (British Tea Table Co., &c.). A bank now occupies the site. Lupton's belief may rest upon facts. No authority has been traced for his reference to Hall House; Wesley simply says, 'a society in Aldersgate Street.' Hutton's society met in Nettleton Court there. The lines of evidence converge to No. 28. The visitor who stands opposite that is probably near the historic spot.

Charles Wesley's evangelical conversion occurred in a house whose site can be nearly located. He returned to England in December 1736. James Hutton got him a home at his own father's house, where he had before been guest in College Street, Westminster. From this, Charles removed to Mr. John Bray's, the brazier, at the west corner of Little Britain, near Christ's Hospital. Little Britain is off the west side of Aldersgate Street. There his spiritual quickening occurred on Whit-Sunday, May 21, 1738.

Bray's house was between Pelican Court and the Town Ditch at the elbow-like bend of Little Britain. The ancient maps above referred to all show these sites. Those of Pelican Court and the Town Ditch are occupied by recently-built portions of St. Bartholomew's Hospital, and by King Edward Street. A visitor standing at the junction of Little Britain and that street is within a few yards of the site of Bray's house, where Charles Wesley lay ill and was spiritually quickened.

An opening, Nettleton Court, is shown on the ancient map-plan of 1739–40, preserved in the archives of St. Botolph's Church, Aldersgate Street Without. A copy, made in 1882, of this plan is preserved in the Wesley Museum, City Road Chapel, London. That copy of the plan has notes connecting buildings with these events. Part of the ancient plan is reproduced in Wesley's *Journal*, i. 473. Visits to the site, paid in 1925, by the Rev. Dr. J. Alfred Sharp and the present writer, as officers of the International Methodist Historical Union (Eastern Section), and by the Rev. George H. McNeal, M.A., of Wesley's Chapel, confirm these statements. Proposals are now under consideration to erect a memorial tablet on the exterior of the Church of St. Botolph, Aldersgate Street, indicating the associations of that district with the spiritual quickening of both Charles and John Wesley in 1738.

⁴⁴ (p. 92) That Wesley here refers to heat as a metaphor for his spiritual feeling is an interesting psychological fact. It was his favourite

form of thought in such accounts and aspirations. Cf. the poem 'Zeal' (*Poetical Works*, i. 13) and *vide infra*, in this chapter, page 103.

⁶⁹ (p. 94) The Rev. Thos. F. Lockyer, B.A., gives valuable details of this historic day in *Wes. Hist. Soc. Proceedings*, viii. 61, and in his *Paul : Luther : Wesley*.

⁷⁰ (p. 96) Two instances of this little-known side of Wesley's nature may be cited. Of scenery at Dawgreen, near Dewsbury, Yorkshire, he wrote : 'All things contributed to make it a refreshing season : the gently declining sun, the stillness of the evening, the beauty of the meadows and fields, through which

The smooth, clear "river drew its sinuous train,"

the opposite hills and woods, and the earnestness of the people, covering the top of the hill on which we stood ; and, above all, the day-spring from on high, the consolation of the Holy One' (*Journal*, v. 375). His description of beautiful expression on human faces is exquisite : 'And now I saw such a sight as I do not expect to see again on this side eternity : The faces of three children, and, I think, of all the believers, did really shine ; and such a beauty, such a look of extreme happiness, and of divine love and simplicity, I never saw in human faces till now' (*Works*, xiii. 311).

⁷¹ (p. 97) The contrast and combination of essentials and accidents in worship which Wesley recognized are shown in his famous declaration as to the usefulness and necessity of open-air preaching : 'I preached abroad, near the Keelman's Hospital, to twice the number of people we have had at the house.' [Newcastle-upon-Tyne.] 'What marvel the Devil does not love field-preaching ! Neither do I : I love a commodious room, a soft cushion, a handsome pulpit. But where is my zeal if I do not trample all these underfoot in order to save one more soul ? ' (*Journal*, iv. 325.)

⁷² (p. 98) Some of these facts are noticed in the article, 'Secrets of Whitefield and the Wesleys' (see Note 29). Wesley's tracing of exceptional powers to God as immediate source has many parallels, e.g. Baxter refusing praise for his literary skill : 'I was but a pen in God's hand. What praise is due to a pen ? '

⁷³ (p. 100) He published an acute study of this physical condition, and offered preventive and remedial advice, 'Thoughts on Nervous Disorders,' *Works*, xi. 509. He had a few grey days, however, e.g. January 5, 1745, when he says, 'I found it absolutely necessary to fly for my life' (*Journal*, iii. 160).

⁷⁴ (p. 108) Cf. *Francis Asbury, the Prophet of the Long Road*, by E. S. Tipple, LL.D., President of Drew Theological Seminary, Madison, New Jersey, U.S.A. Both Houses of U.S. Congress authorized the erection of an equestrian statue of Asbury, on public land near the White

House, Washington, D.C. This memorial was dedicated in 1924. Bishop J. W. Hamilton and President Calvin Coolidge pronounced eulogies on Asbury. Cf. also an article, 'Wesley and Asbury, New Estimates of World Leaders,' in *Methodist Review* (New York) January-February 1924, by the present writer.

⁷⁵ (p. 109) Much of it is easily available in *The Heart of Asbury's Journal*, ed. by Dr. E. S. Tipple. Asbury's *Journal* does not offer records of self-analysis, &c., like Wesley's diaries, nor has it the literary power and charm of Wesley's *Journal*. The Emory collection of confirmatory documents as to Asbury is invaluable. I found this readily accessible (1914) in the Library of Drew Theological Seminary, Madison, New Jersey, U.S.A.

⁷⁶ (p. 111) *Raithby Hall, or Memorial Sketches*, by Mrs. Richard Smith.

⁷⁷ (p. 111) *An Account of the Life and Dealings of God with Silas Told*, written by himself (1785). Cf. the similar work of Sarah Peters (1748), and the life-stories and moral transformation wrought in John Lancaster and other malefactors (Wesley's *Journal*, iii. 381). Wesley reprinted this in *Arminian Magazine* for 1782, p. 128. Wesley's diary (November 8, 1738) shows that he accompanied a malefactor to Tyburn, sang and prayed with him, and preached to the mob gathered at the public execution. He often preached in Newgate prison, Bristol.

⁷⁸ (p. 112) See R. Bourne's *Christian Sketch* (1819) and Lancaster's *Life of Darcy, Lady Maxwell* (1826); also chapter x., 'To Lady Maxwell,' in *Letters of John Wesley*.

⁷⁹ (p. 114) A selection from these instances of Christian experience secured by Wesley has become a classic in Christian philosophy and psychology. This is a group of 'lives' of the early Methodist preachers, *circa* 1739-91, which were collected and published in 1848, in six volumes, under the title of *The Lives of Early Methodist Preachers*, chiefly written by themselves; new edition, edited by Rev. John Telford, B.A., as *Wesley's Veterans*. This collection was examined in 1909 by the Professor of Moral Philosophy in King's College, London University (the Rev. Alfred Caldecott, D.D., D.Litt.). The result was read at the Aristotelian Society, London (*Proceedings*, N.S., viii.). It was 'listened to with great interest and discussed.' It is entitled, *The Religious Sentiment: An Inductive Enquiry, illustrated from the Lives of Wesley's Helpers*. He discovered the following features: (1) The dominant emotional element is the reference to the thought of an Omniscient Being. Reference to the Infinite is at the root of the knowledge of the self, in each case. Man after man states this as fact of experience. (2) This central emotion organized other elements. It opposed and expelled lower ones and established control over all. Fear, Anxiety, and Pride were overcome. Instead, the emotions of Gratitude, Hopefulness, Humility, Confidence, Trust, Respect, Reverence, and Awe were evident. (3) In addition, the Intellectual Sentiment,

the love of truth and knowledge, was won over, and engaged chiefly in the contemplation of the supreme truth. Some of these men had considerable enjoyment of the intellectual life and became leaders in speech and action. (4) The limitation of a reference of all experience to the approval of an Omniscient Being also affected the Aesthetic Sentiment in them. External Nature and symbolic forms of spiritual things attracted them. They appreciated the poetical and rhetorical parts of the Bible, and the Wesley hymnody. They developed an ability to admire such noble and gracious features as appeared in the lives and characters of the quondam rude and illiterate people to whom they often ministered. (5) The Social Sentiments are observed as being strong, and thoroughly organized, and likewise controlled by the same dominant sentiment. Family affection was re-enforced. They were keenly concerned for a reformation of society by a reconstitution of it as a religious fellowship, and for the actual sharing of their spiritual privileges with others. (6) Considerable force of Will was evident. The transformation and elevation of character was due to the conscious exercise of volition, stimulated and controlled by religious desire. It is also evident that an uprising of energy had occurred in them : indeed it seems as if a new intensity had been conferred. ' Plain tradesmen, mechanics, and labourers became moral and spiritual forces acting powerfully on other minds.' (7) In one third of these cases, after a prompt achievement of spiritual harmony, there was a clear current for the remainder of the life. In two-thirds, there was a series of vicissitudes, after the first victory is recorded, before the final victory. In some cases the central emotion was reduced ; in some, it disappeared for a time. Intense despair afflicted some in these periods. Dr. Caldecott notes as a fact of great significance ' this inability of the Religious Sentiment to maintain the hold of the field, even after a very striking and impressive victory.' He infers that the central emotion was not yet in command ; and that fixity of tenure of the central emotion is secured only when it is supported and allied with other emotions. (8) Final stability was reached by them with Joy as an important element. The steady health of the whole mental nature is seen in the presence and pre-eminence of Joy. Not only occasional ecstasy, but a fund of solid happiness came to be theirs. Nor was this the result of physical conditions or organic sensations. Only in a few instances was there any seeming connexion between the outward and the inward conditions. Often the natural tendencies were completely reversed. They rejoiced in tribulation. The reference of the self to the Infinite, noted at the commencement of this examination, touched the very centre of the mental nature of these men. The central emotion succeeded in acquiring control over the other emotions, both singly and as sentiments. At length it completely organized them. By this means it was associated with the attainment of an intellectual ' fixed idea ' and with the chief mental activities.

NOTES AND AUTHORITIES 269

¹⁰ (p. 114) A valuable collection of such material has become available by a publication of the Wesley Historical Society entitled *An Index of the Memoirs, Obituary Notices, and Recent Deaths, together with the References to the Local Histories of Methodism as contained in the Arminian Magazine, 1778–97, The Methodist Magazine, 1798–1821*, and the *Wesleyan Methodist Magazine*, 1822–39. These contain more than 6,000 short biographies. A large number of other autobiographic and biographic studies can be traced by the Index to Wesley's *Journal*, with his attestation, and his interpretation of their significance, e.g. the account of the experience of ' W. B.' in Wesley's *Journal*, iii. 158. This is probably William Briggs, who became the first officer of Wesley's publishing house, City Road, London.

¹¹ (p. 116) See *Journal*, v. 118 ; cf. *Farther Appeal*, iii. 132, also Wesley's letters to his brother Samuel (*Works*, xii. 30), to Furley, and ' Mr. John Smith ' (*Works*, xii. 60).

¹² (p. 116) *Life of W. E. Gladstone*, J. Morley, 3 vols. (1903), also Morley's *Recollections*, 2 vols. (1917) ; *Life*, ed. by Wemyss Reid ; G. W. E. Russell's *A Pocketful of Sixpences*. Cf. my vol., *From Alfred to Victoria*, ' Nineteenth Century, Gladstone.' Gladstone is there regarded as representing his century, with Lincoln and Victoria.

¹³ (p. 118) See his *Life*, by his son (1903). In addition to his works cited in the text, his Christian philosophy is stated in his commentaries on St. John's Gospel and Epistles. The essays at the end of the latter are important.

¹⁴ (p. 120) *The Life of General William Booth*, by Harold Begbie, 2 vols (1920), based on Booth's journals and letters.

¹⁵ (p. 120) See H. Begbie's work, *Broken Earthenware, the wonderful Story of Twice-Born Men : a footnote in Narrative to Professor William James's. Study in Human Nature*, ' *The Varieties of Religious Experience* ' (1909). See also *In the Hand of the Potter* (same author) ; also Professor George Jackson's vol., *The Fact of Conversion*. A study of a single subject of the same kind, which the student should by no means omit, is the work entitled *A Gentleman in Prison, the Story of Tokichi Ishii, written by himself in Tokyo Prison*; translated by Caroline Macdonald, with a Foreword by John Kelman, D.D.—' The most realistic vision I have ever seen of Jesus Christ finding one of the lost.'

The experience of ' Saul Kane ' in Mr. Masefield's narrative poem, *The Everlasting Mercy*, is a similar human document of much importance. A classic work of English fiction, *Adam Bede*, by George Eliot, should also be carefully studied. It is the work of a critical genius and an alien hand, which yet pays tribute to the reality and significance of Christian mystical experience, moral transformation, and redemptive service, as seen in many Methodist life-stories. The period of the novel is the opening years of the nineteenth century. The central figure, 'Dinah Morris,' had for original Miss Elizabeth Tomlinson (1774–1849), afterwards Mrs. Samuel Evans of Wirksworth, Derbyshire. She was wife of the uncle of Mary Ann Evans (George Eliot). The pulpit used by 'Dinah Morris' is in Wirksworth United Methodist Church, and a memorial tablet is in the Wesleyan Methodist Church (see article by Mr. J. E. Cooper, in *Methodist Recorder*, Christmas No. 1896, and *George Eliot's Life*, by J. W. Cross, 254). The novelist visited her uncle and 'Dinah Morris.' Students are pointed to the prayers and sermon of 'Dinah Morris' in *Adam Bede*, chapters ii. and xlv., to her statement as to her 'call' to preach (chap. viii.), and especially to her letter to 'Seth Bede' in chapter xxx. Its phrases, 'I spoke the words that were given to me,' 'it was borne in upon me,' 'I wait to be taught,' show the interplay of the objective Ideal, God, and the subjective human personality. This Mystic also believed herself to be in God. She had a deeper sense of resting on the divine strength; and 'It is as if I was out of the body and could feel no want for evermore.' Union with God was completed in the action of her suffering love for the needy : ' all the anguish of the children of men, which sometimes wraps me round like sudden darkness, I can bear with a willing pain, as if I was sharing the Redeemer's cross. For I feel it, I feel it—infinite love is suffering too.' The ethical result of this mystical unity with God is finely brought out in 'Dinah Morris's ' altruistic service, and her sharing of the shame and suffering of the sinner and criminal, 'Hetty Sorrel,' and others.

[46] (p. 121) This was the Methodist New Connexion (now in the United Methodist Church), of which he was a minister, 1854–61. His theological statements for the Salvation Army show indebtedness to that Church (see *A New History of Methodism*, i. 540).

[47] (p. 122) *Life of George Cadbury*, by A. G. Gardiner (1923). Matthew Arnold's 'lesson' from Nature expressed in his sonnet, 'Rural Work,' seems to have been learned by Cadbury :

> One lesson, nature, let me learn from thee ;
> One lesson, which in every wind is blown ;
> One lesson of two duties kept at one,
> Though the loud world proclaim their enmity :
> Of toil, unsevered from tranquillity ;
> Of labour, that in lasting fruit outgrows
> Far noisier schemes, accomplished in repose
> Too great for haste, too high for rivalry.

[48] (p. 124) *Life of Alexander Whyte, D.D.*, by G. F. Barbour (1923), is a great biography. Additional sources are ' A Self-Review,' by Whyte, published after his death (*British Weekly*, June 14 and 21, 1923), and a valuable article, ' The Services of the Imagination to the Christian Minister ' (*ibid.*, April 4 and 11, 1912); also W. R. Nicoll's study in *Princes of the Church*.

⁸⁹ (p. 127) Professor Frederic Platt, M.A., D.D., has urged this convincingly in his *Certainty and Christian Faith*, ii., 'The Certainties of Christian Experience': 'Religious consciousness is a phase of activity of personal consciousness, and it possesses precisely the same value as ultimate authority for religious faith as the consciousness of realities outside the sphere of religion possesses for them.' Cf. R. W. Dale's summary of this argument in *The Living Christ and the Four Gospels*, chaps. i.–iv., and the important work by Principal H. Maldwyn Hughes, M.A., D.D., *The Theology of Experience*.

CHAPTER V.—IMPLICATIONS FROM CHRISTIAN EXPERIENCE

⁹⁰ (p. 131) Dr. E. H. Sugden points out (*Wesley's Standard Sermons*, i. 304) that Wesley was the first to use the word 'reaction' in this sense, 'the influence which a thing, acted upon by another, exercises in return upon the agent.' *The Oxford English Dictionary* credits this to Wesley.

⁹¹ (p. 134) Principal H. B. Workman, M.A., D.Lit., D.D., shows the evidential value of the experience of persecuted Christians (*Persecution in the Early Church*, v., and his notes).

⁹² (p. 136) Scheffler took the name Angelus Silesius on joining the Roman Catholic Church. His use of Augustine's words comes out especially in the verse which opens, in Wesley's translation, with the words,

> Ah, why did I so late Thee know,
> Thee, lovelier than the sons of men!

⁹³ (p. 138) This discourse, 'Scriptural Christianity,' was the last sermon Wesley preached before the University of Oxford (1744). Dr. E. H. Sugden (*Wesley's Standard Sermons*) thinks there is nothing in religious literature to rival this portrayal of Christian experience.

⁹⁴ (p. 138) This is the first hymn in Wesley's standard hymn-book. The original is entitled, 'For the Anniversary Day of One's Conversion.' The personal affirmation of the first verse, 'my God,' is brought out in verse 5 of this poem of eighteen verses (*Poetical Works*, i. 299):

> Me, me He loved—the Son of God,
> For me, for me, He died.

⁹⁵ (p. 140) This aspect of Christian truth is expounded at length, and very impressively, by the Rev. J. Scott Lidgett, M.A., D.D., in his work, *The Fatherhood of God in Christian Truth and Life*.

⁹⁶ (p. 141) Dr. John Watson, in his vol., *The Mind of the Master*, shows the neglect of the doctrine of the Divine Fatherhood in church teaching generally. He held it as 'the final idea of God.' Dr. Watson overlooks Wesley's work in the restatement of this truth (p. 266).

[97] (p. 143) Cf. *The Spirit, the Relation of God and Man*, ed. by Canon B. H. Streeter ; articles by Professor A. Seth Pringle-Pattison and others.

[98] (p. 146) Cf. *John Wesley and the Religious Societies*, by John S. Simon, D.D.

[99] (p. 146) From *Poetical Works*, v. 475. A poem, 'Communion of Saints,' has 312 lines (i. 356). Part V. of Wesley's hymn-book has four sections, entitled 'For the Society: meeting, giving thanks, praying, parting.'

[100] (p. 150) Wesley told Moore that he believed God had overruled the misery caused him (Wesley) by his wife for his good, and that of the great work to which God had called him. Cf. many entries under the title 'Providence, interpositions of,' in *Journal*, viii. 443.

[101] (p. 153) This exposition was thirty-four years later than that in his *Notes on the New Testament*.

[102] (p. 153) Cf. *The Tripartite Nature of Man*, by J. B. Heard, M.A. Wesley insisted on the function of the Will and its freedom ; see *Thoughts upon Necessity* and *A Thought upon Necessity* (*Works*, x. 455–80).

[103] (p. 157) This is the opening phrase of his noble hymn (translated from Scheffler) beginning 'O God, of good the unfathom'd sea!' Cf. Wesley's tribute to spirit and beauty in facial expression, seen at Everton in 1759 (*Journal*, iv. 320).

[104] (p. 157) Wesley was a loyalist ; but his comments on George II and his robes, and on the House of Lords, are very shrewd and candid (*Journal*, iv. 145).

[105] (p. 161) M. Halévy is quite inaccurate when he writes of Wesley's 'doctrine of perfection that a sinner once saved can never relapse' (*History of the English People in 1815*, published in 1912, English translation, 1924).

CHAPTER VI.—CRITICISM OF THE PHILOSOPHY OF CHRISTIAN EXPERIENCE

[106] (p. 165) Cf. that masterpiece among statements of the evidence for historical Christianity, Dale's *The Living Christ and the Four Gospels*.

[107] (p. 169) Cf. Heb. i. 1, 2, and Lecture ix., 'Is Faith in Christ Necessarily Conscious?' in Dr. D. W. Forrest's Kerr Lectures, *The Christ of History and Experience* ; also *Jesus in the Experience of Men*, by Dr. T. R. Glover.

[108] (p. 170) Wesley was shocked by 'some improprieties' in Homer, but he noticed 'the vein of piety which runs through' the *Iliad* (*Journal*, iii. 366).

[109] (p. 171) In detail, the inward conditions which Wesley said must be fulfilled were the exercise of repentance towards God and faith in the Lord

Jesus Christ; the outward conditions were the use of the word of God and prayer, fasting or abstinence, worship, the two sacraments, fellowship with other seekers, together with suitable Christian conduct; cf. *Rules of the United Societies*, noticed in Chapter III.

[110] (p. 173) Notwithstanding these admissions and corrections by Wesley, which were available, Baring-Gould repeated false accusations against Wesley and his teaching. In his *Evangelical Revival*, Baring-Gould says, ' Justification by Faith with Wesley and the Methodists is often nothing other than Justification by Feelings ' (p. 55). Again, by Christian Perfection, Baring-Gould states that Wesley ' meant instantaneous acquisition of Sanctity by Conversion ' (p. 58). It is a novel but gravely reprehensible way of stating a man's teaching to offer what he ' meant ' according to his critic, and this without any support by quotation or reference. Baring-Gould's gravest inaccuracy is, perhaps, his contrast of apostolic succession, and its claim to give absolution from sin, with an entire misrepresentation of Wesley's teaching. Baring-Gould says, ' The fatal blemish in Wesley's teaching lay in his making Instantaneous Conversion to be accepted as Self-Absolution from all sin . . . every man was qualified to absolve himself ' (p. 27, cf. p. 75). Baring-Gould was entitled to assert his belief that our Lord, before His departure, made special provision for the remission of sins and communicated His authority to ' bind and loose ' to His Apostles, and to their successors; but he was not entitled to state, what the merest tyro among students of Wesley's teaching knows, that in his maturity Wesley did not teach such views as above, which are condemned both by Scripture and experience. Wesley's final teaching on the points can be gathered from his chief sermons entitled, ' The Witness of the Spirit,' ' On Sin in Believers,' and ' The Scripture way of Salvation.' Baring-Gould cites no authority for his grave misrepresentations. The nearest Methodist minister or local preacher would have supplied corrections. Students are referred to *Standard Sermons of John Wesley* with Dr. E. H. Sugden's annotations.

[111] (p. 174) Dr. R. McCheyne Edgar, in *The Genius of Protestantism* (p. 245 *et seq.*), shows the alliance of Reformed Christianity and the modern scientific mind. Modernism, at its best, is not incompatible with wholehearted allegiance to Jesus Christ and the teaching of His Christian Faith. Cf. *The Scientific Approach to Religion*, ed. by Rev. H. D. A. Major, D.D. (Oxford); *Modernism and the Christian Faith*, by Professor J. Alfred Faulkner (Drew Methodist Episcopal Theological Seminary, Madison, N.J., U.S.A.); *Christianity at the Cross Roads*, by President and Professor E. Y. Mullins, Baptist Theological Seminary, Louisville, Ky.; and an important work by Professor Arthur S. Peake, M.A., D.D., published in 1908, which reached its tenth edition by 1915, *Christianity, its Nature and Truth*.

[112] (p. 176) For the ethical results of Christian emotional experience,

cf. instances cited above (p. 267); also in Methodist history, as to Slavery, Social Conditions, Christian Socialism, &c., *in loc.* A recent statement by an author, who is not a Methodist, may be quoted. Mr. Sidney Webb says : ' No one can doubt, it would indeed be hard to over-estimate, the enormous improvement which has been wrought by the Methodists in their century of persistent effort in all parts of the county (Durham). What they aimed at was primarily the salvation of the soul. But the change of heart which accompanied conversion was habitually marked, though often with backslidings, by a change of life. The Methodist, whatever his shortcomings, became a man of earnestness, sobriety, industry, and regularity of conduct ' (*Story of Durham Miners*, 1662–1921).

[113] (p. 178) Cf. ' God as an Inference from Experience,' in Professor E. S. Waterhouse's study, *The Philosophy of Religious Experience*; also *Is Christian Experience an Illusion ?* by Henry Balmforth, M.A.

CHAPTER VII.—THE PHILOSOPHY OF CHRISTIAN EXPERIENCE SINCE WESLEY

[114] (p. 182) *Vide* his *Reden über Religion* (1799) and *Der Christliche Glaube* (1821), also Principal W. B. Selbie's article, ' Schleiermacher,' in Hastings's *Dictionary of Religion and Ethics*, and Professor J. A. Faulkner's *Modernism and the Christian Faith*.

[115] (p. 187) Professor in Williamstown University, Mass., U.S.A. This work was published in 1920.

[116] (p. 190) In the *Yale Review* (circa March 1923) Professor Pratt says that religion and life can get on, and can continue to exist, without the traditional forms of religion ; but ' it does not necessarily follow that they can get on *just as well*.' He considers that definite faith, a sacred book, a religious sanction for morality, and regular cultivation of the spirit and life by private and public worship, are of high importance.

[117] (p. 190) Published 1921. Contributors : Professor A. Seth Pringle-Pattison, LL.D., D.C.L., 'Immanence and Transcendence'; Miss Lily Dougall, ' God in Action ' and ' The Language of the Soul '; Captain J. Arthur Hadfield, M.A., M.B., ' The Psychology of Power '; Professor C. Anderson Scott, M.A., D.D., ' What happened at Pentecost '; the Rev. C. W. Emmett, B.D., ' The Psychology of Grace ' and ' The Psychology of Inspiration '; Mr. A. Clutton-Brock, ' Spirit and Experience ' and ' Spirit and Matter '; and the Rev. Canon B. H. Streeter, ' Christ the Constructive Revolutionary.'

[118] (p. 193) Cf. *The Nature of God and His Purpose for the World*, vol. i. of the Report presented to the Conference on Christian Politics, Economics, and Citizenship held at Birmingham in 1924. Cf. also the chapter entitled ' The Irreducible Christ,' in *Christianity at the Cross Roads*, by Professor

E. Y. Mullins, D.D., LL.D. Cf. also Dean Inge's Roscoe Lecture (Liverpool Literary and Philosophical Society, March 1924) on 'The Platonic Tradition in English Religion.' Dr. Inge outlined the type of Christianity which is needed to-day, and which has the promise of the future. '(1) It is a spiritual religion, based on a firm belief in absolute and eternal values as the most real things in the universe ; (2) confidence that these values are knowable by man ; (3) the belief that they could nevertheless only be known by whole-hearted consecration of the intellect, will, and affections to the great quest ; (4) an entirely open mind towards the discoveries of science ; (5) a reverent and receptive attitude to the beauty, sublimity, and wisdom of the Creation as a revelation of the mind and character of the Creator ; (6) a complete independence of the current valuations of the worldling.'

Book II.—WESLEY AS CHURCH FOUNDER

Chapter I.—Wesley's Thought as Related to His Churchmanship

[119] (p. 204) The Methodist Churches, or Denominations, conform generally to the Presbyterian type of polity. The fissiparous tendency which appeared among the Methodists in Wesley's lifetime, and several times since, resulted in the creation of further Methodist Churches, which followed the Presbyterian type with varying degrees of closeness. Strict Episcopalianism or Congregationalism has had little attraction for Methodists. The large Methodist Episcopal Churches or Connexions of America are not hierarchical nor prelatical in their ministry. They are presbyterial, and susceptible of popular influence. It was recognized as natural that in the constitution of the new United Church of Canada (1925), composed of Presbyterian, Methodist, and Congregational Churches, Presbyterian polity predominated, along with the doctrine of evangelical Arminianism, which Wesley gave afresh to the world.

Chapter II.—Wesley's Acts as Church Founder

[120] (p. 209) Cf. *Wesley and Kingswood* (1911), 21, 123, with plan of site of Wesley's first English preaching-station.

[121] (p. 210) Cf. *A New History of Methodism*, i. 323 *et seq.* ; also the chapter, 'Conflicts with the Law,' in *John Wesley and the Religious Societies*, by Dr. J. S. Simon.

[122] (p. 210) December 24, 1739, is regarded as the birthday of the first Methodist society or local Church. Wesley's meeting-room, the Foundery, in Windmill Street (now Tabernacle Street), London, near his chapel in City Road, E.C., was probably the place. Cf. *Journal*, ii. 316, 328, and Dr. Simon, *op. cit. supra*, 329, and his *Wesley and the Methodist Societies*. There

were several earlier beginnings of Methodism, as shown in Wesley's *Ecclesiastical History*, iv. 175; but the date at the beginning of this note is that of the beginning of Methodism as history knows it.

[123] (p. 212) Cf. Note 122; also Rev. J. Telford's *Wesley's Chapel and Wesley's House* and *Two West End Chapels*; also Stamp's *Orphan-House of Wesley* (Newcastle-upon-Tyne). All Saints' Church, West Street, Seven Dials, London, W.C., contains several memorials of Wesley's possession.

[124] (p. 213) Their office and duties were defined by Wesley and his Conferences; e.g. ' What is the office of a Helper ? ' (*Works*, viii. 309), and the *Minutes*.

[125] (p. 214) A notable instance of the 'mixed' character of Wesley's Conferences is that of 1748. There were clergymen, 'assistants' (superintendents), 'preachers,' 'stewards,' 'local preachers,' and others. Conference numbered twenty-five persons (Bennet, *Minutes*, 52-7). An interesting feature of the first Methodist Conference at the Foundery, London, in 1744, is that the Countess of Huntingdon was its hostess, at her city mansion in Downing Street. She invited there the six clergymen and four lay Methodist preachers of the Conference, and to them and her friends and servants Wesley preached (*Journal*, iii. 143).

[126] (p. 215) The proceedings of Wesley's Conferences are summarized in ' Minutes of Several Conversations,' *Works*, viii. 299-338, and in *Minutes of the Methodist Conferences* (1812). Volume I. gives those of 1744 to 1798. Important additions are given in the edition issued by the Wesley Historical Society, *Publications*, i. Wesley's Agenda of the first Conference (1744) was copied into Richard Viney's Diary (Ibid., *Proceedings*, xiv. 201), which the Rev. M. Riggall discovered in the Moravian archives, Fetter Lane, London.

[127] (p. 215). Q. Upon what principles do you act, while you sometimes obey and sometimes not ? A. It is entirely consistent. We act at all times on one plain, uniform principle ; ' We will obey the rules and governors of the Church, whenever we can consistently with our duty to God : whenever we cannot, we will quietly obey God rather than men.'

Q. But why do you say you are thrust out of the Church ? Has not every minister a right to dispose of his own church ? A. He ought to have, but in fact he has not. A minister desires I should preach in his church, but the Bishop forbids him. That Bishop then injures him, and thrusts me out of that Church.

Q. Does a Church in the New Testament always mean a single congregation ? A. We believe it does. We do not recollect any instance to the contrary.

Q. What instance or ground is there in the New Testament for a national Church ? A. We know none at all. We apprehend it to be a mere political institution.

NOTES AND AUTHORITIES

Q. Are the three orders of Bishops, Priests, and Deacons plainly described in the New Testament? *A.* We think they are, and believe they generally obtained in the Churches of the Apostolic age.

Q. But are you assured God designed the same plan should obtain in all Churches throughout all ages? *A.* We are not assured of this, because we do not know that it is asserted in Holy Writ.

Q. If this plan were essential to a Christian Church, what must become of all the foreign Reformed Churches? *A.* It would follow, they are no parts of the Church of Christ—a consequence full of shocking absurdity.

Q. In what age was the divine right of episcopacy first asserted in England? *A.* About the middle of Queen Elizabeth's reign. Till then all the Bishops and Clergy in England continually allowed and joined in the ministrations of those who were not episcopally ordained.

Q. Must there not be numberless accidental varieties [variations] in the government of various Churches? *A.* There must in the nature of things. As God variously dispenses His gifts of nature, providence, and grace, both the offices themselves and the officers in each ought to be varied from time to time.

Q. Why is it that there is no determinate plan of Church government appointed in Scripture? *A.* Without doubt because the wisdom of God had a regard to this necessary variety.

Q. Was there any thought of uniformity in the government of all Churches until the time of Constantine? *A.* It is certain there was not; and would not have been then, had men consulted the word of God only.—*Minutes of Conference*, 1747, John Bennet's copy (Wes. Hist. Soc., *Publications*, i. 47).

[128] (p. 216) Lord King's work is scarce. Dr. Harrison's article makes available a useful summary of it. Hatch, *Early Organization of the Christian Church* (p. 144), shows that not until the fourth century did the clergy become a separate and governing class. Cf. also Professor P. Carnegie Simpson, *Church Principles*, chap. iii., ' People and Ministry,' a very cogent statement. Cf. the following, from a very valuable study, *The Genius of Protestantism*, by the Rev. R. McCheyne Edgar, M.A., D.D. (1900). Wesley, as already shown, was spiritually quickened by Luther's teaching, and held his New Testament Protestant principles. Dr. Edgar says, ' As regards the ministry, the Confessions are unanimous upon the subject. The ministry is not a special *priesthood.* The priesthood is recognized as belonging to *all* believers. But all are not in consequence to exercise " the ministry of the Word." This is to be reserved for men who have been found fit, and who are consequently called to the ministerial office. Luther was quite clear on this important subject. Thus he says in 1523, in a discourse on 1 Peter ii. 9, " Christ is the eternal High Priest, anointed of God Himself, who has offered for us His own body, and prayed for us on the cross, and also preached the gospel, and taught all men to acknowledge God and Him. These three offices He had given us all.

Since He is Priest, and we are all His brethren, all Christians have the authority and command to preach and proclaim God's grace and virtue, and to go before God, that one may intercede for the other, and offer himself to God. Nevertheless, as St. Paul says that everything should be done in order, not every one should teach and administer the Sacraments in the congregation, but those only who are called by the congregation, and to whom the office is entrusted, and the rest should listen in silence." . . . In another sermon on Psalm cx. 4, and in the year 1539, he says, " For while all are priests, yet not all are to preach or teach or govern, but some must be chosen, from the entire body, to whom such office is to be entrusted. He who administers it is, with respect to his office, not a priest as the rest are, but a minister of all the rest ; and when he can or will no longer preach or minister he returns to the common body, hands his office to another, and is nothing more than any private Christian." '

[129] (p. 218) For Wesley's ' Model Deed' see *Works*, viii. 330 ; ' Deed of Declaration,' *ibid.*, iv. 503 ; cf. references in Rev. John Elsworth's edition of Dr. J. S. Simon's *Summary of Methodist Law*. On Wesley's doctrinal standards see Dr. E. H. Sugden's edition of *Wesley's Standard Sermons* ; also Dr. H. Maldwyn Hughes's booklet, *Wesley's Standards in the Light of To-day* (1921).

[130] (p. 220) Wesley's letter, in 1784, constituting the American Methodist Church :

' *To Dr. Coke, Mr. Asbury, and our Brethren in North America.*
Bristol, *September* 10, 1784.

' DEAR BRETHREN.—1. By a very uncommon train of providences many of the provinces of North America are totally disjoined from their mother-country, and erected into independent States. The English Government has no authority over them, either civil or ecclesiastical, any more than over the States of Holland. A civil authority is exercised over them, partly by the Congress, partly by the provincial Assemblies. But no one either exercises or claims any ecclesiastical authority at all. In this peculiar situation some thousands of the inhabitants of the States desire my advice ; and in compliance with their desire I have drawn up a little sketch.

' 2. Lord King's " Account of the Primitive Church " convinced me many years ago, that bishops and presbyters are the same order, and consequently have the same rights to ordain. For many years I have been importuned, from time to time, to exercise this right, by ordaining part of our travelling preachers. But I have still refused, not only for peace sake, but because I was determined as little as possible to violate the established order of the national Church to which I belonged.

' 3. But the case is widely different between England and North America. Here there are bishops who have a legal jurisdiction : in America there are none, neither any parish ministers. So that for some hundred miles together, there is none either to baptize, or to administer the Lord's Supper. Here, therefore, my scruples are at an end : and I conceive myself at full liberty, as I violate no order, and invade no man's right, by appointing and sending labourers into the harvest.

'4. I have accordingly appointed Dr. Coke and Mr. Francis Asbury to be joint superintendents over our brethren in North America ; as also Richard Whatcoat and Thomas Vasey to act as elders among them, by baptizing and administering the Lord's Supper. And I have prepared a liturgy, little differing from that of the Church of England (I think the best constituted national Church in the world), which I advise all the travelling preachers to use, on the Lord's Day, in all the congregations, reading the Litany only on Wednesdays and Fridays, and praying extempore on all other days. I also advise the elders to administer the Supper of the Lord on every Lord's Day.

'5. If any one will point out a more rational and scriptural way of feeding and guiding these poor sheep in the wilderness I will gladly embrace it. At present, I cannot see any better method than that I have taken.

'6. It has, indeed, been proposed to desire the English bishops to ordain part of our preachers for America. But to this I object. (1) I desired the Bishop of London to ordain only one ; but could not prevail. (2) If they consented, we know the slowness of their proceedings ; but the matter admits of no delay. (3) If they would ordain them now, they would likewise expect to govern them. And how grievously would this entangle us ! (4) As our American brethren are now totally disentangled, both from the State and from the English hierarchy, we dare not entangle them again, either with the one or the other. They are now at full liberty, simply to follow the Scriptures and the Primitive Church. And we judge it best that they should stand fast in that liberty, wherewith God has so strangely made them free.' (*Letters of John Wesley*, p. 263.)

For further authorities on Wesley's churchly actions, cf. *A New History of Methodism*, ii. 83 *et seq.*; Rigg, *Churchmanship of John Wesley* (1886) ; and Professor J. Alfred Faulkner's vol., *Wesley, as Sociologist, Theologian, Churchman*, 85 *et seq*. For contents of Wesley's Service Books for American and also British Methodists, see Green's invaluable *Bibliography of the Works of John and Charles Wesley* (2nd ed., 1906).

[131] (p. 222) A list of acts of Ordination by Wesley is given by Rev. John Telford, B.A. (*Life of John Wesley*, revised ed., 1924, p. 883); cf. also *Wes. Hist. Soc. Proceedings*, vii. 8, ix. 145–54, x. 157, xii. 67, xv. 34. To these must be added Wesley's ordination of Mathew Lumb on August 6, 1788. The certificate of ordination is dated August 7. The original, discovered in 1925, is in the possession of Mr. Edmund S. Lamplough, of London, and reads as follows:

KNOW ALL MEN by these Presents, that I, John Wesley, Master of Arts, late Fellow of Lincoln College in the University of Oxford, did, on the Sixth day of August, in the year of our Lord one thousand seven hundred and eighty-eight, by the Imposition of my hands and prayer, and in the fear of GOD (being assisted by other ordained Ministers) set apart Mathew Lumb for the Office of an Elder in the Church of GOD : whom I recommend to all whom it may concern, as a proper person to administer the Holy Sacraments in the Congregations, and to feed the Church of GOD. Given under my hand and seal the seventh day of August in the year above written.

JOHN WESLEY. (L.S.)

The following important statement by Henry Moore, concerning the famous 'Korah' Sermon, is often overlooked. Moore was Wesley's travelling companion, amanuensis, and one of his literary executors. He was later President, twice, of the Conference. Moore says, 'I was with Mr. Wesley in London, when he published that sermon. He had encouraged me to be a man of *one book*, and he had repeatedly invited me to speak fully whatever objection I had to anything which he spoke or published. I thought that some things in that discourse were not to be found in the BOOK, and I resolved to tell him so the first opportunity. It soon occurred. I respectfully observed that I agreed with him that the Lord had always sent by whom He would send, instruction, reproof, and correction in righteousness, to mankind ; and that there was a real distinction between the prophetic and priestly office in the Old Testament, and the prophetic and pastoral office in the New (where no Priesthood is mentioned but that of our Lord); but I could not think that what he had said concerning the Evangelists and the Pastors, or Bishops, was agreeable to what we read there : viz. that the latter had a right to administer the Sacraments, which the former did not possess. I observed, " Sir, you know that the *Evangelists* Timothy and Titus were ordered by the Apostle to ordain *Bishops* in every place : and, surely, they could not impart to them an authority which they did not themselves possess." He looked earnestly at me for some time, but not with displeasure. He made no reply, and soon introduced another subject. I said no more. The man of *one book* would not dispute against it. I believe he saw his love to the Church, from which he never deviated unnecessarily, had, in this instance, led him a little too far. He had foreseen that the increase of the Societies, so far beyond all that he had looked for in his own days, would necessarily oblige the people to assemble in their own chapels, and, at length, to have all the privileges which the Holy Scriptures secure to all Christian believers' (*Life of Rev. John Wesley, A.M.*, by the Rev. Henry Moore, 1825, vol. ii. 340).

The most recent Anglican pronouncement on the Ministerial Office as it is exercised in churches other than the Church of England appears in Documents on Christian Unity, compiled by the Dean of Canterbury (Rev. G. K. A. Bell, M.A.) and Rev. W. L. Robertson, M.A., published in 1925

NOTES AND AUTHORITIES 281

in connexion with the Lambeth Appeal for Christian Unity—*The Church of England and the Free Churches*. Anglican representatives stated that ' it seems to us . . . that the ministries which imply a sincere intention to preach Christ's Word and administer the Sacraments as Christ ordained, and to which authority so to do has been solemnly given by the Church concerned, are real ministries of Christ's Word and Sacraments in the Universal Church ' (p. 46).

This is, however, qualified by a Second Memorandum from the Joint Lambeth Conference, given on p. 68 : ' In our judgement it does not follow that because certain ministries are admitted to be real ministries of Christ's Word and Sacraments, they must thereby be considered as in themselves sufficient. . . . These considerations affect the question of the authority of the ministry. Spiritual efficacy is one thing, due authority is another. The latter is not involved in the former.'

CHAPTER III.—WESLEY'S REGULATIVE PRINCIPLES

[133] (p. 229) Q. Can he be a spiritual governor of the Church, who is not a believer, not a member of it ? A. It seems not : though he may be a governor in outward things, by a power derived from the king.

Q. What are properly the laws of the Church of England ? A. The rubrics : and to those we submit, as the ordinance of man, for the Lord's sake.

Q. But is not the will of our governors a law ? A. No. Not of any governor, temporal or spiritual. Therefore if any bishop wills that I should not preach the gospel, his will is no law to me.

Q. But what if he produce a law against your preaching ? A. I am to obey God rather than man.—*Minutes* of Conference, 1745, John Bennet's copy (Wes. Hist. Soc., *Publications*).

Wesley's attitude on the consecration of buildings or burial-grounds showed the same freedom. He said, 'Where do we find one word in the New Testament enjoining any such thing ? . . . I never wished that any bishop should consecrate any chapel or burial-ground of mine. Indeed, I should not dare to suffer it ; as I am clearly persuaded the thing is wrong in itself, being not authorized either by any law of God, or by any law of the land. In consequence of which, I conceive, that either the clerk or the sexton may as well consecrate the church or the church-yard, as the bishop. . . . I take the whole of this practice to be a mere relic of Romish superstition. And I wonder that any sensible Protestant should think it right to countenance it ; much more, that any reasonable man should plead for the necessity of it ! Surely, it is high time now that we should be guided, not by custom, but by Scripture and reason ' (*Works*, x. 510). Hence the irony of circumstances against the wishes of his brother Charles on this matter. Notwithstanding Wesley's wishes, Charles Wesley requested that his remains might be interred in ' consecrated ' ground.

After this had been done, as was supposed, it was discovered that that part of the graveyard had not been 'consecrated.'

¹³³ (p. 229) These and other important statements by Wesley occupy four pages of a report of a day's proceedings in the Conference not given in the *Minutes* commonly cited.

¹³⁴ (p. 231) It is curious to note the slur cast upon Wesley's lay itinerants as ignorant men. This has persisted, and has been repeated by a writer, generally well-informed and accurate, M. Halévy. In his valuable work, *History of the English People in* 1815, he describes them as 'rude, fanatical, and unwashed.' On the contrary, Wesley's statement has never been contradicted that there was not one of them who could not pass 'such an examination in substantial, practical divinity, as few of our candidates for holy orders, even in the University, are able to do' (*New History of Methodism*, i. 297). The writings of many of these men can still be examined. The reader is referred to the examination of some of them in the *Proceedings* of the Aristotelian Society summarized in Note 79 in the present work. At his first Conference (1744) Wesley issued a list of books to be read by his preachers who were 'assistants.' It includes the Greek New Testament, classics like Plato, Homer, Virgil, Epictetus, Horace, Caesar, Erasmus, and Pascal, as well as his 'tracts.'

¹³⁵ (p. 232) Dr. Sugden's summary of the facts and his comments are relevant (*Standard Sermons*, ii. 120): 'Wesley held to the end that only an ordained priest could administer the Sacrament; though he so far altered his original view as to hold that episcopal ordination was not necessary, ordination by a presbyter being valid; and so he ordained some of his helpers for the full ministry, including the administration of the Sacrament, both for America and for Scotland' [and later for England too]. 'But it was not until after his death that the Conference took the responsibility of permitting all its ministers to administer the Lord's Supper in England. A further step has since been taken by giving authority to the President of Conference to allow probationers to administer the Sacrament, where it is desirable; and in Australia, home missionaries, or any other person of good character and standing, may receive such permission, renewable from year to year. So the last relic of the Romish conception of the Lord's Supper has disappeared from Methodism.' The British Wesleyan Methodist Conference annually give this authority to unordained ministers, in the same way. After Wesley's death it was frequently found necessary to authorize persons who had not been ordained to give the Lord's Supper in Methodist churches, in order that there might be a regular and frequent observance. The same principles have generally governed Methodism—orderliness and scriptural liberty.

NOTES AND AUTHORITIES 283

¹³⁶ (p. 232) Cf. Principal Sugden, *Standard Sermons of Wesley*, i. 237-60, and Principal H. Maldwyn Hughes, *Wesley's Standards* (p. 23). These works bear also on the next section of the present chapter.

¹³⁷ (p. 236) Wesley's efforts as Bible expositor were followed in the next generation by those of three Methodist ministers, Joseph Benson, Adam Clarke, and Joseph Sutcliffe, each of whom produced a commentary on the whole Bible. Others followed with monographs on portions. A widely-used commentary on the whole Bible, representative of modern biblical scholarship, was issued in 1919, under the editorship of a Primitive Methodist, Professor Arthur S. Peake, M.A., D.D. He and other British Methodist scholars made considerable contributions.

¹³⁸ (p. 239) The Rt. Hon. Lloyd George, in an *obiter dictum* at a breakfast-table conference, commended the English type of mind in its discharge of a juryman's duty. He said, 'The Englishman's mind is the juryman's mind. If you give him the facts you can trust him for the verdict.'

¹³⁹ (p. 242) On the separation of Methodism from the Church of England the statement made by Dr. J. H. Rigg in 1886 is confirmed by the fuller knowledge concerning Wesley and his acts now available, and used in the present work. Rigg says, ' so far as respects the separate development of Methodism, Wesley not only pointed but paved the way to all that has since been done, and the utmost divergence of Methodism from the Church of England at this day is but the prolongation of a line the beginning of which was traced by Wesley's own hand' (*Churchmanship of John Wesley*, 109). Cf. Dr. J. S. Simon, in *John Wesley and the Advance of Methodism*, chap. xii.

¹⁴⁰ (p. 244) Such ' reasons ' Wesley gives in his *Appeal to Men of Reason and Religion*, Pt. II. iii., and Pt. III. iii. 10. On these grounds Wesley justifies preaching and pastoral work by laymen. The clearest declaration of Methodism ever given of the doctrine of the ministerial office, harmonizes with this and the preceding principles of Wesley's work as Church Founder. The pronouncement referred to was made by the British Wesleyan Conference in 1908. It is known that one of the most eminent and saintly biblical scholars who have served Methodism, the late Rev. Professor George G. Findlay, B.A., D.D., helped to this decision. This instruction is provided for every minister and every member of that Church. It reads thus : 'Christ's ministers in the Church are stewards in the household of God, and shepherds of His flock. Some are called and ordained to this sole occupation, and have a principal and directing part in these great duties; but they hold no priesthood differing in kind from that which is common to the Lord's people, and they have no exclusive title to the preaching of the gospel or the care of souls. These ministries are shared with them by others, to whom also the Spirit divides His gifts severally as He wills' (*Summary of Methodist Law and Discipline*,

5th ed., 1924, p. 10). In the United Committee on Methodist Union, in 1923, the inclusion of this paragraph in the section 'Doctrine,' in the Scheme for Methodist Union, was suggested. It was unanimously accepted by all sections of British Methodism as an authentic definition. Cf. the statement by the Rev. F. Luke Wiseman, B.A., in the Wesleyan Methodist Conference, 1925 : ' they in that Pastoral Session represented a very important but, nevertheless, a sectional interest. They were not the whole Church. There were communions in which the clergy were the Church. That was not so in Wesleyan Methodism ' (*Methodist Recorder*, July 30, 1925).

[141] (p. 245) Dr. C. Ryder Smith continues (*Methodist Times*, December 11, 1924) : ' Methodists have one kind of government in the United States and another in England ; we have a purely pastoral Conference in one generation, and a Conference of two sessions in the next ; we alter our machine, indeed, in some degree every year.' The same writer (*ibid.*, May 8, 1924) writing on ' The Challenge of Catholicism—Minister and Layman,' says ' the plain facts are that the Methodist ministry grew up " pragmatically " ; that it grew out of the societies, and was not derived from bishops ; and at first it was not sharply distinguished from the other spiritual officers of Methodism, as appears, for instance, from the fact that it was quite common in Wesley's day for a " travelling " preacher to become again " local " ; that, as a consequence of these facts, it has never been easy in Methodism to answer the question, " What is the theoretical difference between a minister and a layman ? " ; and that, apart from the repudiation of sacerdotalism, there has never been an agreed Methodist answer to this question.'

[142] (p. 246) Cf. an excellent introductory work, *Religion and Natural Science*, by E. Haigh, M.A., B.Sc. (1925); also a devout study of the theory of evolution, by Sir Oliver Lodge, D.Sc., F.R.S., in his volume, *Making of Man* (p. 143) : ' The greatest mystery of the Christian religion is the recognition, as a positive fact, that God is in close relation with humanity, has entered into the strife and turmoil, has taken our nature upon Him, and henceforward, now and always, is active and energizing and suffering and helping, sorrowing and rejoicing and inspiring, and, in spite of all, loving and willing to undergo sacrifice for the disappointing creature upon whom He has conferred the privileges of existence and freedom. . . . Yes, God so loved the world that He gave the Being we are taught to call, in a special sense, His Son.'

INDEX OF NAMES AND SUBJECTS

AMERICAN University, 262
America, War with, 45; Methodism in, 107, 219
Anselm, Philosophy of, 25, 131, 251
Apostolic Succession, 220
Aristotelian Society, 251; and Christian Experience, 251, 267; Papers at, 251, 259, 282
Arminianism, Evangelical, Wesley's, 58, 114, 154; Spread of, 246
Arnold, M., quoted, 270
Art, Jesus Christ Inspires, 196
Asbury, Bishop F., 107, 219; U.S.A. Memorial to, 266; Historic Letter to, 278
Assurance, Christian, 171, 172, 175; Imprisonment for Asserting, 179
Atheism, 252.—*See* Theism
Augustine, 62, 95; quoted, 136, 153
Auto-Suggestion, Experience and, 177

BACON, LORD, 51, 58, 59, 154; quoted, 252; Cipher of, 256
Barber, Dr. F. L., 263
Baring-Gould, S., Mis-statements by, 49, 171, 258, 273
Bath, 31; Beau Nash at, 255
Baxter, R., 42; as 'a pen,' 266
Bernard, St., of Clairvaux, 179
Beauty, References to Natural, 97, 266; Spiritual, 136, 157, 266; Jesus Christ and, 194
Begbie, H., 120, 269
Bell, Dean G. K. A., 280
Bennett, J., 56; his *Minutes of Conference*, 276, 277, 281
Benson, J., and Free Inquiry, 61
Berkeley, G., 19, 20; Philosophy of, 22, 152; and Elemental Fire, 102; and God as Father, 141; as Spirit, 142, 250
Bett, Prof. H., 261
Bible, as a Book, 74, 280; Authority of, 236; Methodist Commentators on, 283
'Bible Christians,' 235
Bigotry, Cautions against, 243
Birrell, Rt. Hon. A., 38, 114
Bishop, the name, 219; Functions of, used, 219, 220, 222; and Methodist Ministry, 283, 284
Blackwall, Dr. R. E.,
Blackwell, Ebenezer, 38
Böhler, Peter, 88
Bonnet, Charles de, 76, 262
Booth, Wm., of the Salvation Army, 120
Bosanquet, B., and Uses of Pain, 283
Brackenbury, Robert Carr, 111, 172
Bray, William (Billy), 184
Brigden, Rev. T. E., 258, 262
Bristol, 31; New Services at, 209; New Building at, 217; and Kingswood, 257
Brotherhood.—*See* Fellowship

Brown, Prof. W. Adams, 60
Browne, P. Philosophy of, 79
Browning, R., Philosophy of, 254
Buchan, Dowager Countess of, 48
Butler, Bishop J., quoted, 19, 21; as Philosopher, 26; and Wesley, 29, 72
Bunyan, J., 175
Byrom, John, 151, 256

CADBURY, G., 122
Caldecott, Dr. A., 267
Calvinism, 141, 154, 228, 246
Cambridge, Platonism at, 54, 259
Carter, Rev. H., 69
Cennick, J., 213
Chapman, Prof. J. A., 263
Children, Tenderness towards, 48
Christian Experience.—*See* Experience
Christian Perfection, 85, 161
Church Buildings, Unauthorized, 211
Church Catholic.—*See* Church Universal
Church Constitution, Types of a, 202; for Methodists, 214, 219; Regulative Principles of, 227; Lay Rights under, 233
Church Founder, Acts of a, 206–16
Church History, Methodists in, 225
Churchmanship, New Testament, 202
Church of England, Separation from, 46, 206–226; Controlled by Bishops, 208; Methodists and, 225, 226; Variation from, 230
Church Principles, Spread of, Methodist, 246
Church Services, Unauthorized, 208
Church Tradition, Tested, 237
Church, Universal Christian, and Methodism, 225, 284; and Unity, 281
Church Workers, Unauthorized, 213; Tested, 245
Cipher, Writing, 256
Clarke, Adam, 25
Clarke, S., Philosophy of, 19, 24; Insufficient, 26, 141; Use of, 62
Clutton-Brock, A., quoted, 194
Coke, Thomas, 110; Re-ordained, 219; Historic Letter to, 278
Collier, Dr. Frank W., 262
Colman, Mr. J. R., his Wesley MSS., 256
Common Sense, Christian, as a Test, 237
Conference, Methodist, and Laity, 214, 242, 276
Conference on Christian Politics, Economics, and Citizenship, 274
Conscience, Butler on the, 28; Kant on the, 253; Christian, as a Test, 226
'Consecration,' of Buildings, 281
Consensus, Use of, 168, 238
Conversion, Religious, 90 *et seq.*; Instantaneous, 172; Proofs of, 243

285

Cowper, W., quoted, 48; and Philosophy, 251
Creation, Evolutionary Theory of, 78

Dale, R. W., 271, 272
Dallinger, W. H., 263
Darwin, C., 76, 262
Davison, Dr. W. T., 252
Death, Physical, 253
Deism, Opposed, 22, 23, 131, 139
Deissmann, Prof. A., 136
Descartes, 26, 54, 59, 136
Determinism.—*See* Necessity
Dissenters, Methodists as, 221, 224
Dougall, Miss L., 191
Drew Theological Seminary, U.S.A., 267
Durham, and Methodist Work, 6, 274; University of, 250
Durham, Bishop of (Dr. H. H. Henson), quoted, 255

Edgar, Dr. R. M., 273, 277
Edwards, Jonathan, 143
Elsworth, Rev. J., 278
'Eliot, George,' and Methodist Workers, 269
Emotion, and Christian Experience, 172, 173
Episcopal Church Government, 201
Ethical and Christian Experience, 162, 273
Experience, Christian, Unity of, 116, 163; Reveals Truth, 127; Aristotelian Society and, 251, 267; Criticism of, 147, 165; Eighteenth Century, 107; Emotion in, 173, 182, 274; Metaphor of, 101; Modern Philosophy and, 181; Recent Types of, 116

Fairbairn, A. M., 16
Fatalism, 154, 228
Father, God as the, 139, 191
Faulkner, Prof. J. A., 274, 279
'Feeling,' Religious.—*See* Emotion
Fellowship, Christian, 61, 142-46; New Forms of, 210; Methodist, 238
Findlay, G. G., 283
Fire, Elemental, 24, 102; Metaphorical Use of, 101
Fitchett, Dr. W. H., 215; quoted, 245
Fletcher, John, 154
'Forward with Wesley,' 245
Free Churches, Growth of, 21; Constitution of, 220; Valid Ministries in, 281.—*See also* Methodism
Freedom, Natural.—*See* Slavery; Spiritual, 228, 234
Freewill, Doctrine of, 154, 160, 228
French, Rev. E. Aldom, 257
Friendship, Need of, 157; *see also* Fellowship, Jesus Christ and, 197

Gardiner, A. G., 18, 123
George, Rt. Hon. D. L., M.P., quoted, 283
German Pietists, 181
Gladstone, W. E., 116

Glover, Dr. T. R., 62; quoted, 105; on Christian Experience, 195
God, Existence of, 22, 25, 131; as Goodness, Truth and Beauty, 15, 132, 136, 163; Manifested in Jesus Christ, 148, 157; Plato on, 249.— *See also* Father
Grace, Divine, All have, 154; Means of, 193
Green, Canon Peter, quoted, 225
Green, R., 260
Grimshaw, William, 218; quoted, 224

Hadfield, Captain J. A, 192
Haigh, E., 284
Halévy, E., 272, 282
Hamilton, Bishop J. W., 267
Happiness, Creatural, 253
Hargitt, Prof. C. W., 262
Harrison, Dr. A. W., 217, 277
Hocking, Prof. W. E., 252
Hoernlé, Prof. R. F. A., Works, 249; quoted, 251
Holiness, Possibility of, 154, 159; as Christian Perfection, 161
Holland, William, 93, 97
Holy Scriptures, 73, 74; Authority of, 62, 234
Holy Spirit, The, in Experience, 142, 144, 179, 190-95; and Psychology, 192; as Orchestral Conductor, 193; Interpreted, 203
Homer, quoted, 39; 'Amazing Genius' of, 81, 117; Piety of, 272, 282
Horton, Rev. S., 262
Hughes, H. P., quoted, 256
Hughes, Principal H. M., quoted, 173, 261, 271, 278
Hume, D., 23
Hutton, James, 92; a Moravian Leader, 264, 265
Hymnology, Contribution by, 70-72; Philosophy in, 72, 259, 261
Hymns, J. and C. Wesley's, quoted: 'Lo! God is Here,' 55; 'My God, I Know,' 61; 'Where Shall My Wondering Soul,' 94; 'O Thou Who Camest,' 105; 'I Thank Thee, Uncreated Sun,' 136; 'O for a Thousand Tongues,' 138, 261; 'O God of Good,' 141; 'O Come and Dwell,' 144; 'Peace, Doubting Heart,' 158; 'All Things are Possible,' 160; 'Turn the Full Stream,' 162; 'Here is Knowledge,' 240; 'O the Fathomless,' 247; 'Open, Lord, Mine Inward Ear,' 256
Hypothesis, in Philosophy, 59; in Wesley's Thought, 130; Exposition of An, 131, 149, 153, 156

Idealism, 102; Christian, 167; Berkeley's, 22, 152, 249; Plato's, 249
Illingworth, Canon J. R., 127
Imagination, Services of the, 270
Immanence, Divine, 191, 284
Inge, Dean W. R., quoted, 132; On Unity of Saints, 164; on Protestantism, 229; on Future Christianity, 275
Intuition, Spiritual, 225; Primacy of, 227

INDEX OF NAMES AND SUBJECTS 287

Jackson, Prof. George, 269
James, William, 172, 183–86
Jesus Christ, God in, 136, 162, 169;
 Love of, The Christian Motive, 155;
 as Alpha and Omega, 196; as Conscience of Humanity, 252
Jevons, Dr. F. B., 139, 175
John, St., as favourite teacher, 178;
 Prologue of, 169
Johnson, Dr. S., 48
'John Smith,' Letters to, 68
Julian, Canon, 260, 261

Kant, E., on Conscience, 253
Kelman, Dr. J., 269
Kempis, Thomas à, 263
Kilham, Alexander, 248
King, Lord, on Church Polity, 216, 277
Kipling, R., quoted, 259
Knox, A., quoted, 257

Lackington, J., 258, 259
Lamplough, Mr. E. S., 279
Law, William, 19, 20; Influence of, 89, 141, 263
Lay Rights, in Church Courts, 233, 283, 284
Lecky, W. E. H., 17
Legal Acts, Church Founder's, 217–26
Leger, Prof. A., 259
Lidgett, Dr. J. S., quoted, 35, 252, 271
Literature, Significant Use of, 64–81
Locke, J., 19, 54, 80
Lockyer, Rev. T. F., 266
Lodge, Sir O., quoted, 284
London, Methodist Chapels in, 212;
 Aldersgate Street, 92, 264; Little Britain, 265; St. Paul's Cathedral, 96; Westminster Abbey Memorials, 16
Lord's Supper, Sacrament of, in Methodism, 222, 231; a Converting Ordinance, 232, 233, 282, 283
Love, Christian, as Motive, 155; Central in Christian Philosophy, 178
Love, Infinite, as Reality, 139, 195, 254
Luther, Martin, his Preface read, 92; quoted, 277

Mackenzie, Prof. J. S., 249
McNeal, Rev. G. H., 265
Malebranche, P., 53
Man, Filial Relation of, to God, 140, 161
Man, Implications in, 152; Explained, 153; and Christian Philosophy, 156;
 Capabilities of, 159; Divine Image in, 254; Creation of, 262
Martyrdoms, as Miracles, 134
Masefield, J., 269
Maxfield, Thomas, 213
Maxwell, Lady, 112, 172
Mechanism, Rejected, 228
Merz, J. T., 252
Metaphysics, Wesley's, 51, 53; hypothesis in, 59; in his *Philosophy*, 78
Methodism, Effect of, 32, 274; Survival of, 245; Spread of, 246; Statistics of, 257
Methodism, New History of, 214, 262, 270
Methodist Church, Constitution for, 214, 219, 277–79, 283; Teaching Standards in, 261; Universals, 167

Methodists, 'The People Called,' 61;
 The Name, 260; Persecution of, 179; Service Books for, 221, 279; Union of British, 284; Preachers.— *See* Preachers
Milton, J., quoted, 81, 123
Minister, Methodist, Office of, 283.— *See* Preachers
Moffatt, Dr. J., Bible Translation by, 250; and Wesley's translation, 262
Moore, Henry, 280
Moral Values, as Standards, 15
Mullins, Prof. E. Y., 275
Murray, Grace, 56.
Music, Influence of, 38; Vocal, 72, 91, 138; Helped by Instrumental, 97, 193; Spiritual Experience and, 147; Jesus Christ Inspires, 196
Mysticism, Society of Friends and, 122; Christian, 164, 228, 229, 240, 259; of the Wesleys, 60, 229, 235, 240; in Hymns, 256, 261; Methodists and, 270

Necessity, Doctrine of, 155, 228, 246
Newcastle-upon-Tyne, 7, 250; Orphan House, 257
Nicoll, W. R., 65
Norris, J., 53
Notes on the New Testament, 72, 218, 249
Nutter, Dr. C. S., 261

Obedience, in Christian Experience, 170
Open-air, Preaching, 209, 266
Ordination, 44; of the Methodist Preachers, 219, 220; Irregular and Temporary, 223; Certificates of, 248; by Preachers, 248
Overton and Relton, on Methodist Movement, 226
Oxford, 44, 46; Disputations at, 139

Pain, Uses of, 39, 59, 157; in the Cosmos, 253, 254; as Misery, Overruled, 272
Paley, W., and Teleology, 27, 252, 253
Pattison, Mark, 20
Paul, St., 17; Comparison with, 62, 83; and 'Adoption,' 144; and the Holy Spirit, 143; and Man's Nature, 153; and a 'New Creation,' 155; and 'Purpose,' 150; and Co-operation with God, 156; and 'in Christ,' 161
Pawson, J., 81, 224
Peake, Prof. Arthur S., and Emotion, 174; and 'Experience' in Scriptures, 179, 273; Commentary of, 283
Philosophy, Christian, in Eighteenth Century, 15; Types of in Religions, 60; *Survey of Wisdom of God*, 75; Metaphysical, 78; Jesus Christ and, 196; Depth in, 252
Plato, 22; quoted, 249, 259, 282
Platt, Prof. F., 271
Pratt, Prof. J. B., 187
Prayer Book, the English, Altered, 202, 219, 221
Preachers, Methodist Itinerant, Experience of, 114; Examined, 267; Not Ignorant, 282

Prelacy, Methodists and, 202
Presbyterianism, Methodism and, 204, 275
Private Judgement, Use of, 229, 241, 242
Protestant Principles, 229, 239, 281
Providence, Divine, 65, 150, 254.—*See also* Pain
Psychology, 153, 154; and Christian Experience, 177; and the Holy Spirit, 192
Purpose, Divine, in Nature, 27, 65, 75; Implications in, 149, 151, 252

Reason, Duties of Human, 38, 61, 66
Reformed Churches, 206, 215, 224
Religious Societies, 44, 91, 264
Riggall, Rev. M., 258
Rigg, J. H., 255; quoted, 283
Robertson, C. Grant, 18
Robertson, Rev. W. L., 280

Sacraments, The, Use of, 231; The Lord's Supper and Conversion, 232
Sanctification.—*See* Christian Perfection
Scheffler, Johann, 136, 271
Schleiermacher, F. D. E., 182
Science, and Christian Teaching, 78, 273
Selbie, Principal W. B., 274
Shakespeare, W., Comparison with, 15; on Conscience, 128; Works of, burned, 81
Sharp, Dr. J. A., 101, 265
Simon, Dr. J. S., 226, 275, 283
Simpson, Prof. J. Y., 262
Simpson, Prof. P. C., 277
Sincerity, Need of, 170
Sin, in Man, 156, 159; Confession of Grace, 86; by Charles Wesley, 263; Deliverance from, 160
Slavery, Discontinued, 114
Smith, J., Cambridge Platonist, 54
Smith, Prof. C. Ryder, 245, 284
Snaith, J., quoted, 255
'Society,' Methodist.—*See* Methodist
Socrates, 16, 180, 249
Sorley, Prof. W. R., 249, 251, 263
Spectator, The, 15, 64
Spirit, Inward Witness of the, 149.—*See* Holy Spirit
Standard Sermons, 72, 218, 249
Stanley, A. P., 16
Stead, W. T., quoted, 15, 17, 257
Stephen, Sir Leslie, 64, 180
Streeter, Canon H. B., 190
Sugden, Dr. E. H., 253, 261
Sutcliffe, Joseph, 241

Taylor, Bishop Jeremy, 86, 101
Teacher-Evangelist, A, 67, 248
Teleology.—*See* Purpose
Telford, Rev. J., quoted, 101, 258, 261
Temperley, Prof. H. W. V., 19
Theism, Arguments for, 22, 25, 27; Chief, 131–35, 252
Thomson, Prof. J. A., 252
Thought, English.—*See* Philosophy
Tillett, Dr. W. F., 261
Tipple, President E. S., 267
Told, Silas, 111
Toronto University, 326

Usefulness, Church Rules, 242

Virgil, quoted, 23, 250

Walker, Samuel, 214
Wallace, A. R., 76, 262
Wallington, Mr. A., 260
Warburton, Bishop, 143
Washington, U.S.A., 262
Waterhouse, Prof. E. S., 178, 274
Watson, John, 271
Webb, Prof. C. C. J., 147
Webb, Rt. Hon. Sidney, quoted, 274
Wesleyana, 7, 8, 256
Wesley, Charles, 45, 230; quoted, 83, 104, 247; a High Churchman, 223, 228.—*See also* Hymns
Wesley Historical Society, 8, 231, 258
Wesley, John, descriptions of, 37, 46, 248, 258; his Depression, 266; Development of, 85; Estimates of, 15; Evangelical Conversion of, 90; Experience, 39, 90 *et seq.*; Energy, 98, 192; Failings and Sins, 86; Good-humour, 47, 49, 257; a Genius, 54; Illnesses, 257; 'Korah' Sermon, 222, 280; Pedigree, 44, 257; Philanthropy, 47; Physique, 46; Versatility, 52
——, As Church Founder: Preaching Standards, 72, 235; and his Thought, 201; his Acts, 206–26; his Principles, 227–45; Deed of Declaration, 218, 233
——, As Philosopher: Qualifications and Method, 43, 51; Hypothesis, 59; and Divine, 66, 67; not Systematic, 72; Summarized, 151, 152, 162; Criticized, 165, 262
——, Sayings: I am a spirit, etc., 59, 130; I am willing to do, etc., 245; Church or no church, etc., 203; Soul-damning clergymen, etc., 231; This is the very thing, etc., 203; We desire to follow Providence, 203; Think and let think, 61, 230
——, *Works of*, 63–81; Bibliography of, 260; his *Appeals*, 66; *Arminian Magazine*, 231; cipher, 40, 256; Diaries, 40, 86, 255; *Journal*, 37, 65; *Letters of*, 49, 51, 219; *Notes on New Testament*, 73, 234; on *Old Testament*, 235; *Philosophy* (5 vols.), 75; Natural History in, 76; Evolutionary Theory in, 77; Metaphysics in, 78; Criticized, 262; *Rules* for Methodists, 68; *Standard Sermons*, 72
Wesley, S. (brother), 134, 206
Wesley, S. (father), 44, 149
Wesley, Susanna (mother), 44, 85
Westley, J. (grandfather), 207
Westcott, B. F., 118
Whitefield, George, 209
Whyte, A., 124–27; and Butler, 252, 254, 263
Williams, John, R.A., 66
Wilson, Woodrow, quoted, 15
Wiseman, Rev. F. L., quoted, 284
Wordsworth, W., quoted, 122; and Philosophy, 250
Workman, Principal H. B., 271

www.ingramcontent.com/pod-product-compliance
Lightning Source LLC
Chambersburg PA
CBHW060555230426
43670CB00011B/1833